EFFECTIVE LIVING

EFFECTIVE LIVING

YOUR GUIDE TO
CREATING A LIFE YOU DON'T NEED
TO TAKE A VACATION FROM

RICARDO MILLER

Rev. date: 03/13/2020

To order additional copies of this book, contact:
Xlibris
1-888-795-4274
www.Xlibris.com
Orders@Xlibris.com
806535

Dedication

I wholeheartedly endorse the truth that we are the sum total of the choices we make on a daily basis. Throughout my life I have made choices that, if given the opportunity to do over, I would do differently. Even still, with the hand that I was dealt, and the decisions I made, I pray that I have been an inspiration to many, most importantly, my son Ricardo Miller, Jr. I live daily with the reminder that you live beyond my words and are watching all that I do. My greatest hope is that I have served as an exceptional example in every area of life. May you grow and become a better man that I could ever be. You are brilliant and filled with unlimited potential. LIVE BOLD, LIVE BRAVE, and NEVER DIM YOUR LIGHT! Son, I dedicate this project to you.

Acknowledgements

I believe that **no one** is self-made, but that a huge part of who we are is attributed to the collective contribution of the people whose paths have intersected ours, resulting in them leaving an indelible imprint. When it's all said and done, I can truly say that I am able to do what I was born to do because over the years God has placed some of the most amazing people on the planet around me. Throughout my journey these people have shared their treasures with me - the secrets of an intentional, impactful, balanced, fulfilling, and joyous life. I call it Effective Living. To each of them, living or deceased, with love, honor, and admiration, I dedicate this book and its impact to the richness of their legacy.

To my dearly beloved mother, Eunice Miller - I say Thank You! Thank you for supporting me and speaking life over me. Your words particularly during our Sunday morning talks have become a major inspiration in my life. Before leaving for Texas nearly 20 years ago you told me wherever I planted myself, I would succeed and prosper. Mom, you were right.

To Apostle Raymond & Olivia Wells (Living Waters Kingdom Ministries), Pastor Danny & Norma Wegman, and Pastor Kelly James (Pathway of Life Church), Bishop Michael Pitts (Cornerstone Global Network), Pastor Jeffrey Smith (Strong Tower Ministries) The Late Bishop Dean Wells, Sr. & Mary Wells (Pentecostal Church of Faith in God), my brother Taurus King, Evangelist Sylvia Turner,

Pastor Bradick Cleare, Dominick Antonino, Franco Charles, and Pastor Mario Ramos.

Thank you for helping this young man from The Bahamas see his potential inside and for your encouragement to maximize every opportunity. You inspired me to live a most intentional, impactful, effective life, and for that, I am eternally grateful.

"Effective Living is doing what you want to do, when you want, where you want, with whom you want, and as much as you want. It is the harmonious balance of enthusiastically doing what you need to do with complete fulfillment of what you want to do."

~ Ricardo Miller

"You must never confuse faith that you will prevail in the end – which you can never afford to lose – with the discipline to confront the most brutal facts of your current reality, whatever they might be."

———————————

Admiral James Stockdale

Contents

Introduction
BE UNCOMMON; APPLY WHAT'S IN THIS BOOK!

This book is about to change your life forever! Take your time. Underline and highlight the things that stand out to you the most. The goal for this book is not for it to be limited to just another good read. Nor am I content with hearing how impressed you are with the content. On the contrary, the objectives are for you to have a reference from which your greatness can be stirred, for you to intentionally work on achieving and maintaining balance, and for you to live your best, most-fulfilled life.

My prayer and greatest hope is that the thoughts in this book stretch and challenge you in every area of your life. I want...No, I need you to be uncomfortable with some of the content, as this is what it is going to take to shift your way of thinking, living, and being. From the onset, I would like for you to understand and deeply believe you were born to win in every area of your life. Yet, you still must prepare to win! To experience the fulfilled, deeply satisfying and rich life you ultimately dream of, you are going to have to challenge yourself like you've never done before.

You're going to have to become very *intentional* about everything you do from this point on. If you want to win, advance and succeed in all that you put your hands to, this is the book for you. Effective Living is deliberate living. Choosing to accept the fact that you are the subtotal of the choices you make on a daily basis. Life comes alive for the person who discovers the truth that they can create the life they desire.

Everything changes for the better, for the person who understands that "life is ten percent what happens to you and ninety percent how you respond to it". So, decide now to read this book as many times as possible to capture all of the truths that are on these pages. **Take it from this Island boy, when I say "Everything that you desire is on the other side of your willingness to live the principles within this book."** The book of 3rd John chapter 2 (KJV) states, "Beloved I wish above all things that you prosper and be in good health even as your soul prospers." As we begin this new decade and I reflect on my childhood growing up here on the island of New Providence, I wish I had learned the importance of embracing the concept of becoming the person that I was created to be. It's very important for you to understand that who you are becoming is more important than what you are accumulating.

STOP! THINK! AND LISTEN TO THE SILENCE! Wherever you are, listening to the silence is an easy and direct way of becoming present. Even if there is noise, there is always some silence underneath lurking in between the sounds. Listening to the silence immediately creates stillness inside of you. Take a deep breath and in the stillness, as you read this book, identify the principles that can help you dramatically change your life for the better. Work on them daily. Hold yourself accountable for doing the work. Read the book, and then read again. Highlight what speaks to you the most. Write notes, grow and evolve. Use this short yet impactful read to lead you to an effective life.

I have always been one to "not let the world see me bleed." This projected a strength that I often tapped into, even when I was personally burdened, or wanted to hide from everything and everyone. One day, without asking too many questions, my insightful and loving mother said to me "Ricardo, be stronger than you look." She somehow knew that in the midst of the strength that I exuded, the grace with which I bore my cross, and execute my assignments, that I have to encompass an authentic strength. A strength that comes from one's inward parts.

This strength has to stare back at me when I look at the man in the mirror. It has to be there when life is exciting and I want to engage at the highest level, as well as when life challenges me and I am left with no option but to push beyond how I feel. This strength she spoke of is crucial when no one was introducing me, calling my name, or cheering for me. It has to be there beyond the personality and the persona of Ricardo Miller.

Effective Living is the lifestyle behind this strength. The harmonious balance between having enthusiasm for what I need to do, coupled with the fulfillment of doing what I want to do. It is nestled in the strength of who I am at my core. It manifests in my relentless commitment to being the highest and grandest expression of who God created me to be. This strength keeps me from settling for mediocrity and keeps me doing what many are not, so that I may become what so few do. I am a dreamer, a doer, a giver, a teacher, a student and a lifelong learner, a mover and a shaker. I lead an intentional and very impactful life and it's all because of this strength. I may seem strong, but know that I am stronger than I look, because I have chosen the path of living an effective life. You have that same strength; use it to create a life you do not need to take a vacation from. This life is one of happiness and gratitude in all things, impact and intentional living. NOTHING in the world will compare to you living effectively!

With Prayers for your BEST,

Coach Ricardo

Chapter One

THE BIG QUESTION

Have you popped the BIG question? No, not marriage, as I am certain that is the first thing that came to mind. There is an even bigger, more significant, and life-altering question. This question determines what you do, where you go, how far you go, and with whom you choose to go. Once asked, this question cannot be ignored until it is satisfied with an honest answer. In meticulous detail and with great eloquence you can write out the master plan for your life and then diligently work on it. But, you still won't get very far for too long without answering the big question.

What is this single question that impacts everything else? What is this question that will keep you up all night, or wake you up and get you going every morning? What is this burning question that demands an answer? Drum roll please...and the big question is... **"What is MY WHY?"** That simple question will be both the catalyst from where you start, and the momentum to keep you going. *Why* exceeds surface satisfaction of the most lavish material acquisitions, social acceptance of the highest order, and political correctness. Your why transcends the approval and limitations of others and challenges you to not accept any less of yourself than the grandest, and highest version of you.

An honest holistic answer to your why, will lend to you living an effective life. I repeat, honest and holistic! You may ask how important is it for the answer to be honest and holistic, or do I have to give a lot of time and consideration to this? The answer

1

is yes because so much is predicated on it. You see, while your and your *how* are based on any number of variables and can change, *your why* is a NON-NEGOTIABLE.

Growing up, I got into what seemed like every possible opportunity for mischief and misconduct. The product of a single-parent home, my mother worked tirelessly to ensure that my five siblings and I never went without life's necessities - food, clothes, shelter, and with very few extra spoils here and there. Life in The Bahamas yielded very limited governmental, civic, or religious group assistance; and when it was given, the impact was miniscule for our large family. This led my mother, a resilient and diligent woman to work multiple jobs to provide for her family. She was not about to wait around for a handout. Instead, she worked and worked, and worked some more.

Needless to say, with my mother working so much, an absent father, and no immediate positive role models, I became my family's nightmare. I skipped school most of my elementary age years, and though I attended school more during my high school years, I was completely disengaged and disconnected from the learning process.

As a teenager, I found myself in a gang and I thrived in it! I was becoming known throughout the island for street fighting, school violence, shoplifting, and drug dealing. The most beautiful and smartest women found themselves attracted to me. I earned the respect and admiration of not only the members of my gang, but a deep fear from the members of rival gangs. The validation and support I needed was readily given. In fact, I lived for that. There was no designated leader in my gang. We all knew our role and held our own, but the strongest among us became the leader. I was among the strongest. It was then that I realized that I was an influencer.

I figured out that I could get people to do what I wanted them to do. Even more fascinating, I somehow impacted the way they saw themselves. If I thought you were a weak pup, I made you believe the same about yourself. On the other hand, if I thought you were a lion, I lead you to function in fearlessness, even if what you were doing was unethical or illegal. I was an innate leader and excelled in being among the head of the pack. I found real fulfillment and deep satisfaction in getting people to feel validated in what they were doing, and about who they had chosen to be. *My why* for choosing life in the gang would go on to have profound effects on the man I would later become.

"Personal growth is not a matter of learning new information but of unlearning old limits." – Alan Cohen

Riding on nothing short of God's grace, I made it out of the gang, not having served any time in prison, or worse, dying a premature gang-related death. Although far removed from the street life and being a gang member, being an influencer has never left me. In fact, the desire to bring out the strength and best in others intensified. As I started to see myself beyond who I was, I used my pain to inspire others. I focused on turning my life around completely. I helped others find their way out of the gang, and mentored young people so they wouldn't succumb to the destructive lifestyle I initially did. At that point *my why*, though the same was more positive and holistic, subsequently yielding a more fulfilling result. *My why* is helping people discover their purpose and maximize their potential with the ultimate goal of creating a life they don't need to take a vacation from; living life to the fullest.

I worked with scores of children, teens, and young adults, and watched as the thing in me sparked something in them, which furthered my resolve. It was big, it was bold, and it was bad. Really bad. But that good/bad dynamic up to that point had never made me feel more alive, so I committed my existence to this. Going on little-to-no guidelines, little physical rest, more street savvy than book-smarts, and limited resources, I watched as a generation was being redefined through me. I became unstoppable! Each hurdle, all of the negative chatter by those who thought I was a fluke or a fleeting pastime. Every roadblock and adversity, all limitations - whether self-imposed or brought on by others would end up in a head on collision with *my why.*

I cannot begin to tell you how many times I wanted to quit, due to fatigue or frustration. Sometimes, my excuses for quitting were not excuses at all, but very legitimate REASONS. Yet, *my why* would not let me. I lost many friends and young people to the streets, prison, or death. As a result, I reasoned that I was not making a significant enough impact, but *my why* would not let up. I went without, so others could have and even in that broken, deprived state, *my why* would not let me walk away.

Life will give you every reason to quit.
Your *why* gives you one good reason to NOT!

With quitting no longer an option, I tried slowing down. That seemed to work, but right before I got too complacent, or started losing momentum; *my why* gave me a nudge. Soon after establishing a rhythm and structuring my *what and how,* I began receiving local and national honors for my efforts. My work with

4

young people started in 1996 through my organization, Words at Work Children's Ministry. By 1998, the Ministry of Youth, Sports, and Culture recognized Words at Work as the Fastest Growing Youth Organization in The Bahamas. In 1999 I was selected for esteemed privilege to represent my community as a part of Youth in Parliament. That same year, the Ministry of Youth named me the Most Distinguished Youth Leader of the Year. And in 2000, I was again named to appear on behalf of my community at Youth in Parliament. Again, these provided more fuel for *my why*. The accolades were more than mere recognition for my pride. They affirmed the truth that I always knew - I was born to change the world. To be celebrated for doing so was not necessary, yet the affirmation felt really good.

In my early twenties, life and love transplanted me from all that I did and all that I knew in The Bahamas to Texas, in the United States. It is said that "Everything is BIG in Texas" and that proved true - including my apprehensions.

Soon, the novelty of exchanging my exciting and purposeful island life for big city living overtook me. I was trying to understand and submerge in this new culture, get acclimated with my new environment, and new role as a husband while experiencing what felt like *my why* gnawing at me. At first, it seemed like too much. Like I just needed to take a minute to wrap my mind around my new realities, but *my why* was moving faster than my reasoning and before long, in a new role, in a foreign country, I found myself right back at it. I served the children and young people at my church and on the days when I was not at work, I could be found through the aisle in the library at the University of Texas, devouring material related to purpose and the idea of becoming the best version of myself that I had been redefined by.

Your why will put a demand on you, requiring you to get better in every area of your life. Periodically, your why will stretch everything you hold dear, challenge every belief you have built on, and question everything you deem to be your truth. When this happens, the only suitable response is to become even more convicted, or persuaded by your why. Then, life will reward you with even more passion and vigor to execute your what and how. It is an ongoing, unending cycle.

The reason why you are burnt out and unfulfilled before reaching your goals or even after setting and crushing them, is because you do not have a clearly defined, honest, and holistic *why*. Have you ever questioned how someone who seemingly has it all could be so sad, broken, or empty? Have you ever felt like even with all of your wins, you are still unfulfilled?

Winning in life means very little if it is only to say you have won. Amassing wealth, for the sake of having more material things than you had growing up will leave a void in your life so big, that you could easily curse being wealthy. Getting that coveted position will leave you angry if you only went after it to prove you could get it. The clothes, cars, and home will be dreaded reminders of how you overcommitted yourself to working hard but missed out on the best years of your life with your spouse and children. Your why will keep you from these pitfalls and frustrations. For many, the answer to your why will not be found on a negative path like mine, or at least I hope not. But if that is where you find yourself as you hold this book, know without a shadow of a doubt - there is hope for living a fulfilled, balanced life.

Your why may not come as early, or late, as mine did. Maybe identifying your "why" never even occurred to you until you read this book. Wherever you find yourself right in this very moment of the day, of the year, or of your life, I pose the big question to you: WHAT IS YOUR WHY?

Stop! Take a moment to respond to that, and then write your answer on paper or in your electronic device. Keep it before you daily. Draw strength from it on the most challenging days. Reflect on it when nothing makes sense. Declare it out loud when life backs you in the corner of hopelessness. Chant it when negativity floods your thoughts. Live it in every moment and in every decision from this day forward.

RECAP & REFLECT

→ Know your WHY?

→ **What** you do and **how** you do it may change, but your **why** is a non-negotiable.

→ Life will give you many reasons to quit. Your why gives you one good reason to NOT!

→ Your why transcends the approval and limitations of others.

→ An honest, holistic answer to your why, will lend to you living an effective life.

→ Personal growth is not a matter of learning new information but of unlearning old limits.

MY THOUGHTS

_____

_____

_____

_____

_____

_____

_____

_____

_____

_____

_____

_____

_____

_____

Chapter Two

WHAT IS SUCCESS?

Ask several different people to define "Success" from Texas to California and you will find that many define success differently. How about internationally? Should you ask someone in The Bahamas or St. Kitts, Mexico or London, China or in Africa, you will perhaps receive just as many different answers. Everyone may have a personal definition of success, but only a few have really considered it in the light of its truest meaning. To an athlete, success may be setting a new record or winning a gold medal. Success to a surgeon might mean performing a heart transplant. A student may consider success the earning of a college degree. A missionary or an evangelist sees success in the winning of souls and the planting of new churches. The prominent businessman sees success as meeting or exceeding projected outcomes.

Success means different things to different people, but true success has only one definition – accomplishing an aim or purpose. It is establishing and maintaining the balance of faith, fitness, family, finances, and fun all with unlimited peace and satisfaction. By this definition, success is synonymous with effective living.

We see a lot of different examples and patterns of what people might perceive to be success. Yet, a more intimate look into the lifestyle of those who are successful, it reveals that there is still much to be desired. Over the years we have discovered that many are wealthy but unfulfilled. They are wealthy but clinically depressed, wealthy but stressed, wealthy but unhealthy, and the list goes on. I want to achieve success in every area of my life without anything missing, lacking, or broken. So, I ask the question, how do you achieve good success? Success is not good within itself. It is possible to be "successful" in different areas, yet still be empty and void of happiness.

As a young boy in Nassau, I saw several men in town who took great pride in cleaning their yard. One of these men was our neighbor Mr. Jacque. Whenever he cleaned his yard, Mr. Jacque had onlookers stop in awe of him. They admired his success at having his own house and a well-kept yard. Though quaint in size, Mr. Jacque took care of his yard as though it were a home behind the esteemed gated communities of New Providence. However, compared to America's standard of prosperity, the owning of a small house on the island was by no means a measure of success. Yet still, even compared to progressive countries around the world, success is not merely a manner of more money or material things.

If you think of these things only, you have a short-sighted view of success because having money doesn't make a person successful nor fulfilled. The late Howard Hughes had amassed more wealth than any American in history. Yet, before he died, he admitted that he was not happy. We must not fool ourselves into believing the accumulation of things is what makes us fulfilled or successful. Success is your faithful commitment to your spouse, your relentless dedication to your children; success is mastering your emotions, going after your goals and crushing them. Success is being able to take the trip of your dreams to countries with names you've only recently learned to pronounce. Success is maintaining a healthy and appealing body; success is waking up hungry and going to bed satisfied with the day and its accomplishments. Success is the determination and execution to not finish where you started.

Success Comes with a Price

All that I am today came at the price of my wins and lessons along the journey. With humility I went from being *the it guy* back home Nassau, Bahamas - to having to work at places like Dollar Tree, Domino's Pizza, and Pizza Hut, and cutting lawns because it was no longer just me that I had to take care of. I had a family that relied on me and I needed to show up for them, every day. Though the compensation was minimal, to say the least, it was what I learned and what was perfected in me at those jobs that proved to be the real jackpot. These invaluable principles, hard work and an unparalleled hustle, catapulted me to success that I continue to experience in so many areas of my life. Lean in as I share what success requires of all those who seek her.

Discipline

No one who is undisciplined in life can be successful. There are too many undisciplined individuals who desire to live a successful life; however they have not established the patterns required to achieve any significant level of success. If you are going to walk in the blessings of God, you are going to have to decide now that living a disciplined life is a criterion for reaching the life you desire. To be successful and live an effective life, you MUST BE DISCIPLINED!!!

My prayer is that as you continue to read this book that you will embrace the idea that God truly wants you blessed. He wants you to embrace the type of success that will lead you to effective living.

Being Ridiculed

If you are uncomfortable with people talking about you, criticizing you, or judging you, you are not ready to be successful. The truth is, successful people are talked about and scrutinized all the time. Being successful sometimes places your life under a microscope with every decision you make. Whether it's what you wore today, or where your children go to school, it's open season at any given time, and in any setting. If you pay close enough attention, you can hear the hissing and see the stares when you walk into a room. Ultimately, what others say or think of you is of less significance than what you say and think of yourself. Can you handle the pressure of being talked about in the beauty or barber shop, around the water cooler at the office, or openly on social media, and resist the need to counterattack or defend yourself?

Risk Looking and Sounding Crazy

One of the biggest risks that most people who claim to want success are not willing to take is looking and sounding crazy – whether to family, friends, or those who they perceive don't understand their vision. To a non-dreamer a dreamer will seem outlandish and far-fetched in their thinking. A non-dreamer may even encourage the dreamer to "get real" or "keep dreaming." On the journey to living a successful, effective life, be mindful of sharing your dreams with small thinkers and others who play life safe. To the person who never moved away from the neighborhood they grew up in, sharing your dream to move to a foreign country, or to launch a great business opportunity is outlandish. They will tell you every reason in the world why you should not. You want to do something no one in your family has ever attempted or did but didn't succeed at, and they seek to remind you of the family you were born into.

Guard your heart, your mind, and your dreams from small thinkers. You have more to lose by playing life safe. Take risks, dream big and don't be afraid if the wrong person gets wind of your dreams. The minute they attempt to speak negative limiting words about you or your dreams, shut them down!

Enjoying Life's Bounty – Sans Guilt

For a long time, I had no idea that I had the power to create the balanced, fulfilled life I wished for, and secretly craved. As with most of us, I found myself in the cyclical lifestyle of accepting an average life of going to church, reading the Bible only from a religious standpoint which seemed to only produce average results. Later on, I learned that it is possible to live life beyond that of the average.

I no longer feel guilty for wanting to have more, do more, and be more. A bountiful life is an effective life. It is from this place of unlimited bounty that I can both enjoy life as I should and use my time, talents, and treasures to enrich the lives of others. Do not allow society, religion, or your family – intimate, nor extended, to guilt you out of the life you desire. When what you do to create the life you don't need to take a vacation from is not illegal or immoral, there is no limit to the fulfillment you will feel as you see who you become.

RECAP AND REFLECT

→ The accumulation of things is not what makes us fulfilled or successful.

→ Success comes with a price.

→ No one who is undisciplined in life can be successful.

→ If you are uncomfortable with, or afraid of people talking about you, criticizing you, or judging you, you are not ready to be successful.

→ A bountiful life is an effective life.

→ Define what Success is for you.

MY THOUGHTS

_____

_____

_____

_____

_____

_____

_____

_____

_____

_____

_____

_____

_____

_____

Chapter Three
THE BALANCED LIFE

"If you don't make the time to work on creating the life you want, you're eventually going to be forced to spend a LOT of time dealing with a life you don't want." - Kevin Ngo

This idea of "creating your life" does not readily go over well with those who believe that a higher being or power is solely responsible for the life we live, and that ultimately we are not calling the shots and making the plays in the "game of life". Now even though I am a God-fearing man, my faith leads me to believe that we are free moral agents who, *along with* God, are co-creating the life we live. That means, through each decision, each action, and each day, we have the power to create the life we wish to have.

"I am creating a life that I don't need to take a vacation from!" - Ricardo Miller

I coined this quote, making it my company's slogan and one of my life's governing declarations when I realized that I had the power to first conceptualize, and then actualize the life of my dreams. Early in my young adult life I knew that God would use me to impact hundreds of thousands of lives globally. Though originally from a small archipelagic nation, there was always an unwavering surety that my reach would be felt worldwide. That was without question. Thankfully I was wise enough to also know that if the impact of my life was going to be significant, a great amount of diligence and intentionality would have to be invested. Realizing this, I got to work with doing what I needed to do. I learned, and then taught. I received, and readily gave. I served. I acquired. I flourished. It was as though the more I worked for what I wanted, the more it would manifest, and the more I would desire to become more.

You may feel like your life is stuck between a rock and a hard place and all of your efforts, as much as they are, just don't amount to much. With all of your possessions and acquisitions, whether materialistic or academic, you may still feel unfulfilled. To have the home, career, bank account or family of your dreams, yet still left feeling unfulfilled and unhappy at your core is an indictment on the one shot at life that you've been given. On the flipside, it is also an indictment to stop putting off pursuing your dream career because of fear of finances. Maybe you're scared to launch your business because the economy in your city is in a sluggish place. Maybe you've put off seeing the world because you're waiting for a dream spouse to join you. Maybe you've given so much of your time to another person's vision or business that you only have scraps of time left to commit to your own. You have to establish the medium between who you seek to be and what it takes to become that.

Dale Partridge said "Stop creating a life that you need a vacation from. Instead, move to where you want to live, do what you want to do, start what you want to start, and create the life you want today. This isn't a rehearsal people. This is YOUR life."

We only have one opportunity to get it right. This means we cannot continue to spend our days stuck. Days are expensive and time is passing us by.

Be Passion Driven

Throughout your life, you may have many passions, but your passion is singular. It is what you are deeply interested in doing. You find that it's that thing, or those things that you are good at and that comes naturally to you. Often your passion is the thing that you make your living doing. It leaves you enthusiastic and craving it. It is an inward impact. If you are blessed, your passion will align directly with your purpose. It is common for your passion to lead you right to the path of your purpose. Remember, a balanced life allows time for what you are passionate about.

Be Purpose Driven

Your purpose is the thing that you were put on earth to do. It is the act of accomplishing God's vision for your life. Often arising out of a struggle that you've overcome, or are in the process of overcoming, your purpose is used to help others through sharing your journey. Your purpose yields an outward reward. It is the thing that you do with such enthusiasm and conviction that you would do it even if you were not getting paid for it. Purposeful, balanced living will give you the strongest desire to keep moving forward, even on your most challenging days.

Family

If you want to change the world, go home and love your family. It is so easy to take those closest to us for granted. We put off family time for work responsibilities, social obligations, and even legitimate reasons like fatigue. If you don't make time, you will never have time. Creating and maintaining a balanced life means prioritizing the things that are important. Nothing is more important than family. When I realized and incorporated this truth, I moved from hoping for time with my family to intentionally creating time for them. I would fly in from an international engagement and take my wife out to dinner or spend time with my son. Life offers a lot, but nothing compares to family.

Social

Life can be extremely demanding pulling us from work, to home, to school and then back again. It is an absolute necessity to be intentional about making time to bond with family and friends through social time together. Bonds are fortified and relationships strengthened when you connect over game night, movie night, a day at the beach or park, a weekend trip, or an evening out on the town.

Finances

The Bible says that money answers all things. There is no greater quality of life to be lived or greater impact to be made without a substantial amount of money. As with everything else in life, when you honor money, it will honor you. You will find your money going further when you are honorable to those you owe. I subscribe to the principle of tithing and have seen the returns thereof. Before doing anything else, I recommend you set aside and give a 10% offering from your earnings as your tithe. That is the money that will be used to bless others. The Law of

Reciprocity says that money may leave your hand, but it doesn't leave your life as it will come back to you.

I've made it a habit of paying my bills out as they come in, but another great option is to have them automated. Either way, taking care of your financial responsibilities may leave little for splurging. It will also help you avoid the headache of being overwhelmed by bills. The next thing I suggest if you haven't already, is to always set some aside for savings. No matter the amount, saving even a small amount of money over a long period of time is advantageous. Then finally, spend a little on yourself! It could be a special meal, or a movie outing, either way, be sure to treat yourself.

Spiritual

I won't attempt to tell you whom to worship or revere. But I will boldly declare that having a relationship with Jesus Christ and maintaining a healthy spiritual life adds incomparable value to my life. Making time to pray, reading and meditating on the word of God cannot be matched to any other experience. I feel stronger and more focused after spending time developing my spiritual muscles. Like all muscles, the more work you put into it, the stronger you will become. Whether first thing in the morning, throughout the day, or last thing in the evening make time to cultivate your spiritual life. The unique and special relationship with the Divine is so vital to your overall wellbeing.

Professional

Maintaining a healthy desire to professionally keep growing and developing yourself keeps what you do from becoming mundane and unfulfilling. Find a course that offers a certification, seek out insight on the requirements for promotions, and get further training and development. Find joy in your work, and if you don't, seek out something that will leave you fulfilled about what you do. You are much better off in a fulfilling job that pays you less, than one that pays you well but is unsatisfying. I understand the financial implications, but what is more important than your joy and your peace of mind? Give wholeheartedly to your work but know when to shut it down. Don't make it a habit of taking work home or working incredibly long hours that end up taking away from other valuable areas of your life.

Community

Make time to serve mankind. Volunteering at a soup kitchen or with your local boys or girls club, library, church, or YMCA is one of the absolute best things you can do for yourself. While those you serve will benefit, the true blessing of servitude is bestowed on the one giving of themselves to serve others. Belonging to an extended community gives you such a rich and gratifying appreciation for life. The lives you impact, whether children or adults, are forever attached to yours. It is a priceless experience. Whether weekly, or monthly, make time to add value to your life by adding value to the lives of others.

RECAP & REFLECT

→ Create a life that you don't need to take a vacation from.

→ Days are expensive and time is passing us by.

→ Your passion is the thing that you make your living doing. It leaves you enthusiastic and craving more.

→ Purposeful, balanced living will give you the strongest desire to keep moving forward, even on your most challenging days.

→ Life offers a lot but nothing compares to family.

→ When you honor money, it will honor you.

→ Whether first thing in the morning, throughout the day, or last thing in the evening, make time to cultivate your spiritual life.

→ You are better off on a fulfilling job that pays you less, than one that pays you well but is unsatisfying.

→ Make time to serve mankind.

MY THOUGHTS

Chapter four
BELIEVE IN YOURSELF

Say this out loud, **"I am not an accident. I am hand-crafted by God and His hand of purpose is upon my life. I am a mover, a shaker, and a world-changer. I am here to live an intentional, fulfilling, balanced life."**

You have to believe you have the right and the ability to be all God created you to be. You have to believe in the power of God living in you. Whether you call it self-esteem, confidence, or self-assurance, it is a deep seated belief that you have what it takes; the inner fortitude, resources, talents and skills to become successful and blessed in all you do.

Battlefield of the Mind

In the fight of your life to live a successful and effective life, the greatest battle you will face is not the one against the doubters, or your family's history, or even others in the same lane as yours. Rather, you will find that your greatest battle will be in your mind. Your mind is a battlefield. The battle in the mind is where life's most critical battles are won or lost. On one side there is the current "limited-thinking" you that's fighting to stay safe and comfortable, and on the other side is the fearless dreamer fighting to emerge. It is a common occurrence to hear from people who have now obtained an effective life, share stories on how they could have accomplished so much more had they gotten out of their own way sooner. Let us learn from their stories sooner than later. Listen to me when I say this. Don't be afraid to go to war with yourself. A lot is at stake! Declare war on your limiting way of thinking, living, and being.

Believing in Yourself is a Choice

Believing in yourself is a choice just like anything else. It is a mindset you develop over time and with experience. Although it helps if you have positive, supportive people around you, the fact is, most of us are surrounded by average people who feed us the same limiting beliefs and negative conditioning they themselves have and subsequently project onto others.

In my early days of ministry, while I knew I was called to impact lives, my self-confidence was very limited. I had a great desire to do God's will and those around me could see it as well. But my limited education kept me from taking authority and being fully confident in my potential. At the beginning, many times when I stood behind the lectern, I would sweat profusely and become a nervous wreck. I'd hold the microphone chest high and speak in a timid voice. One day I said, "This is enough. I will no longer allow fear to be my dictator." I joined a Toastmasters Club to practice and refine my speaking ability. I enrolled in night school and began teaching myself the things I needed to learn in school. It was tough, but my will was strong and my belief in what God purposed me to do matched it. I couldn't allow myself to get in the way of fulfilling my own destiny.

The past is the past. There is no payoff for blaming previous circumstances for your current level of self-confidence. It is now your responsibility to take charge of your own self-perceptions

and beliefs. You must choose to believe t
you set your mind to. You can do all thin
you strength, wisdom, understanding,

Combined with training, coachir
can learn to do almost anything. I
most gifted, nor talented in anything
anything was possible through Christ. ι ɔ.

material and messages. I worked harder than others and that yo
me to where I am. If a boy from Soldier Road, Nassau, Bahamas
who lived the life of a gang-banger and robber, having only
received an attendance certificate from High School can do
it, then you can to! If this same boy, after giving his life to Christ,
could be used to help thousands do all of the amazing things
that I've been privileged to do, then you too can accomplish
anything if you will simply believe it is possible.

You Have to Give Up "I Can't"

If you are going to live an effective life you will have to give
up the phrase "I can't" and all of its relatives. The phrase "I can't"
actually disempowers you and makes you weaker every time you
say it. There is a technique called kinesiology that tests people's
muscle strength as they say different phrases. For instance, put
your left arm out to the side and have someone push down on
it to see what your normal strength is. Then, pick something you
think you can't do such as "I can't play basketball" and say it out
loud. Then have the person push down on your arm again. It will
always be weaker. However, when you say aloud "I can do it,"
Your arm will always be stronger. Your brain is designed to solve

and reach any goal that you give it. The words you say actually do affect your body.

see this in small children. When you were a small child, e was no stopping you. You thought you could climb on anything. No barrier was too big for you to attempt to overcome. But little by little, your sense of invincibility is conditioned by the limiting beliefs your family, friends, teachers and others put upon you. Albeit some of those things are precautionary to help you know how to set proper boundaries. However, if a person is conditioned to believe that you should be afraid of flying in an airplane and they are constantly sharing that belief with you as a child, you are more likely to develop a fear of flying as well. You must take responsibility for removing "I can't" from your vocabulary. Write down every "I can't" that you can think of and throw them away. Step out on faith and do the impossible. Just like the child that says "I can't" learn how to ride my bike, eventually learns that this is a lie and becomes the next Lance Armstrong to win the Tour de France, you can get rid of any limiting belief hindering you from living an effective life. But you have to believe in yourself. If no one else does, you have to believe. It is a critical ingredient to living your best life.

Take the Limits Off

You cannot be afraid to go where you, your family, your countrymen, or even your mentors and those who inspire you have never gone before. In a world where so many are accomplishing remarkable things, you have to ask yourself, "Why not me?" Why shouldn't big things happen for you? Why can't you be the first to do something great? Why can't you achieve and maintain a highly successful and effective lifestyle? Whatever the limitations you have placed on yourself, I challenge you, no I DARE YOU to shake them loose! Whatever your age, gender, ethnicity, nationality, religion, education, family history, economic status, or social position in life, refuse to be hindered or stopped. The only thing that is truly holding you back is you. The only reason why you are not successful is you. You are the only thing standing between you are and where you want to be.

RECAP AND REFLECT

→ You have to believe you have the right and the ability to be all God created you to be.

→ Your greatest battle will be in your mind.

→ Believing in yourself is a choice.

→ Write down every "I can't" that you can think of that you have and throw them away.

→ You are the only thing standing between where you are and where you want to be.

MY THOUGHTS

_____

_____

_____

_____

_____

_____

_____

_____

_____

_____

_____

_____

_____

_____

_____

_____

Chapter five

THE CRIPPLING EFFECT OF EXCUSES

"Ninety-nine percent of all failures come from people who have a habit of making excuses." – George Washington Carver

By design, no matter where we find ourselves in any given time or season of our lives, no matter our status, there is an innate desire to be, do, and have more. Many of us have dreams, desires, and goals. So why aren't we seeing more of what we desire? Why aren't we having the experiences we yearn to? Can I tell you, more often than not, that the excuses you make are absolutely the only things stopping you. You see, a made-up mind cannot be stopped. A determined heart is unstoppable. At the core of every excuse is the good and pure intention of keeping you safe. We've heard these excuses from some of our friends and relatives. Some of them goes as follows…"Now is not the best time to start a business, and with the overwhelming increase in human trafficking it's just too dangerous, or traveling to a foreign country to serve children isn't the best idea," and the list goes on. The fault does not just lie on friends and relatives. Here are some common excuses we tell ourselves.

- The timing is not right
- This may not work out
- I am from a challenged or disadvantaged background
- I am too short/tall/old/young
- I am shy

- I am not good enough
- I am scared
- Others won't like me
- Others won't support me
- Things won't work out
- I was born in the wrong gender/nationality/race/family

The truth is, whether imposed by self or others, excuses will always be presented to you. But what is also true is that you, and only you, have the power to accept or reject them. The choice is yours. When you seek excuses and justification for your inaction, or affirmation for your poor choices, you will always be given one. In an attempt to protect your ego and validate your limiting, or negative beliefs, your untrained nature uncovers ways to describe how you have been victimized, why you cannot, have not, or did not. This negative practice sabotages your will, your drive, your productivity and stifles your truest and highest potential. When an individual can live and operate above excuses, they are well on their way to living the abundant and effective life.

Have you ever heard someone give a "reason" for why they've not attained or seen the success they would have liked to have seen in life? Well, the answer is simple. You have to give up all your excuses. You have to take the position that you've always had the power to make it different, to get it right, and to produce the desired results. For whatever reason, whether ignorance, lack of self-awareness, fear, needing to be right, the need to feel safe – you are the one who chooses not to exercise that power. Your why behind your choice not to act doesn't matter. The past is the past. All that matters now is that you choose to be 100% responsible for your actions from this moment forward. Whatever happens or does not happen is determined by you. Yes, that's right, it's a choice. You can choose to take responsibility and that is the first step to relinquishing excuses completely. If something does not turn out the way you planned, ask yourself these 7 questions:

1. What did I do to create this result?
2. What was my frame of thought?
3. What did I believe about the situation at that time?
4. What did I say or not say that made a difference?
5. What did I do or not do to create this?
6. What did I do to get the other person to respond that way?
7. What do I need to do next time to get the desired result I want?

I once heard someone give a very simple formula about taking responsibility and getting rid of excuses. The gist of the idea is that every outcome you experience in life (whether it is success or failure, wealth or poverty, health or illness, joy or frustration) is the result of how you have responded to an earlier event or series of events in your life. So, one must ask themselves, "Do I like the outcome I am currently getting?" Whatever your answer to that question is, you have two basic choices to make. You can either take responsibility or play the blame game. You can choose to blame all the outside forces like the economy, weather, lack of money, education, racism, gender bias, ageism, your wife, your husband, your boss, the lack of support, the church, the Pastor, and so on. If you are a Christian you've probably even blamed God, or the devil. No doubt all of these factors do exist, but if any one of them were the only deciding factor, nobody would ever succeed. Billy Graham would have never become a world-wide evangelist, William J. Seymour would have never lead the Azusa Street Revival, Jackie Robinson would have never played major league baseball, Michael Jordan would have never won 6 championships, Bill Gates would have never founded Microsoft, Steve Jobs would have never started Apple computers.

For every reason and circumstance in which we say it is not possible, there are hundreds of people who have faced similar circumstances and succeeded. If this is the case, then your preconceived notions of why you can't do something aren't actually the limiting factors that keep you from achieving your goals and vision. It's not the external conditions and forces that stop you. It's you! We stop ourselves. We think limiting thoughts and engage in self-defeating actions and behaviors. We even go so far as to defend our own self-destructive habits. We ignore useful feedback. We fail to continuously educate ourselves and learn ways to improve. We waste time on unproductive activities, engage in idle gossip, and eat unhealthy food. We spend more money than we make. We fail to exercise and prepare for the future. We fail to tell the truth and avoid unnecessary conflict. We don't ask for what we want and then wonder why our life is not as effective as we imagined it would be; and then we sit and wonder why we're not living our best life.

But this, by the way, is what most people do. They place the blame for everything they can't do on outside forces. At the end of the day, there's an excuse for everything. But you have the power to overcome excuses. By simply shifting your perspective and actions you can put excuses to rest. The only thing you really have control over in this life is yourself. So, it is best to make the necessary changes within and everything else around you will begin to take form.

As I began to take inventory of my life, I noticed that I still had some habits and behaviors that were reflective of my formal life. While they were not completely detrimental, I realized that I wanted something different; I wanted a different result from what I was seeing. I wanted more. Unfortunately, most of us are so driven by our habits that we never change our behavior. We get stuck in our conditioned responses to our spouses, our children, those we interact with, or those we lead. We are a bundle of conditioned reflexes that get into the groove of the "same 'ole, same 'ole". But you have to decide to regain control of your thoughts if you are going to live an effective life. Your imagination and creativity, your dreams and your actions all have to line up with the highest and greatest truth. Everything you think, say, and do needs to become intentionally aligned with your purpose, your values and your goals. Upon doing this, you will most definitely be positioning yourself to live your best life. It's possible, you can do it. Don't you dare make another excuse! The more you make excuses, the easier it will become to make more excuses. Don't believe me? Think about it, the more you do something, the better you get at it. This is the truth of repetition. The same is true for excuses. Overcoming one excuse makes it easier to overcome another one. So, do you want to overcome the excuses that limit you from living an abundant, fulfilled, effective life? Work on execution! That's it. EXECUTE.

RECAP AND REFLECT

→ At the core of every excuse, is the good and pure intention of keeping you safe.

→ Whether imposed by self or others, excuses will always be presented to you.

→ In an attempt to protect your ego and validate your limiting, or negative beliefs, your untrained nature uncovers ways to describe how you have been victimized, why you can not, have not, or did not.

→ Choose to change your response to what happens, or the way things are – until you get the outcomes you want.

→ Everything you think, say and do, needs to become intentional and aligned with your purpose, your values and your goals.

MY THOUGHTS

_____

_____

_____

_____

_____

_____

_____

_____

_____

_____

_____

_____

_____

Chapter Six

MASTERING TIME

Time management is one of the major components to effective living. Time is both a gift and currency; a slave and a master. The very essence of life is predicated upon what we do with the time we are given. Have you ever wondered how someone living an ultra-productive, effective life, manages to get it all done; where do they find the time to do and be all things? They are given the same 24hours yet are able to get more done before lunch than you do in an entire day. At the end of the day, you will give yourself and your time to whatever you highly value. If you don't seem to have enough time, it is because you have not made enough time. The tasks, or habits, though important and valuable to you, are just not a priority. It is human nature for people to make time for the people and things that mean the most to them. Furthermore, whatever you honor is what you will be drawn to. This is true of time. If you honor time by managing it properly, you will be given more time.

Tips for managing your time effectively

Plan your days in advance – Get a jumpstart on your day by planning days, or at a minimum, the day before. This allows you to give clear thought and consideration to what needs to be done and how best to get it executed. Become organized. Being organized, helps with efficiency and productivity. Organizing your living and working spaces, your purse, your files, and your car means you do not lose time trying to find things because what you need is already in its place. Subsequently, you become less stressed and irate and much easier to live and work with.

Automate tasks – The use of systems and technologies to reduce or eliminate the amount of human engagement needed to complete a task or process greatly helps in managing time effectively. Where related to your home, work, family, or personal life, automate small but necessary tasks so that you are readily available to work on larger, more detailed ones.

Use 'don't disturb on your phone' – One phone call can take you completely off course, throwing the things you need to get done out of the window. Social media notifications can do the same. Have you ever gotten a ping to your phone, you open it, and two hours of aimless scrolling went by before realizing it? When seeking to get the most out of your day, both small chit-chat with family and friends, as well as social media notifications can wait.

Do important work only – with a prioritized list of what needs to get done, activities/tasks of higher value can be focused on more specifically. Activities/tasks of lower importance can either be looked at later when the highly important work is done, or either delegated to someone else.

Create and stick to a routine – Routines create repetition. Repetition creates ease.

Ease enhances productivity. Productivity lends to proper time management, and proper time management helps to create an efficient effective lifestyle.

Work in blocks – Do not try to take on everything all at once. Pair activities and tasks together based off of what is needed to complete each task. Get a block done, then take a short break to stretch, eat or drink some water before starting another block. When working in blocks, avoid multi-tasking. (Examples: Set a specific time of day to answer emails. Handle one piece of paper one time – if you pick it up, deal with it.)

End procrastinating – "Procrastination is the thief of time." This poor practice robs you of time you will never get back. Do not put off for tomorrow what you can do today or put off for later what can be done right now. Both later today and tomorrow will have its own share of things to get done that requires your time and attention.

Daily Recap – At the end of each day, go over the day. Celebrate all that you have accomplished. Look at the areas where you may have missed the mark and determine what you can do differently or better tomorrow. Then do it.

Time is your most precious commodity

Time wasted is time you will never have again. Your time is more valuable than money. This invaluable lesson became a governing principle for my coaching client Rachel. When she was dating her "now" husband, who at the time lived in a different state, she would always look for fun things for them to do together during her short, but much anticipated visits. Rachel decided to introduce Max to the card game "Uno," a favorite pastime of hers. In the days leading up to her visit she kept talking about it. With each conversation, the excitement for enjoying this game grew. One day while at the mall, Rachel saw the cards. She felt the rush of joy come over her as she reached for deck. However, she stopped and looked at the price and thought the sticker read for a little more than what she would normally pay in comparison to the price at her local superstore (two dollars more to be exact), so Rachel decided to wait. Excited to see Max, she flew out to Atlanta.

Unfortunately, within hours of her arrival, she spent the majority of her time shopping around for Uno cards to no avail and wasted precious time with Max. What's worse, during her persistent pursuit over something as minuet as Uno cards, a loose cart ended up banging into Max's vehicle leaving a significant dent in his bumper. Needless to say, both Max and Rachel ended up quite irritated and what was supposed to be precious time spent together turned into a day of frustration for both of them! This simple example speaks to each of us in so many areas of our lives whether we want to believe it or not. Just in case you thought you would have never wasted the time Rachel did, let's look at the ways we do waste this precious commodity we call time.

Common Time Wasters to Avoid

Social Media – In a day and age where everyone is seeking relevance and attention, social media and reality has captivated the world who seems overly obsessed with keeping up with the lives of others.

Too Much TV – I do not have a television in my home. It's not that I do not like the occasional crime shows, a good documentary, or shows like The Profit, and Shark Tank, just to name a few, but my time does not allow for a lifestyle of commitment to anything that does not serve me in my pursuit for growth in some facet of my life. The average person has multiple televisions throughout their home and engages in a lot of screen time. It has been reported in the US alone, an estimated 119.9 million households that consumed television in 2018-2019. According to a Nielsen report, United States adults are watching five hours and four minutes of television per day on average. That's 35.5 hours per week and slightly more than 77 days per year. Needless to say, that is a lot of TV watching.

In speaking to The Late Dr. Myles Munroe about legacy, he shared with me something his mother told him. "People who spend a lot of time watching TV will never be on TV." WOW! That solidified my position living in a home with no TV. Though being on TV was not an obsessive thought or an overwhelming desire, what Dr. Myles shared with me that day never left me. It sustained me when I craved exchanging precious time for a binge watch of my favorite shows. Dr. Monroe reminded me that I couldn't just focus only on the idea of who I wanted to be, but that I needed to commit to the work of becoming.

Planning – Yes, even planning can be a major time waster. You have read enough books to get you on your way. You have listened to enough people on how they got started. You have done your research. You have attended so many conferences and have heard so many motivational talks that you're busting at the seams! You do not need to take another screenshot for inspiration. Planning in these instances can be such a time waster. Your moment is now. Stop planning to do it and just do it!

Not Maximizing Moments
*"A man must be a master of his hours
and days, not their servant."*
- William Fredrick Book

Making the most of every moment requires special attention to your intentions. It takes a deliberate and intentional consideration to what you do with the minutes, hours, days, weeks, months, and years, that you are given. This can be easier said than done, but with consistent application, healthy habits and a subsequent lifestyle it can be formed.

Neglecting to Seize Opportunities – Success occurs when preparation meets opportunity. If you are going to live the life of your dreams; the life that you don't need to take a vacation from, you are going to have to be able to identify when to close in on an opportunity. The truth is, good opportunities seldom come by, and great opportunities can be a once in a lifetime deal. The time spent thinking, talking, and wondering about an opportunity needs to be given over to actually seizing it. Maximizing opportunities eliminates repeated cycles, subsequently saving time.

MINDLESSLY Driving/Sitting in Traffic or Standing in Line – With an hour- long commute to and from work, I am intentional about making the best use of that time to indulge in activities that lend tackling the important tasks on my to-do list. I tend to not listen to music. Sure, that can be enjoyable, but instead, I use my drive for critical thinking, praying, making declarations over my day, an upcoming event/project, coaching clients, or listening to an audio book. As a result, I position myself to meet goals before I've even reached the office.

RECAP AND REFLECT

→ Time management is one of the major components to effective living.

→ Time is both a gift and currency; a slave and a master.

→ If you honor time by managing it properly, you will be 'given' more time.

→ Time is your most precious commodity. It is more valuable than money.

→ Avoid common time wasters at all cost.

→ Be intentional about making the most of your days, hours, and minutes.

MY THOUGHTS

_____

_____

_____

_____

_____

_____

_____

_____

_____

_____

_____

_____

_____

_____

Chapter Seven

HEALTHY HABITS

PHYSICAL-MENTAL-EMOTIONAL

"Take care of your body, because when it expires, your time is up."
- Ricardo Miller

You only have one body. You can't turn it in for a newer or upgraded model when it stops functioning at its optimal level. I am committed to taking care of my body. The truth is few people consider the ramifications an unexpected toll on their health can have on their overall assignment and purpose. Life happens. However, some of this can be eliminated if you would simply take note and make adjustments in addressing the following eight keys of taking care of your health.

Know Your Risk Factors

Do you know your family's health history? Did your great-grandmother, grandmother, or mother have high blood pressure? Despite good eating habits, if you're not careful, you may eventually develop it as well. Has someone in your family had cancer? If you don't know, find out right away. Many illnesses are hereditary and it's best to know the devices that could work against you sooner than later. It is best to get ahead of them rather than having to play catch up and believe God for healing for something that would have otherwise been preventable. You can feel just fine now and still be carrying risk factors, like hypertension, that will cut your current life expectancy in half. Don't assume you are fine just because you feel fine. Step one is to see your doctor for a check of your blood pressure, blood sugar, and cholesterol. It is a requirement for any of the mentees that I have to get an annual physical. Besides, if you are not on top of your health, who will be? Know your risk factors.

Exercise

There's no substitute for a healthy exercise regimen. Whether at home, outdoors, or at the gym, calories burned or miles covered is always a plus. With your doctor's approval, get out there and do some form of exercise. Rarely do medical doctors say exercise or elevating your heart rate in some capacity is bad for you. Physical activity is a must to maintain your stamina. It will lower your cholesterol and promote healthy blood flow. Running, walking, tennis, swimming, biking - it doesn't matter. As long as you do an activity that raises your heart rate on a regular basis, you will be well on your way to achieving optimal health. Remember, when your body expires, your time is up. So, take care of it and exercise.

Watch What You Eat

There is no greater contradiction than a person who wants to live an effective life, but has a diet filled with oily, fattening foods. Good eating habits are a major contributor to maintaining great health. You can try loading up on vitamins, but truthfully, you are more likely to live longer if you just focus on eating a well-balanced diet in reasonable quantities. So, what's a reasonable quantity? If you are at a restaurant, try eating only half of the serving on your dinner plate. Most people are unaware that the portion size of a standard meal in a restaurant is a serving for two. You should never eat the entire meal, nor should you eat until you feel full. The human body doesn't recognize that it is full until 30 minutes after food consumption. Therefore, eating just shy of full is a great way to ensure you do not overindulge. In addition to maintaining a well-balanced diet, eating multiple nutritious small meals throughout the day, according to some studies, can actually boost your metabolism. More than short term diets, we should be giving thought and effort to long term lifestyle changes. This is effective living.

Adequate Rest

Getting the appropriate amount of uninterrupted sleep one needs to engage their REM patterns is of vital importance. REM sleep is your nervous system's way of restoring, healing and refueling your body. If you find yourself tired throughout the day, yawning continuously or feeling overly sluggish, you are likely not reaching REM sleep throughout the night. Take a short power nap or sit and rest. Chronic sleep deprivation and sluggishness problems should be reported to your health care provider. There could be something beyond your sleep patterns affecting your metabolism and you should investigate this area of your health.

Live in the Present

Feelings of regret or worry about a past event, or anxiety about an upcoming one are not only a waste of precious time, but it also adds stress to the body, which makes you more susceptible to disease. Be intentional. Intentional living is focusing your attention on the beauty and gifts this life is offering you. The next time you are tempted to worry, allow God's peace which surpasses all understanding to guard your heart and mind. When things feel difficult in the moment, it's okay to take a deep breath and try again. You don't have to have everything figured out. You just have to remind yourself how you've made it through before and how you'll make it through again. Do your best and be content. Be anxious for nothing and maintain a thankful heart and present mind.

Businessman, motivational speaker, and president of High Point University, Nido Qubein once said, "Your present circumstances don't determine where you can go; they merely determine where you start." In the same token, "What we achieve inwardly will change outer reality." – Plutarch.

Life changes. You lose love. You lose friends. You lose pieces of yourself that you never imagined would be gone. And then, without you even realizing it, those pieces come back. New love enters. Better friends come along. And a stronger, wiser you is starring back in the mirror.

Mental Exercise and Stimulation

A healthy physical body includes a sound and sharp mind. Keep challenging your mind to expand, grow, learn, experience, decipher, and explore. The person who wants to live an effective life must take advantage of every opportunity to stimulate his or her mind. For example, one mental exercise I do during my one-hour commute to work is "Automobile University," a term coined by late motivational speaker and author Zig Ziglar, referring to the time we use in our cars to increase our productivity. Layovers at airports or drives in the car can be put to good use by listening to podcasts, teachings, or empowerment CDs. Sure, music is great way to perk up any commute, but that should take up very little of your time when compared to the invaluable activity of developing your mind.

Find Some Quiet Time

Of course, too much of anything is not good. Balancing mental exercise with non-active activities and quiet time is equally important. Not only is quiet time simple and fun, it also has been known to reduce your heart rate and stress level. It can also help keep you present in the moment, increase your feelings of peace, serenity, joy, and faith. It is a good habit to practice once per day to completely clear your mind. Get away from everything and for at least 30 minutes close your door and be in solitude. Trust me, this does the body good!

Surround Yourself with Positive People

Keep yourself surrounded with positive-minded, healthy people who are on your team. Your team will always consist of people who care for, support, love, respect, and appreciate you. It is said that your life is a reflection of the five people you spend the most time with; if you want to know where you are going examine the lives of those five people. If you don't like what you see, it may be time to change associations. Sometimes changing associations is not easy, especially if you're dealing with life-long friends, or even family. Separating from those closest to you, no matter how toxic, is a tall order but is also one that is not always necessary. In many instances, maintaining a healthy distance will serve in keeping their toxicity out of your life. However, if you find that limited distance is not enough, by all means, cut negative people out of your life completely. Once gone, let them stay gone. Letting a toxic person back into your life is like reopening a portal to hell. Don't do it. Some people are better left in your past no matter how bad you want them in your present.

The people you spend time with influence your attitude and thoughts more than you think. The positive people – family, friends, and mentors – I like to call them your tribe, will go a long way in serving you on the most challenging days. Your tribe will remind you of your greatness, they will challenge you when you are dormant, and they will remain receptive to how they can add value to your life. No one has ever succeeded alone. I believe and continue to experience the truth that someone is assigned to help me. The same is true for you. Someone is assigned to help you. You will not live an effective, impactful life without the help of others. Be receptive to the help around you while keeping toxic people at bay. Personal, more intimate relationships can sometimes breed the most toxic and negative situations you will ever find yourself in. Never settle for someone who keeps lying to you, hurting you, making excuses, disrespecting you, or treating you like a second class citizen. If you are not valued and honored in your personal relationships, love yourself enough to get out.

Your value is not predicated on what they can or cannot see. You are worthy and deserve so much more.

Laugh Loud. Laugh Often

Proverbs 17:22 (KJV) says, "A merry heart doeth good like medicine." I wholeheartedly believe this. When you share a healthy belly-laugh, it opens you up and releases tension. Besides, what is life without joy, happiness and laughter? Be intentional about laughing. Laugh out loud and often. Recent studies have shown that laughter, fun, and mirth help in keeping people healthy. Laughter has also been known to serve as a healing agent for sick bodies. Laughing or even anticipated laughter raises endorphin levels in the body. So, laugh long and laugh often. Everyone really is a unique, hilarious person. Look for the hilarity in every situation and keep laughing.

KEEP YOUR THOUGHTS POSITIVE

Watch your thoughts, for they become words.
Watch your words, for they become actions.
Watch your actions, for they become habits.
Watch your habits, for they become character.
Watch your character, for it becomes your destiny.
- Margaret Thatcher

This speaks clearly to the power of your thoughts and how they can chart the course for your life. What you see today is a direct result of what you thought yesterday. What you will see tomorrow is exactly what you're thinking today. There is no way to separate your thoughts from your destiny. I often tell my business and personal coaching clients; I can only help them to the degree to which they are willing to relinquish their limiting beliefs or thoughts that have gotten them to the unhealthy place they have found themselves in. Even the best of the best coaching or personal development program cannot break beyond the barriers of a negative thinker.

> **"I can't change the direction of the wind but I can adjust my sails to always reach my destination."**
> **- Jimmy Dean**

A positive person can look at any situation, no matter how dire and find something to rejoice and give thanks over. There's nothing like being in the company of a positive person. They can bring positive energy into any situation. They simply have a way of brightening the room and filling it with cheer. Always remember what you put out comes back. If you want to feel and be great, monitor your thoughts closely to ensure that you are thinking only positive, forwarding thoughts. If you catch yourself thinking a negative thought, simply turn it around into a positive one. Find a way to put a positive spin on that very thought. Seek the 'brighter side' of every presumably bad or negative thing.

> *"Casting down imaginations, and every high thing*
> *that exalts itself against the knowledge of God*
> *and bringing into captivity every thought to the*
> *obedience of Christ." (II Corinthians 10:5, KJV).*

This scripture admonishes us to do away with the toxic thoughts that contradict the truth of what God says about us.

Positive Self-Talk

In the Bible, the book of Genesis recounts how God said, "Let there be...," and there was. Imagine how all of creation was created by just a word. How fascinating! Our words carry the same immense power. We have the same superpower to create our desired outcome for our own lives. Coupled with our thoughts and positive self-talk, our words frame our entire world and have the power to determine the very outcome of our lives. The words "I AM" determine who we become, what we accomplish, how we show up in the world, and ultimately the legacy we leave when we exit. It's like a self-fulfilling prophecy. Whatever you say about yourself is what you will continue to see about yourself as you attract more and more of it. Rather than saying "I am broke," or "I cannot afford that," say "That is not a financial priority at this time." Instead of "I am unlovable," say "The right person will love me with ease." Stop saying, "My business is failing," and start saying "My business is growing because I am learning from my mistakes." In other words, speak what you seek, until what you see, is what you seek. Beyond what others think and say about you, it's what you say about you that becomes your truth. Many of you are not living the effective lives you desire because of the self-defeating things you are saying about yourself. "Michael is fortunate to be where he is," or "I was not raised in that kind of family so that could never happen to me." Okay. If you say so! Remember...

"Words have energy and power with the ability to help, to heal, to hinder, to hurt, to harm, to humiliate, and to humble."
– Yehuda Berg

Manage Your Emotions

Our emotions are our feelings or reactions to life's occurrences. These occurrences set off triggers that can range from light to extreme, having our emotions going one way or the other. Life by design, sends mountain and valley experiences. These experiences can take us from pure bliss to absolute mayhem, sometimes without warning. If we lived in a bubble alone, this would be easier to manage. Having to co-exist with others at home, work, school, church, the grocery store's checkout line, and the mall parking lot means we will be challenged on some days in ways we may not always want to deal with.

Have you ever determined, I mean completely purposed in your heart that "Today is going to be epic," only to go out into the world and the very first human you encounter makes you throw all of that feeling of splendor out the window? Effective living is both understanding and mastering your emotions, feelings, and reactions.

"Instead of worrying about what you cannot control, shift your energy to what you can create." - Roy T. Bennett

You are not at the mercy of your emotions, nor do you have to be governed by them. When your ability to live an exciting, fulfilled, and effective life lie in the state of your emotions, you will find yourself in and out of happiness, not having experienced true joy. This manifests in our lives as being very happy one moment, then completely angry or irrational the next. You may be having a great day, then we get a phone call from someone or see a subliminal social media post that completely enrages us. It's the going from what I like to call, the 0 to 100 Syndrome. Not dealing with negative emotions that surface in your life can result in unwanted ramifications in other areas. Unchecked emotional energy is stored somewhere. Science itself has proven that our emotional state can take a toll on our heath. So, learn to face your feelings in a way that's healthy. The worst thing you can do is stuff them away. My grandmother used to say, "Pressure bursts pipes." In other words, anything not dealt with and released improperly will only result in lasting damage. Living effectively is paying close attention to the people, places, things, and circumstances that invoke feelings of anger, resentment, sadness, brokenness, and hopelessness. It's addressing them internally, as well as externally. It is also ensuring that we are not stuck on the people, places, things, and occurrences that conjured up unhappiness.

Although true happiness is one of the derivatives of effective living, staying stuck on a specific circumstance keeps us out of the present moment.

It's important that when dealing with your emotions you learn to communicate well and clearly. Not in anger or in a disgruntled manner. One policy I have used is to never deal with a situation in the moment. Confrontation in the moment will usually lead to an emotionally charged response that you will regret later, often not yielding the desired results. Step away from the situation, clear your mind, gather your thoughts, and respond appropriately.

You may find that what you wanted to say at first was not the most effective way to handle the situation. It's important to not burn bridges by the way you negatively deal with your own emotions. I have seen many individuals, have an "I'll show them" attitude and completely cut off someone who they felt did them wrong. While I do not condone mistreatment of anyone, I am a firm believer that God will fight our battles and the wrong people do will only come back to bite them in the end. That is the law of reciprocity; a law that works irrespective of political, religious, gender, or socioeconomic status. By this point you may have noticed that I have talked extensively on the subject matter of managing your emotions. That was not by chance. It is because so many of you are not winning in your marriage, parenting, careers, businesses, health, and finances, because you have not mastered your own emotions. If you get nothing else from this chapter remember this... people cannot MAKE you angry, unhappy, or unfilled. Only YOU have that power. Where you go wrong is when you relinquish or surrender that power to others. The irritable parent, spouse, irrational boss, compulsive shopper, overeater, and substance abuser, all have the same problem at their core. They have not learned to master their emotions.

Work done on your physical, mental, and emotional well-being is an invaluable investment in you that others consequently will benefit from.

You will find that you are:

A better lover
A better friend
A better parent
A better earner
A better leaner
A better partner
A better listener
A better communicator
A better role model

RECAP AND REFLECT

→ Take care of your body, because when it expires, your time is up.

→ Know your family's health history.

→ Live in the present.

→ Time is your most precious commodity. It is more valuable than money.

→ You will not win in your marriage, parenting, career, business, health, joy or finances, if you do not master your own emotions.

→ People cannot MAKE you angry, unhappy, or unfilled; only YOU have that power. Don't relinquish that power to others.

MY THOUGHTS

Chapter Eight
THE BOOMERANG PRINCIPLE

Commonly known as karma, the Law of Reciprocity greatly supports the idea that what you get out of life is tied to your negative or positive thoughts, words, and actions towards others. Despite this law, many think nothing of highlighting and overtly discussing the inadequacies of others. Regardless of your belief system, this serves as a universal truth. There's not one thing you put out there that doesn't come back to you. Every act and intention is followed closely by an equal or greater reaction. Though it may not come back from the same person or in the same manner, be assured, that just as a boomerang is thrown out and returns, so will your actions and decisions come back on you. The good news is, this principle also works vice versa! The positive things you do will always return to you as well.

When you exude kind thoughts, give positive and encouraging words, or share in the act of kindness, it boomerangs right back to you. Whether in public or in private, shared with others, or within yourself, the energy of the boomerang is directly linked to the decisions we make on a daily basis. Life is an echo. You put out a sound, and that sound comes back to you magnified. In the same way, life is a seed, you plant it, and it comes back to you multiplied. All of life is an on-going cycle of giving and receiving, putting out, and drawing in. Furthermore, you have to ask yourself if what you see in others through your judgment lens, exists in you. Don't want to be scrutinized or critiqued? Simply don't do it to others.

Radiate and give love and love will come back. Constantly we are entering a new decade, a new year, a new month, a new day. I challenge you to an intense and intentional private introspection. This requires that you stop and consider what you are putting out? What do you think of others who aren't like you? How are you when others are winning? What comes to mind, or out of your mouth when you see others fail? How do you respond when others are at odds with you, whether justifiably so or not? Learn to always think and speak of others what you would want others to think and speak about you. Let love be the chief motivating factor in all that you do. If you do what is right, God WILL bless you and life will honor you. If you are honest towards others, life will reward you. You will see bountiful blessings boomerang to you. Genuinely be kind to others and watch as people go out of their way to be kind and favorable towards you. Sincerely work hard for others, and you are guaranteed to experience others relentlessly working for you.

If this strongly resonates with you, it could be that you are already doing the work of becoming better. If that is true, you may want to consider getting a coach to help you structure your behaviors to ensure that you are best positioning yourself to reap the positive return from your daily activities. But Ricardo you may say, I've been doing all of the right things with the right intentions for a very long time and still haven't seen the return. Why hasn't what I have thrown out come back to me yet? Think about that boomerang. Think about the skill and precision you must develop to hit your target and the process it will take to return with the same precision with which it was sent out. When you throw out a boomerang for the first time, it is highly unlikely that it will go anywhere, much less hit your target and return. Even with your best attempts, the first few times it may hit the ground. But that's when practice makes perfect. You continually have to work on the angle and the speed. You develop momentum, and before long, it becomes less about hitting the target and more about strengthening your throw. Day after day, you give a little attention to practicing, becoming consumed by how fascinating the entire process is. Then one day without plan or thought, you find yourself sending out the boomerang and it hits the target and comes back to you.

In 2003 when I relocated to Texas from The Bahamas, I sought to reestablish my organization and become a national voice in the United States. Wanting to convey my professionalism in a new environment, I wasted no time in having flyers, business cards, pamphlets, and customized t-shirts. I purchased a business phone. I immediately applied all of the appropriate principles I knew to get the word out about the work that I was doing. I was no stranger to this, as I had perfected it back home leading a very successful platform. Unfortunately, that gave me the hope and confidence that it would happen for me with relative ease in my new environment. First a few months went by, then that turned into a year, then two years. I was doing everything right but was not seeing the reward or the return on all of the effort that I was putting in. It felt like nothing was breaking. However, I did not quit.

Persistently applying strategic principles and practices, I continued to work on getting the word out and rebuilding my platform. I made the commitment to keep making phone calls, keep sending out the emails, and keep making the appointments on any and every lead I came across. Finally, I got a call from a gentleman who wanted more information on the services I had offered. He was interested in inviting me to be a presenter at a National Conference. All of the work that I had put in amassed in that one phone call, that one moment. That invitation shifted the momentum and things began to change for me.

Though it may take a while, remember, what you put out will always come back to you. But you must be persistent and relentless. After all these years later, I am still a believer that there are some things that just come natural to you. However, going to the next level demands unwavering diligence. Where most people go wrong is that even when they are doing all of the right things, applying the right principles, and giving their very best efforts, they stop just short of seeing it all pay off. They don't keep going, growing, and strategizing to ensure that all of their efforts and sacrifice yields a return in the form of tangible manifestations. The return will come but you have to be intentional and relentless about learning, adjusting, implementing, and evolving.

Remember, everything you put out there will come back to you. Every act and intention will be followed closely by an equal or greater reaction.

RECAP & REFLECT

→ Life is an echo. You put out a sound, and that sound comes back to you magnified.

→ Persistently apply the strategic principles and practices.

→ It may take a while, what you put out will always come back to you!

→ You have to be intentional and relentless about learning, adjusting, implementing, and evolving.

MY THOUGHTS

Chapter Nine

STUDY THE PAST

"Sometimes going back is the only way forward"
- Ketaki Sane

Going back in strength and with a soundness of mind is the only way for you to learn, heal, and evolve. As emotionally taxing as it almost always proves to be, revisiting the past is a healthy and holistic way of redirecting your present to a brighter and happier future. The past can no longer hurt, only heal. It can no longer break, only mend. The only power the past has over you is the power given to it—BY YOU. While the past does not have to determine or define your future, going back is crucial to the quality of your growth and your development.

Revisiting the Past of Others

Sometimes we are given the opportunity to hear another person's past so that it doesn't become our future. I spent many days on the streets of Soldier Road in Nassau, Bahamas with my fellow gang members. Nothing productive ever happened there but little did I know that one day I would have a life-altering visit to the past. I was 17 years old and ruthless. With just a few years in the gang, I was untouchable. My temper and patience were both short and my hands were big. It didn't take much for me to approach anyone and without cause plant a five-finger slap across their face.

People in the area knew not to cross me. One day while hanging out in the front of Sugar Kid Bowe's store, a guy from the streets, a former thug, now a worn out gangster who once held a reputation of being one of the lead guys in the gangs had approached us. He said "Hey, what's up? I was wondering if you guys could give me a dollar?" With a forceful voice and a face that was even stronger, I told him to leave before I took care of him. That was street talk for leave now or you'll wish you did. Walking away, he looked at me, his eyes locked into mine, piercing through to what felt like my soul and said, "Twenty-five years ago, I was you. I use to run these streets." For the next day, I couldn't shake his words or the conviction with which he said them. He was right, I pondered. He once was the guy who used to run the streets. Like a broken record, this played in my mind repeatedly.

This acknowledgement led me to realize that if I kept up in what I was doing, I would get what he got. I didn't want my future to look like his. I didn't want to be a product of the streets. I didn't want that for my life. I wanted more. To this day I believe that that encounter was a divine intervention. Whether it was or not, it was the catalyst from which I started to turn my life around. A visit to his past completely redirected my future and propelled me into a purposeful and impactful one. The national recognition, international organization, global reach, my unwavering walk with God, and my commitment to become my absolute best self, can in great part be attributed to that afternoon encounter.

Revisit Your Generation's Past

Attached to your generation are blessings and curses, habits and practices that have caused outcomes for you, oftentimes without your knowledge, or that you would have otherwise chosen differently. These things can be extremely dark, and unfathomably painful. However, it is important that you ask the right questions to get necessary answers.

"My people are destroyed for a lack of knowledge.
- Hosea 4:6, (KJV)

Your financial, relational, spiritual, and mental wellbeing are all a part of your family's past. It goes beyond a coincidence when your family does not get married, and if they do, they don't stay married. Before getting married yourself, try getting answers from within your family and encourage your expected spouse to do the same. Don't assume or remain in ignorance. Ask questions. Should you find the answers unbearable, seek professional help with addressing and overcoming them.

Revisit Your Past

The past cannot be changed, forgotten, edited, or erased; it can only be accepted. It is so easy to lose years being stuck in an unpleasant memory from the past. Without notice, this memory intrudes on your peace, and your joy. It robs you of the present and future, along with all beauty and potential that they both contain. Facing the past and accepting it, void of seeking to forget, edit, or erase it, only empowers you. There are times when the people, places, things, and experiences of your past seek to keep you there. There are times when despite your greatest effort, you cannot seem to pull yourself away from an experience. The very thought of its painful grip paralyzes you. To free yourself of this, you bury the experience with the hope that it never resurfaces. The truth is, it does resurface as all things undealt with do. It resurfaces in the way you view yourself and others. It resurfaces in your lack of confidence and faith. It resurfaces through your intimidation of the present and apprehension about the future. Until you freely allow the difficult experiences of the past to come to light and be thoroughly addressed, you will find yourself in a fight against yourself.

Sadly, this is a "lose-lose" situation. Forgive yourself for the poor decisions you may have made. You did what you did based on where you were at the time. But now you are committing yourself to live the effective life. You are no longer that person. Decipher the lesson, forgive yourself, and move forward in grace and healing. You are not defined, limited, nor disqualified by your past. Revisiting the past, whether somebody else's, or yours, holds powerful insights that can help you in your present and future. With boldness and fearlessness, seek the teaching moments gained from every experience. Going back in strength and with a soundness of mind is the only way for you to learn, heal, and evolve.

RECAP & REFLECT

→ Sometimes we are given the opportunity to hear another person's past so that it doesn't become our future.

→ The only power the past has over you is the power you give to it.

→ The past cannot be changed, forgotten, edited, or erased. It can only be accepted.

→ Until you freely allow the difficult experiences of the past to come to light and be thoroughly addressed, you will be in a fight against yourself.

→ You are not defined, limited, nor disqualified by your past.

MY THOUGHTS

Chapter Ten

THE PRINCIPLES OF PROGRESSION

Progression as defined by the Oxford Dictionary is "the process of developing or moving gradually towards a more advanced state." By now you have figured out effective living speaks to progression. For progression to be long-lasting and effective, there are some principles that must be adhered to. These principles are not bound, nor are they limited to a selected few. Rather, in concert with life, these principles will work for you if you work them, regardless of whom you are and where you are in your life. Progression is not a matter of knowledge only, but a matter of knowing and moving in unity with the abundant, impactful and effective life that can be yours when you do the work to attain and maintain it.

Progression Principle 1: *"Love thy neighbor as thyself."*
- *Luke 10:27 (KJV)*

Selfless acts of kindness and love towards others helps us to progress as the very acts stretch our heart, causing us to do more and be more. The incomparable joy we receive when we serve others from a pure place sends a rushing thrill of adrenaline to our heart. Loving others is like making a deposit into our own love bank. Without fail, when we need to make a withdrawal in our time of need, life will be there to offer the same. To "love thy neighbor" does not mean just to have a good inward feeling toward someone else. Love without service is not love at all, it's make-believe. The story told in the Bible of "The Good Samaritan" was not merely about a man who just happened to have a good inward feeling, but it spoke of a man so filled with compassion that he went out of his way to serve someone else. The account of this event can be found in Luke 10:30-37.

Progression Principle 2: *Pure motives*

Let your desire for success be driven by pure motives. Rid your heart and life of these contaminants:

- Greed or lust for power - This toxic laced desire causes men to over-extend themselves and end in failure.
- Fear of poverty - This driving force is behind many moderately successful men, but no man ever achieved the blessed life through fear of poverty.
- Pride - The desire to keep up with your neighbor. Operating out of this kind of pride is dangerous, mainly because it manifests itself into fear which leads to inefficiency.

Excessive love for work - Because of a person's ability to create and receive reward for their creativity, they can get so inflamed with ZEAL that their work becomes a great joy. Even though this can be a good thing, there is a danger in such a driving force if one is not careful. Such fervor can cause a man or woman to neglect their health and family. From the beginning of my Christian walk, I have been reminded by some great and incredible people who have been in my life about the critical importance of trying to pursue success from a balanced perspective. I can remember the late Bishop Dean Wells saying to me "Take care of your family. Always take care of your family."

It was Apostle George W. Jobe who from the first day he met me, encouraged me to make sure that I took care of all structure and legal aspects of our young and fast growing ministry.

Progression Principle 3: *Uplifting Others*

Uplifting others is a sure way to build both you and the receiver. Concentrate on uplifting at least one person each day. When this desire becomes an enduring passion for serving, you will be directed by God to do everything necessary to help others succeed; then, your success is eminent. Those who are passionately devoted to giving more and better service to people can ordinarily expect success. Such service and devotion is best motivated by an authentic love for people. This rule of progression should be applied by every individual wanting to live an impactful and effective life. It is a law that is in harmony with every law of God and man.

Progression Principle 4: *Be Solution Centered*

Identify a problem. End the blame. Take responsibility and accept the challenge of every situation, then move on to find and implement solutions. Be willing to learn from what doesn't work. Keep working on finding and applying solutions. This formula will guarantee more wins and a well-lived life. Remember the difference between being progressive and regressive.

- A progressive person explains. A regressive person explains away.
- A progressive person seeks to find a way. A regressive person says, "There is no way."

- A progressive person goes through the problem. A regressive person seeks to go around it.
- A progressive person says, "There should be a better way to do it." A regressive says, "That's the way it's always been done here."
- A progressive person shows he is sorry by changing his behavior. A regressive person says, "I'm sorry," but repeats the behavior.
- A progressive person works hard and has more time. A regressive person is always "too busy" to do what is necessary.
- A progressive person makes commitments and fulfills them. A regressive person makes promises and forgets them.

Recognize Your Greatness

You are capable of more than you know. More than you were born into, more than you have experienced, and are experiencing now. You have within you the capability to do and be so much more than you are now. Recognizing and actualizing your greatness is the awakening of your highest expression. It is living a life without fear; it is acknowledging that limits lie before you but choosing to move forward anyway. Greatness is not reserved for the few but is available to all who dare to seek it out. You come from a linage of men and women who have carried humanity's burden on their backs. Men and women who dared to tear down the barriers that came up before them. Men and women who failed countless times yet emerged from their defeat with the victory. On the inside of you lie dormant gifts and abilities that have yet to be released into the world. All you need to do is activate them. Owning your greatness is nothing more than your willingness to put everything on the line for the sake of experiencing the fulfillment of your dreams. Do not continue to wear the garment of ordinariness because no one else has told you that you are great. I am telling you right now. YOU ARE GREAT! Go achieve greatness. Your only limit is You.

RECAP & REFLECT

→ Progression is not a matter of knowledge only, but a matter of knowing and moving in unity with the abundant, impactful, and effective life that can be yours when you do the work to attain and maintain it.

→ Let your desire for success be driven by pure motives.

→ Be willing to learn from what doesn't work.

→ You are capable of more than you know.

→ Greatness is not reserved for the few but is available to all who dare to seek it out.

→ Your only limit is you.

MY THOUGHTS

_____

_____

_____

_____

_____

_____

_____

_____

_____

_____

_____

_____

_____

_____

Chapter Eleven

THE FAITH FACTOR

There will be times when you have to fight through the bad days to get to the best days of your life. Bad days give you a greater appreciation for the good ones. The idea of better days being ahead in the midst of the pain I was experiencing and the hope that things would somehow, and in some miraculous way turn around for my good is exactly what kept me together as I walked through what proved to be the darkest, most painful, and challenging time of my life.

Faith in Adversity

Prior to early 2019, I had experienced a few brushes with death, I fought many personal fights that seemed designed to silence my voice or push me to give up the work I undoubtedly knew I was called to do. Yet, nothing could prepare me for the extreme brokenness and intense pain of losing my marriage, family, home, cars, investment property, and even some friends that I held dear. Nothing could have prepared me to witness the stability of my global organization, my life's work, rocked to its core.

With nearly two decades of marriage under our belt, and not just any marriage, but one where we built, worked, and served together. It was in that difficult season, that my then wife and I found ourselves in a union with issues that could not be reconciled. Even with all of the creative effort, unceasing prayer, and wise counsel given towards our reconciliation, we would later find ourselves divorced. The burden and shame of divorce for a frontline minister is unimaginable. This was amplified even more as I served as the Family Pastor of our church. I never saw myself as a divorcee. It was never even a consideration. As far as I was concerned, we were going for the long haul, "till death do us part." The product of a single-parent home, I made a commitment to myself very early in my life that I was not going to allow my children to have that same experience. I believed, and still believe in the strength of a healthy, nuclear family. I never imagined my wife and me in separate homes raising our son. Spousal and child support were never a part of even my most far-fetched thoughts. Dividing assets. Living alone. Starting over! None of this was the way I saw my life unfolding. Yet here I was, faced with this new reality.

What do you do when life hits you with a category 5 storm you were not prepared for? In September of 2019, I helplessly watched from my home in Texas, as Hurricane Dorian decimated two of the major islands of my homeland. Though I was not there physically, I walked through many difficult emotions, namely fear, hopelessness, confession, frustration, and anxiety. What was set to hit the first of the two islands, Abaco as a Category 3 hurricane, in a matter of 24 hours became a category 5 hurricane that no one, and I mean no one, could have prepared for. Dorian, then took his savage and brutal rains and maximum sustained winds of 185mph (295 km/h), tying with the 1935 Labor Day hurricane for the highest wind speeds of an Atlantic hurricane ever recorded at landfall. This storm was no small event. The catastrophic natural disaster ravaged and completely defaced most of Abaco and

East Grand Bahama leaving countless casualties in its path including many who are still missing and feared dead.

Like the people of those two islands searching for answers no one seemed to have, walking through the aftermath of my failed marriage, tore me apart. It was then that the pain of my new reality hit me. How was I going to rebuild my life? Where would I go? What would I do? Where would I even start? What would become of the little that was left of my ministry? It was my life's work. Over two decades in shambles and hanging in the balance. Everything in my life was unrecognizable to me, except for my faith.

"Storms make trees grow deeper roots."
- Dolly Parton

Left in the aftermath was the debris of my broken heart and my faith. Built on the solid foundation of God's unwavering love and His promise to never leave me nor forsake me, my faith would help me withstand the brutality of my experience. In the lowest of times I held on to the truths of God's word and meditated on them daily. There were days when I did not want to get out of bed and see the light of day. Yet, my faith assured me that if I could just fight through the bad days, I would get to the best days of my life. My faith in God assured me that if I could stand firm in Him, that I would see the restoration of everything that I lost. In the times of weariness and weakness, my faith ushered the way to rest and power. I used that power to start eating better, reading and exercising more. I made a habit of going to bed early and rising early. I set myself up to be rejuvenated and ready for all that the day held for me, good or bad. I worked on me and allowed God to do the same.

Through faith, I partnered with Him to rebuild my life. Soon I watched as my mind, body, and spirit came into alignment with my complete healing and wholeness.

"The circumstances and events that we see as setbacks are often times the very things that launch us into periods of intense spiritual growth."
- Charles Stanley

The pain of my divorce expedited my growth and accelerated me to the place of exponential increase in so many intangible areas of my life. I lost a lot, but I gained even more. I can say with unshakable confidence that I would not be where I am in my life, in peace, in my mind, in my new platform, and where I am in serving humanity, had it not been for my divorce. I don't hover around the memories of what was, but instead, I take joy in what is still becoming. That setback, as painful as it was, helped me in more ways than it hurt me.

Everyday requires intentional work and a recommitment to remain partnered with God to create my best and most impactful life. After having lost so much, I am unapologetically adamant about creating the life of my dreams. The life that I don't need to take a vacation from. My faith is stronger, so I see with more precision the life God has in store for me. I have partnered with Him and am working diligently to live, work, and enjoy life at the highest level.

The Significance of Faith

The Bible says, "Without faith it is impossible to please God, for he who comes to God must believe that He is, and that He is a rewarder of those who seek Him." - Hebrews 11:6 (KJV). Faith needed to be the foremost thing in living the life I desired. First, there needed to be an unwavering belief that God is who He says He is. This steadfast assurance is what keeps me in times of trouble. It stabilizes me, setting my focus on a being higher than myself. It fills me with the hope that is found in His promises. If I can believe that God is who He says He is, then I know that He will do what He says He will do. Without a shadow of a doubt, I must believe that his highest intent for me to is to live a life of abundance and not lack or insufficiency. A life of wholeness, not brokenness or hopelessness. Faith in God affirms that the adversity I have or am experiencing is only a temporary state. I affirm within my heart that He hasn't left me and that if I can work alongside Him to rebuild my life from the inside out, I will be restored. That is such a great hope! I needed that hope and clung to it like my life depended on it, because the reality is, IT DID! Author and Pastor, Joel Osteen said "Don't focus on the adversity; focus on God. No matter what you go through, stay in faith, be your best each day, and trust God will use your experience to position you for greatness."

I knew that I could not stay in that place of brokenness, feeling hopeless and lost. I knew that I somehow had to get beyond losing my wife, or the joy of coming home to my son. I knew that I had to rebuild my global organization because though I had done so much, there was still even more to be done. I allowed myself the time to grieve all that was lost but, I did not stay stagnant losing vitality over it. I got to work on purging my heart, my mind, and my life of the need for answers, the need for an apology, and the need for blaming another including myself. My faith in God also meant it was imperative that I forgive her, and myself, releasing ALL bitterness or resentment toward everyone. I won't tell you that it was easy. It wasn't. But more than staying resentful or angry, I wanted to live an effective, abundantly blessed, and joyful life. Abundance and frustration cannot simultaneously coexist. Joy and unforgiveness won't occupy the same space. Faith and hate won't show up at the same time.

So, I coupled my faith in God with professional therapy and got it done. Just as I could not get better or be better without God, God would not do anything for me without me. Faith, no matter how much, is dead without works. I had to add work to my faith in Him and His promises. That work shifted my focus from my circumstances to God and the turnaround that I knew I would experience as a result. Less than a year later, things did turn around and are still turning around. That's not a lot of time, and it won't happen as quickly for everyone. But I was willing to do what many are not. So, I am experiencing the results at a level that not everyone will. Walking in the newness of my redefined normal, with my faith fortified, I am creating a life that can withstand a Category 5 storm. With all that I learned in what I lost, I am wiser, stronger, more driven, and a lot more intentional.

Faith Trumps Failing

No matter how many times you get it wrong, remaining steadfast with your faith in God and with the vision you have for your life will unarguably lead you to greener pastures. Continuing in faith and remaining a believer of life, love, or success is not easy, especially when in spite of your greatest efforts, things don't appear to be going right or coming together. However, you cannot allow failures to define you or the years you have left.

A failed marriage does not make you a failure. The same is true for a failed business, or a failed plan. You have to see beyond the failures. See your desired outcome. Keep that in the forefront of your heart and mind. Let that motivate what comes out of your mouth. If you can experience one massive failure, or even multiple failures, yet remain in faith—you haven't failed at all.

Take all that you've learned in that unsuccessful experience and use it towards your growth and development. Use it towards your next attempt. Seek the principles in the lessons of life. Principles don't change even when circumstances do. Apply those principles the next time around. If you remain in faith and do the work, success is imminent! I have mentioned doing the work multiple times because it's important to understand that despite our greatest intentions and our greatest belief in God's divine's power, faith without works—diligent, intentional actions—is dead. At the end of the day, it's your commitment to work, not just your faith that exposes just how strong you are. So, take heart when it comes to difficult circumstances. Your strength is revealed by how you handle life's greatest challenges. It's time to embrace the effective life.

RECAP & REFLECT

→ Faith trumps Failing.

→ Failing does not make you a Failure.

→ You cannot allow failures to define you or the years you have left. Only allow faith to do that.

→ Faith in God affirms that the adversity you have or are experiencing is only a temporary state.

→ Your strength is revealed by how you handle your greatest challenges.

MY THOUGHTS

_____

_____

_____

_____

_____

_____

_____

_____

_____

_____

_____

_____

_____

_____

_____

REFUSE TO BE A VICTIM!

Life has a way of throwing curveballs our way. These curveballs are the people and experiences we didn't see coming, and are meant to derail us from our game plan. Always unannounced, these curveballs can take you out of the game and leave you enraged at your misfortune.

After a series of misfortunes whether big or small, the best of us can feel angry, frustrated, and resentful. "Why is this happening to me?" you may ask. Or "When will I catch a break?" "Bad things are always happening to me." "If it weren't for bad luck, I'd have no luck at all." "Nothing ever goes right for me." These are the cries of a person who has become a victim of life's circumstances.

In all fairness, it's not difficult to find yourself in an unfortunate, negative, or unbecoming situation. But what is most important, is the mindset we take on having had these misfortunes.

Over the years, I've taken some pretty strong blows from life. However, I can accredit where I am today due in part to my mindset. Despite what I've endured, whether through introspection, or through an angel set to cross my path at a divine moment, I heard or saw the right thing, in the right moment, which upon reflection, shifted my focus from a victim to that of a victor. With that, I was able to walk away from each presumably negative experience knowing that I had absolutely nothing to complain about.

I am on a mission to create the life of my grandest dreams; one that I don't need to take a vacation from. Where I am going, regret and frustration has no place, and complaining will only prolong the time it takes for me to get there.

NEWSFLASH: Life can be quite challenging sometimes - even for a Life Management Coach. In the midst of it all, I work even harder, and I'm more adamant and relentless to move forward and grow. I refuse to play the victim role. I own my life and I make no excuses for myself. Adopt, or enhance that same mindset. Decide to become the person you are destined to be by engaging with daily practices that will allow you to move forward and to win in life.

Here are 7 Things to Remember to Keep You from Adopting a Victim Mindset:

1. Life Happens to Us All.

None of us are exempt from life's curveballs. The happiest, most accomplished, wealthiest, and most notable among us, all have their share of obstacles, disadvantages and unfair incidences. This is no excuse to not be your best, nor does it disqualify you from living a victorious and effective life.

2. Change is Inevitable.

There is no way to avoid change. Things change, people change, circumstances change; time changes and that change impacts everything. You cannot get around it, so get over it! The sooner you prepare for and adapt to change, the sooner you are able to continue to in building and living the life you desire. Don't allow a change in your circumstances or status send into you into the downward spiral of the victim mindset.

3. Happiness is a Personal, Inside Job.

Other people are not the answer to your happiness. While they can add to your happiness, your soul-mate, children, family, friend, therapist, or spiritual leader are not responsible for making you happy. When you emancipate others from the obligation of making you happy—which by the way, is solely yours, you also free yourself of disappointment, anger, and resentment.

4. Your Mistakes Don't Define You.

Move through life with the understanding that your mistakes are not the final factor in who you are and the life you can live. See each mishap, misstep, or poor choice as a lesson on the way forward and upward. Those with a victim mindset voluntarily allow their mistakes to keep them in desolate places, long after the experience as they relive it over and over; allowing their present and even future to be defined by a past experience. Don't allow your future to pay the price for something your past already is. Learn the lesson, then let tenacity and resilience define you.

5. Timing is Everything.

Know that everything takes time and timing is everything. You can't rush that which is intended to go through a process. Avoiding process and due diligence, keeps you from being processed and adequately prepared for all that you fully desire to do, have, and be. A victim mindset will impose on you the belief that everyone else is living the life that you desire, but it's not happening for you. But know with all assurance, that if you continue to show up for your life every day, and relentlessly do the work, you will experience your heart's grandest desires in the fullness of time.

6. Keep Growing.

Keep growing and never stop working on yourself. Who you see yourself to be is a mere fraction of all that you have the potential to be. A victim mindset will condition you to believe that you've already lived your best days, and had your best experiences. Challenge that mindset with the notion that you're getting better with age.

7. You are a Beautiful and Powerful Being.

You are a beautiful and powerful being capable of so much. Rejection, hardships, mistakes, and loss will only have the power that you give them. Remind yourself that you are amazing. Daily tell yourself that you are worthy; that you are enough. Tell yourself you don't have to be anything beyond your incredible and unique self. Believe that you have the capacity, ingenuity and power to create the amazing life you desire. Know that God and life has so many wonderful things in store and that just ahead, are people, places, and things that are aligned to help you live a life you don't need to take a vacation from.

These seven things are always on my mind. They each serve in reminding me that everything has a season and reason in my life. Reject at all costs adopting the victim mindset. Instead, let your heart and mind always be overly consumed with gratitude. Be grateful always for who you are, where you are, and how far you've come. Yours is a unique and amazing journey; embrace it!

Stop complaining, take on this week as an opportunity to begin a more intense and intentional effort to creating an incredible life.

**I am cheering you on. I join you in believing
that you are NOT a victim!**

RECAP & REFLECT

→ Life can be quite challenging sometimes but refuse to be a Victim.

→ Life happens to us all.

→ Change is inevitable.

→ Happiness is a personal, inside job.

→ Your mistakes don't define you.

→ Timing is everything.

→ You have got to keep growing.

→ You are a beautiful and powerful being.

MY THOUGHTS

Daily Declaration
for Living an Effective Life

I was not born to be broke, sick or frustrated

I am blessed in every area of my life

*From this day forward I will be the head and not
the tail, above ONLY and not beneath*

I am the lender and not the borrower.

Whatever I put my hands to prospers.

All things are working together for my good.

My future is brighter than my past.

*My heart, my mind, and my spirit are all free of negativity,
toxicity, limiting thoughts and limiting beliefs.*

*Because God is my creator, Jesus is my Savior
and the Holy Spirit is my guide, I am becoming
unshakable in times of shaking.*

*I am maximizing my potential and living out a
fulfilled, impactful, and intentional life.*

I practice habits that will bring me closer to living life by design.

MY BUCKET LIST

Life Management Agency Services:

Coaching

Our one-on-one coaching provides you with step-by-step strategies tailored to suite your personal needs in accomplishing your goals. With our coaching program, you show us the target, and we will help you hit it. GUARANTEED!!!

Personal & Professional Development Events

Our Effective Living Mastermind Classes and Annual Life Management Retreat are two of our intensive programs that give you an in-depth learning experience to strategically expose you to the practices of winning at life.

Keynote Speaking

On an annual basis Coach Ricardo speaks to more than 150 private and public meetings for corporations, companies, churches, and community organizations. Both riveting and exciting, he is a well sought-after speaker at conferences, workshops, seminars, and retreats throughout the United States and around the world.

For more information or to book go to our
website www.RicardoMiller.com

About The Author

Ricardo Miller is the CEO and Founder of Effective Living LLC., which specializes in Life Management Coaching and Personal Development Training. For decades, Ricardo has been equipping people of all ages, guiding them with the ultimate goal of discovering purpose, and optimizing their highest potential. He is the host of the weekly radio talk show, "Effective Living with Ricardo Miller" on Fishbowl Radio Network every Monday night at 7PM CST, which was nominated for Best Radio Show of 2019.

Annually Ricardo's voice is heard across a variety of platforms and settings as a keynote speaker or trainer to over 150 events annually, both nationally and internationally.

His passion to train and develop clients seeking to enhance their lives and the lives of the people they serve, is demonstrated through his riveting one-on-one coaching of the finest leaders across various industries, and extends to his quarterly Success Mastermind Classes, his annual Effective Living Life Management Retreat, and The Influencers Summit - the largest meeting of its kind in The Bahamas.

In addition to authoring 5 books, Ricardo is a popular guest speaker on national and international radio and television programs. In recognition of his 20 years of contributing to the nation's youth in The Bahamas, the government declared October 11 – Ricardo's birthday, as National Children' Ministry Day. In 2018, Miller was inducted into his High School's Hall of Fame.

Ricardo Miller is dedicated to sharing the message of discovering your grandest purpose and optimizing your highest potential as you work to create a life you don't need to take a vacation from.

HOW FORGIVENESS AND *A COURSE IN MIRACLES* CAN SET YOU FREE

BREAKING
FREE

LORRI COBURN

BALBOA
PRESS
A DIVISION OF HAY HOUSE

Balboa Press books may be ordered through booksellers or by contacting:

Balboa Press
A Division of Hay House
1663 Liberty Drive
Bloomington, IN 47403
www.balboapress.com
1-(877) 407-4847

Because of the dynamic nature of the Internet, any web addresses or links contained in this book may have changed since publication and may no longer be valid. The views expressed in this work are solely those of the author and do not necessarily reflect the views of the publisher, and the publisher hereby disclaims any responsibility for them.

The author of this book does not dispense medical advice or prescribe the use of any technique as a form of treatment for physical, emotional, or medical problems without the advice of a physician, either directly or indirectly. The intent of the author is only to offer information of a general nature to help you in your quest for emotional and spiritual well-being. In the event you use any of the information in this book for yourself, which is your constitutional right, the author and the publisher assume no responsibility for your actions.

Any people depicted in stock imagery provided by Thinkstock are models, and such images are being used for illustrative purposes only.
Certain stock imagery © Thinkstock.

Quote from the *Song of Prayer* pamphlet used by permission from The Foundation for *A Course in Miracles*®.

ISBN: 978-1-4525-3306-3 (e)
ISBN: 978-1-4525-3305-6 (sc)

Library of Congress Control Number: 2011902646

Printed in the United States of America

Balboa Press rev. date: 8/23/2011

For Rod
Your unconditional love
symbolizes God's love for me.

For Gary Renard
Your courage and honesty in
The Disappearance of the Universe
were the inspiration for this book.

CONTENTS

INTRODUCTION

Much sheer effort goes into avoiding the truth;
Left to itself, it sweeps in like the tide.
~Fay Weldon

I discovered *A Course in Miracles* (ACIM) in the late eighties, and it went right over my head. Though I did get something out of it: the habit of using affirmations every hour, and the notion that if I attack my brother I'm really attacking myself. Other than that, I decided the *Course* was too wordy, convoluted, and difficult to understand, so I put it down for seventeen years.

In 2003, I came upon a book called *The Disappearance of the Universe*, by Gary Renard, which is based on the teachings of Jesus as expressed in *A Course in Miracles*. Gary wrote that we are dreaming our lives and that God did not make this world. What a bizarre concept! I initially dismissed this as another ridiculous religious teaching that made no sense. As I studied further, however, the idea that God did *not* create this world answered the questions that had haunted me my entire life. It made perfect sense! I had always felt a loving presence greater than me, had felt assistance in my life, and had longed to experience heaven, which I believed was my true home. I just could not reconcile that love with the awful, dreadful conditions on earth.

Our Judeo-Christian culture teaches that, "In the beginning God created the heavens and the earth" (Gen. 1:1). This is an indoctrinated belief that many of us never even think to question.

1

A *Newsweek* survey on religious beliefs showed that 80% of respondents believe God created this world.[1] Who else but an all-powerful, awesome God could create the majesty of mountains, sky, and sea, along with the intricate order of the stars, sun, and moon? While most of us assume God created the earth, we also assume that He is somehow in charge of what goes on. Hence, natural disasters like tsunamis, hurricanes, and earthquakes are called "acts of God." The image of a negative, wrathful God is woven tightly into the fabric of our Western culture, right along with the completely contradictory idea that He loves us. Do you know anyone who doesn't know the story of Adam and Eve? Even those who have never attended church know what happened to them when they disobeyed God! According to the Bible, women for all eternity suffer in childbirth because of just one woman, Eve. The idea that God will punish us for wrongdoing is so deeply ingrained that we only half-jokingly say, "God will get you for that!"

I grew up in a fundamentalist Protestant church, and it was beneficial in many ways. I learned that Jesus loved us so much that he died for us, and I felt Jesus' friendship. I learned to be kind and loving to others, to do unto others as I would have done unto me, to forgive, and to see everyone as a child of God. Church taught that there was something bigger than us, and that life goes on after death. This was very reassuring. As a teenager I had a positive experience with the church youth group and have several friends from that group to this day.

However, my church also turned me away from God with negativity that went hand in hand with love. I was horrified by the story of Abraham and Isaac in the Old Testament, but I don't think I ever spoke up, because that would be questioning God. To test Abraham's faith, God commands him to sacrifice his son Isaac on the altar, as one would kill an animal. Since Abraham is willing to do it, God rescinds the command, and tells Abraham that He was just testing his faith. I always thought this was inordinately cruel of God. The story of Job is even worse. God rains horrible illnesses upon Job and inflicts death upon his family, simply to prove to Satan that Job will stay true to God. In the back of my mind I was suspicious of God, yet I tried to ignore these feelings, because I also loved Him. Today, as I read the Bible from a metaphysical view, the horror and fear dissipate, and God is once again the loving, benevolent Father.

My experience with the Protestant religion was not necessarily the same as that of many others. There are many Christian churches that are more loving than they are negative and frightening. However, my church was on the far end of the strictness scale, and we weren't supposed to dance, play cards, roller-skate, or wear makeup and jewelry. I did all these things anyway. My church also believed that Catholics and the more liberal Protestants were doomed to hell, because they were not firm enough in teaching the saving blood of Jesus. My religion taught that unless we believed that Jesus died for our sins, *and* we accepted him as our personal savior, *and* we continued to live a sanctified life, we would go to hell. Thus, I was terrified that almost everyone I knew would burn in eternal fire.

I was *told* that God loved me, but what I *experienced* was that God only loved me if I obeyed the rules. If I made one wrong move and happened to die that night in a car accident without first confessing my sin, then I would go to hell. If, however, I had confessed my sin and asked forgiveness, then I would get into heaven. That was scary! I constantly prayed quickly when I did something wrong, for fear of eternal damnation. My church held "altar calls" during which you came forward, embarrassed and in front of everyone, to kneel at the altar. The invitation, which felt more like a demand, was to confess sins and recommit your life to Christ if you had backslidden. It was also an opportunity for non-Christians to get saved. I always sat shaking in my seat until I either went up or the tense waiting period had passed. Often I went forward just to be on the safe side. Then I felt tremendous relief because I knew I was saved and would get into heaven. I once heard a radio preacher refer to this as "fire insurance."

Being a born-again Christian comforted me from the fear of death. Eternal life was possible if I just confessed my sins and accepted Jesus as my savior. I loved Jesus, and I still love Jesus to this day. I experience him as gentle and loving, yet strong. When I was young, Jesus felt different than God did. God was big and mean and stern. Jesus was the fall guy for God's wrath, and I was grateful that he died for me. To this day, the word "God" occasionally evokes dread, doom, and disapproval, but only warmth and wisdom come from "Jesus."

In spite of being born again, I found it hard to believe that God was so wrathful that He would remand us to hell. But, I was afraid not to believe for fear that I *would* be sent to hell. At the age of seventeen, I developed enough courage to question my minister and not automatically swallow what I had been taught. I debated with him that a loving God would not let people gravitate toward Judaism, Hinduism, Buddhism, Islam, and other religions, only to send them to hell because they didn't believe in Jesus. I was told not to question, and that if I did question, then I, too, would be sent to hell. I asked why God would create me with a thinking brain and then tell me not to use it. I was told to have faith. Faith in what? A vengeful, irrational God?

With this, I left the church for ten years, disillusioned and directionless. During those years I often felt panic. What if I was wrong? What if there really was a hell? My heart seized on hot summer days when I stepped into my scorching car, as I thought that hell must burn a million times worse than that.

During my ten-year absence from the church, I continued to wonder about God. What kind of God would create us and send us to hell if we didn't correctly follow the rules? What kind of God would create us with constant temptations to behave in certain ways, and then label those behaviors "sinful" and punish us for them? Would God give us brains and then ask us to suspend logic and simply obey? Isn't this how Hitler succeeded in turning normal people into mass murderers? It reminded me of my college professor who gave an essay test on World War II; I knew that if I disagreed with his political opinion, my grade would be lowered. Why attend class? Why think at all? Isn't college supposed to be a place where educated debate is encouraged? Shouldn't it be the same with God? Why be alive and think logically about God, if the wrong opinion leads you to burn forever? We were taught that we had free will, yet if we used it we would be damned.

For years I swore that when I got to heaven I was going to give God a piece of my mind. I planned on telling Him I could have done a better job than He did with this world, as I'd make a happy place, free of death, destruction, and darkness. I often raged at God, to the amazement of one of my friends, who expressed fear that if he got mad at God he'd be sent straight to hell. But I figured that if God loved and created me, He'd understand my anger and doubt. Other questions I had for God included why Jesus suffered on the cross, given his powers as God. Since Jesus was God, why didn't he just jump off the cross? Why didn't he dissociate from his body so he didn't feel pain? Why did God require that His only Son be murdered? Apparently suffering was part of the deal, in order to sufficiently atone for man's sin.

Once again, it wasn't until I read *The Disappearance of the Universe* that my lifelong questions were answered. God does *not* require sacrifice, has never condemned us, and never will. Jesus was not sent to die to atone for our sins and he was not the *only* Son of God. The message of Jesus' crucifixion was to show that the body is not real and there is no death. Jesus *willingly chose* to be crucified to teach us that we are *all* the Sons of God, we are *all* innocent, and we can *all* attain the same level of oneness with God that he did. Jesus did *not* suffer on the cross because he was one with the Mind of God and did not identify himself as his body.

A Course in Miracles says that we humans have projected onto God and Jesus all of our guilt, fear, and anger, and that's why God and this earthly life appear so cruel. This explanation made sense to me, given my background in psychology. I'd seen the destructive effects of projection in the lives of my psychotherapy clients for years. I'd witnessed many clients destroy their lives with their false beliefs and become completely irrational in the face of overwhelming emotion. I'd seen countless examples of how we create our lives with our beliefs, and how others' behaviors and attitudes toward us had more to do with our attitudes toward ourselves than it did with them. In other words, everyone and everything that shows up in our lives reflects our own level of self-love.

I have not been the same since reading *The Disappearance of the Universe.* It completely changed my life and set me on a path of discovery that has been nothing short of miraculous. It set me on fire to learn about *A Course in Miracles* and now to teach it.

It is my hope that the teachings of ACIM will free you as they have freed me. The idea that God did not create this world has been the single most liberating concept in my life. The miracle is waking up to the love, joy and peace that have always been *within* you, but that you sought through things outside of yourself. This freedom is real, tangible, and joyous, something that you already have. Your acceptance of the truth and light within you automatically releases you from the dark dream. As Jesus says in the Bible, "You will know the truth, and the truth will make you free" (John 8:32).*

* Throughout this book, Bible verses are from either the King James Version or the Revised Standard Version.

CHAPTER ONE

A RADICAL NEW WAY OF BEING

God, if Thou livest, Thine eye on me bend, And stay my grief and bring my pain to end: Pain for my lost, the deepest, rarest friend.
~Robert Nichols

Autumn is exquisite in Michigan. My soul warms to Indian summer days, breathtaking crimson and golden trees, and the musky smell of fading leaves. Bold orange pumpkins dot the patch and champagne parchment cornstalks sway in the breeze, making me glad to be alive.

I was born on the quintessential fall day. What should have been an enchanted time, however, was marred by dual tragedies in my family. Two weeks before I was born, the unthinkable happened. My cousin Sally, who was four at the time, was holding hands with her seven-year-old sister as they crossed the road. She felt her sister's hand slip from hers, as her sister was hurtled into the air.

Here is my cousin Sally's description of what happened:

> I can tell you what a four-year-old remembers. In my memory, I remember "feelings" and how I felt rather than the actual account of events. Intertwined with that are the events that were told to me at a later date.

It was a warm fall Sunday, on October 5, 1958. It was a busy morning and we were late for church (as usual). We had to sit up in the balcony so our lateness wouldn't be obvious. I remember being hungry and cranky and was picking on my older sister Carol. In fact, everyone was in a cranky mood and back at home each person had his own version of how to spend the sunny afternoon. My mom wanted to wash the curtains, my dad wanted to listen to the ball game on the radio, and my sister Carol wanted to accept the invitation to go out on the neighbor's boat (it was her best friend's family). Because everyone was cranky, my mom decided to leave the curtains in the washer and piled all six of us in the car to go for a ride in the country.

The country west of Port Huron, Michigan, was always beautiful in the fall. The rolling hills and changing tree colors took one's breath away. It was also the time of year that nuts were ready for picking. My dad stopped the car on the side of the road while my mom, sisters Barb and Carol, and me walked across a two-lane paved road to pick hazelnuts, leaving my dad listening to the ball game on the car radio and watching my two-year-old brother.

The wind picked up and four-year-old me, who was prone to ear infections, complained about my ears hurting. My mom asked Barb to go get a hat out of the car for me. Barb refused and Carol piped up, "I'll go!" Of course I had to join her. (It was more fun than standing under a tree picking up stupid nuts.) We walked across the road and were headed back when I heard my mom scream "CAROL!" Carol stopped and I felt her hand pull out of mine. Then the next thing I remember was my dad carrying Carol in his arms. He had retrieved her from the ditch where she landed after being hit by a sixteen-year-old male driver. I remember lots of blood and people showing up and standing around. Carol was still alive when the ambulance arrived thirty minutes later. My mom rode in the ambulance and my dad and the rest of us were driven home by a nice couple. Sitting in the back seat of that car, I remember laughing and acting silly and saying, "Didn't Carol look funny?" Then Barb slapped me and I started crying. I didn't understand anything, but that slap made me cry.

The funeral home wasn't scary. I remember Carol had a bruise on her arm and the scent of flowers was very overpowering, almost making it hard to breathe.

Two weeks after Carol's death I was born. The phone rang at 6 a.m., and my sister dragged herself out of bed since it shrilled incessantly. Upon knocking on my parents' door, she found they had gone to the hospital. The phone call was from another cousin, a different family from Carol's. My uncle had been killed in a car accident that night, leaving my aunt widowed with three children still in school.

Why does a joyous birth have to be coupled with senseless tragedy? Does God send us to earth simply to lose everyone and everything we love? What kind of God would allow a little girl to get killed right in front of her family? Why would God saddle my aunt, a devout Catholic and one of the sweetest women in the world, with widowhood? No matter how strong our spiritual foundation is, tragedies such as these shake our faith. They rock our world, and in order to go on, we have to find a category or compartment for them or they will drive us mad.

Any intelligent person has had to question the meaning of life and the suffering in this world. When tragedy strikes, we desperately search for reasons. Somehow, if we understand *why* the trauma happened, we believe it will lessen the grief. We've heard the usual answers: God has a divine plan and everything happens for a reason; earth is a place of suffering but heaven is a place of peace; we can't understand the mind of God. We've been taught that light and dark, good and bad, and all opposite polarities are perfect expressions of the divine oneness. These answers bring comfort to many, but leave others with deep feelings of emptiness, anger, and disbelief. These answers fall short, don't feel right, and often leave even more questions unanswered. *Why* does every good thing have to have a bad side? *Why* does there have to be suffering at all? Can God really love us and still have created this kind of world?

Traumas aside, daily life alone is enough to make us anxious, depressed, and uncertain. There is no safety in life. The rug can be pulled out from under us at any moment, and many of us experience momentary happy times only to wonder when the ax is going to fall. Most of us worry about losing our loved ones, and there is a background level of anxiety carried with us at all times. We want to escape this earthly life, wake up to our spiritual selves, so we no longer have to endure the constant travails that are inherent in this plane.

Have you had a tragedy in your life that has made you lose faith? Have you longed for a relationship with Spirit, but just can't believe in the God you learned about in church? Have you explored different spiritual paths only to keep looking for one that makes more sense to you, one that works better?

There has been a resurgence of Eastern spirituality in our culture since the Beatles introduced us to their Indian guru. Many of us have resonated with the Hindu and Buddhist teachings that suggest that this world is ephemeral, an illusion, and we have found inner peace from meditation. At the same time, having grown up in the United States, we have had difficulty meshing the calm, receptive Eastern nature with our Western action and goal-oriented lifestyle. The thought of a guru to which we surrender is anathema to proud individualism. Many of us also find it tough to calm down in our hectic society, and somehow feel we've come up short if we do not still our minds perfectly in meditation.

Enter *A Course in Miracles* in the mid-seventies. The perfect bridge between East and West. The answer for many of us here in the U.S. and now around the globe.

As one of my clients to whom I introduced the *Course* said, "It's the only thing that makes sense to me." Like many of us, she knew there was some force in the universe that held everything together, but could not buy any of the spiritual paths that she'd explored. She found some good things in all of them, but they did not meld together for her like the *Course* did.

A Course in Miracles makes many promises, all of them true and attainable. We are promised tranquillity here and now, banishment of fear, loving relationships, and a jump start on our path to enlightenment. Where we were once filled with anxiety and despair, our lives now become filled with zest and joy. The *Course* claims that we can save a thousand years or more in our path by practicing the Workbook lessons. We don't have to meditate perfectly or burn off all our karma to achieve enlightenment, because enlightenment is simply a recognition and acceptance of our divine self. Unlike the meditative techniques of the East that direct focus to the third eye and let thoughts float through without attachment, ACIM uses our minds to actively choose truthful thoughts and deny false ones. It is a concerted effort in mind training, reversing our false thinking so we can wake up to truth.

A New Theology

Every new truth begins in a shocking heresy.
~Margaret Deland

A Course in Miracles is a spiritual self-study course that we can do completely on our own. There is no organized religion that tells us what to do; we don't have to believe in any particular doctrine, go to church, or follow rules someone else made up. We all have our own inner teacher, which ACIM calls the Holy Spirit. This is our higher Self; this is the Love that is the center of our Being. We need listen to no other voice, for this Love will guide us to our highest good. We can converse with It anywhere, anytime. If we want to be happy, all we have to do is listen to Its guidance, and our peace is ensured. When we are in touch with the love, serenity, and radiance that come from within, we automatically make loving choices.

Currently we see this world completely upside down. We see a world of fear, wrought with death and destruction, because we view it from the vantage point of the ego. The ego is our fear-based, false self, the part that forgets our connection to God. When we begin to look at the world through the eyes of God, the eyes of our inner loving Self, we see a totally different world. Through better choices, we begin to experience love instead of suffering. We recognize the ego masks of guilt, doubt, fear, and hatred, and instead see ourselves and others as we really are. We become conscious of the majesty within, and we glow, feeling gentler and lighter. We love ourselves and others—gone are the fears that life can destroy us or take our loved ones from us, for we know there is no death. We know we are safe and warm in truth. No one and no thing can take what is our essence.

A Course in Miracles may initially shock with its tenets, but as we ponder them, they make perfect sense and answer questions about the nature of life, the meaning of life, and the inherent suffering of life. The nature of life is that God did *not* create this world, but we did. The meaning of life is that we are dreaming this world. The dream is not real, and we find meaning only when we reconnect to our true home, which is the presence of God within us. The suffering of life is part of the illusory world and is overcome when we recognize truth. Because God is pure Love, He did not create a world of death, suffering, and separation. God would *never* cause us to suffer or learn through pain, and it is only our belief that we are separated from God that causes suffering.

The central teaching of *A Course in Miracles* is that we are home with God right now, asleep to our true nature and dreaming about life on earth. We are like Dorothy in *The Wizard of Oz*, dreaming a horrific nightmare that we are lost and can't find our way home. Like Dorothy, we long for home, also called heaven (or Kansas). Even though Dorothy thinks Oz is a beautiful place, she keeps trying to find her way home. When Dorothy awakens, she finds she is indeed at home with her loved ones. Moment to moment we have the opportunity to click our heels and go home, to choose between love and fear, between the truth that we are still with God or the illusion that we have separated from Him. The *Course* refers to this as the choice between the ego's way of thinking and the Holy Spirit's view of the world.

This world, since it is filled with fear, is an illusion, as God creates only love. All problems arise from one error, the mistaken belief that we are separated and alone and that God has abandoned us. This false belief appears to cut us off from our Source, much like a kink in a water hose prevents the source of water from flowing to its destination. We are unable to receive God's love when there are kinks in our thinking. Forgiveness is the primary tool that opens us to the flow of love and peace. Forgiveness is stressed over and over in ACIM as the main way we find our way back home.

A Course in Miracles states that God is pure Love, and as Love would never create hell or punish his beloved children. Because this earth is a dream, and dream occurrences aren't real, no one has ever sinned. However, in the illusion we see ourselves as flawed individuals, guilty of numerous sins. We think ugly thoughts and do ugly things. But that comes from our false self, the ego, and therefore it is not real. The ultimate truth is that only God and Love, which are the same thing, exist. Love is actually another name for God.

We are taught in the Bible that man's sin keeps him from God, so God had to send Jesus to die in atonement. However, ACIM says that Jesus did not die as a sacrificial atonement for man's sins, because God was never angry with us to begin with. Since we have never separated from God, there is no sin to be atoned for. It's all our bad dream. Jesus willingly chose to be crucified to teach us that the body and death are not real. He did not suffer on the cross because he knew he wasn't his body, and his mind was solely identified with God.

A Course in Miracles was revealed to a woman named Helen Schucman. Helen was a research psychologist and professor at Columbia-Presbyterian Medical Center in New York City. She had been raised Jewish and had searched for God in the Catholic and Baptist religions, but had concluded that there was no God and that she was an atheist. Helen and a colleague at Columbia, Bill Thetford, had a very conflicted relationship, which made working together difficult. Exasperated, Bill finally stated, "There must be another way" to get along. They made a commitment to treat each other with kindness. Shortly thereafter, Helen heard an inner voice tell her, "This is *A Course in Miracles*, please take notes." She thought she was going crazy and told Bill about it, and he suggested that she go along with it and take the notes. Bill sensed that the notes had something to do with their commitment to get along better. Hence, *A Course in Miracles* was dictated over seven years, beginning in 1965. Helen took the notes and Bill transcribed them. The Voice of the *Course* identified itself as Jesus of the Bible, and Helen believed that it was indeed Jesus. However, she had many doubts and internal conflicts about the entire process. The lives of Helen and Bill changed so dramatically, though, that their experience convinced them this was of great value.

Many people will question the authenticity of the voice of Jesus, even as Helen did. How do we know Helen wasn't just crazy? We don't. But how do we know if Moses really heard the voice of God from a burning bush, or if the Apostle Paul, whose letters form the basis of the Christian religion, really saw the light of Jesus on the road to Damascus? We don't. But the power of the teachings speaks for itself, as do those of ACIM. God did not stop communicating with us two thousand years ago. He speaks to us every moment of every day, in every way imaginable. The evaluation of any spiritual teaching should come from whether it enriches people's lives. *A Course in Miracles* has done just that, radically improving many lives. It has sold two million copies by word of mouth alone since it came out in the seventies. There are several thousand study groups in over fifty countries, and scores of books have been written about it. It is rapidly rising in popularity, as it satisfies the quest for a usable, practical spiritual path that also accelerates enlightenment.

A Course in Miracles has three sections that are all contained within one book. The Text forms the theoretical basis, the Workbook provides daily lessons designed to shift your thinking toward miracles, and the Manual for Teachers clarifies important points. It is the *experience* of ACIM's teachings that lead you to see the world differently and to open to your true loving and peaceful nature. Therefore, don't believe what I say; test the ideas on your own. As you read this book, you may find that you doubt or disagree with what I am saying. Good! Think for yourself.

Throughout this book, *A Course in Miracles* quotes are in bold print. The parentheses at the end identify their location, and the nomenclature is explained in the appendix. Also, the traditional use of "He" for God will be used here, but feel free to substitute "She," It," "Spirit," or whatever you are comfortable with. God does not care what words you use.

This book is a guide to the primary principles of *A Course in Miracles* as I have experienced them myself, and with friends and psychotherapy clients. We will explore the nature of this world: how we are caught in a dream by our false self, the ego. We will ascertain the difference between the false ego self and our true Self, and how to awaken from the dream by practicing true forgiveness.

In chapter 3 we will explore why we heap suffering upon ourselves in spite of God's wish that we only have peace and happiness. We will examine how we erroneously came to believe that we are separate from God. We'll learn that this earthly life is but a dream, and that we are still safe in the arms of God. Chapter 4 will show us that we have only one Self, our true Self, but we forget this and identify with a false self, the ego, which causes all of our problems. In chapter 5 we will look at the use of forgiveness as the way to wake up and go home to God as well as to reduce suffering.

If you are one of the many people who have been turned off by the religious tradition around Jesus, you may want to skip directly to chapter 6. There we'll discern what Jesus really taught compared to what has been promulgated by the church. Jesus' teachings will be examined in light of his clarifications from ACIM. The earlier chapters explain many of the terms used in chapter 6, so look to them for further elucidation. If you did not read the introduction, you may want to refer back to it, as it addresses how I was disillusioned with church doctrine as well.

In chapter 7 we will learn to identify the Voice of God within us, which is our intuition, and develop a closer relationship with Spirit.

If you would like a quick overview of ACIM, go to my website, http://www.lorricoburn.com, and download the free audio titled *The Basic Principles of A Course in Miracles.* This talk will save beginners a lot of time in their understanding of the *Course* and will help current students deepen their understanding and application of its principles.

CHAPTER TWO

WHAT IS GOD?

It is fear that first brought gods into the world.
~Petronius

Most of us have heard the words, "God loves you." For most of us, that is exactly what they are—words. We can barely grasp the fullness of their meaning, and except for isolated incidents in our lives, we don't usually *feel* God's love.

In our Judeo-Christian society we tend to perceive God as a Being *outside* of us, whom we need to beseech for life's favors. We are not taught what God *really* is, that God is a force *inside us*, in the center of our Self. This is not a force given only to people who believe a certain way or who go to church. This force, which is love, is inside every one of us. It is part of us, yet it is bigger than us and goes beyond us. It is actually what we are made of. *Love, joy, and peace are the essence of our Being!* We are adrift on the sea of life, oblivious to the life raft right inside us. There is so much power available to us, but we ignore it. Most of us do not seek God's healing because it has been intertwined with the notion of a disapproving and angry God. We leave the Big Guy alone until we absolutely have to call on Him. We think that to get God's love we have to live a pristine or holy life, go to church all the time, or never have fun again. So we push the idea of God to the side. When we do that, we are pushing our true Self, our own nature, to the side. We are giving up our life force, surrendering it to outside things that we think will make us happy. We forget who and what we are, and chase after accomplishments and possessions. All the while, our inner Self patiently awaits our return, knowing the day will come when we'll realize all the things we sought didn't make us happy after all.

When I ask my clients what they believe about God, most answer by repeating parrot-like what they learned. "I believe in heaven and hell." "I believe God is in charge of everything." "I pray for others, but not for myself, because my problems are too little for God, and He has bigger things to deal with." "I believe that I'm a nice person, so I'll go to heaven." "I believe that since I have accepted Jesus as my savior that I am going to heaven." "I believe God allows bad things to happen so we can learn." "I believe that God allows bad things to happen to punish people who are not following His will." "I believe everything happens for a reason."

As I explore further with my clients, however, they have difficulty specifically recognizing how God does or does not intervene in their personal lives. Most have an abstract, vague concept of a big person in the sky that does *something*, but it's hard to say what. Most assume God created them but never ask why, or for what purpose. In other words, the majority has an unclear sense of who or what God is, how He works in their lives, and why. If people believe they experience a loss for a reason, they usually have difficulty finding a *good* reason. Unable to figure God out, most people put Him on the back burner until a crisis strikes.

For those who do seek and question, God means different things to different people. Most people in our society picture a white-bearded, powerful old man on a throne in the sky, an anthropomorphic God that feels love, anger, and jealousy like humans do. Some think of God as a benign energy force, the creative power behind the universe. Others believe God is a force of love, healing, and light.

A Course in Miracles defines God as pure Love—pure Love and nothing else. No form, no anger, no judgment. We are taught in *A Course in Miracles* that we have been created as the same

Love that God is. Most of us don't know that we are this Love. In my work with thousands of clients, I have noticed that the central problem every single person has is a lack of self-love, also called a lack of self-esteem. *A Course in Miracles* refers to this as guilt. Guilt is so ingrained in our nature that we don't even realize we're feeling guilty. We have pervasive guilt about almost everything, from minor thoughts to major infractions. We think we're not doing well enough as parents, partners, workers, sisters, and brothers. We think we should handle things better. We don't feel as successful as we're "supposed" to be, and then when we are successful, we feel guilty because others haven't arrived at the same level. We fear that if others knew what we were really like they wouldn't like us. We think we're bad people for the personal problems we experience. We feel guilty for our feelings and opinions. We don't like our bodies. We're ashamed of our negative personality traits. Again, we often don't even realize that we're feeling guilty or bad about our selves because it's such a normal part of our existence.

The secret is that we *really* feel guilty because we're unaware of our true identity as beloved, innocent beings. Inside of us is a place of love, joy, and peace. These are not feelings, but actual states of being that are the substance of what *we are*. Every single person walking this planet has this inside. We don't know it, though, because of the guilt that blankets our true state. The majority of us are not plugged into our Source. We wonder why our lives don't run smoothly, why we stall, why we sputter, when all the while we've left the plug dangling half out of the socket. When we fully connect, we tap into phenomenal power and love. We accomplish anything we desire and are centered and peaceful rather than anxious.

I explored the nature of God with my client Kim,* who grew up Catholic and had an uncle who was a priest. She said she didn't like going to church anymore, as she wasn't sure what she believed about God and didn't want to be a hypocrite. We discussed how

---

* Names and identifying information have been changed to preserve confidentiality.

God is the highest place within her, and I asked her if she had ever had a time when she felt a magical, loving peace. She said she felt it when she returned to graduate school for her special education degree. She just "knew" she was supposed to get her degree from a particular school, but she wanted to complete the program in seven months instead of the normal two years. She contacted the school and made her proposal, which was initially rejected. She persisted due to her strong sense of being right about her plan. She got accepted and indeed completed the program in seven months. When she teaches, she is in her best zone. She intuitively knows how to connect with the most difficult children, and her supervisors tell her that she naturally uses techniques that most teachers don't know without advanced training.

Kim started realizing that this part of her is God. God is her highest, best Self, where everything flows without effort, where she feels peaceful, loving, and intuitive. She taps into wisdom beyond herself, yet within her. This wisdom is inside all of us, and we can all live lives of effortless joy when we tap into this place, this Self. This is the way life is *supposed* to be, and the way life *becomes* when we practice forgiveness.

Where do you shine? What are you doing when things fall into place for you? What is it that brings out the best in you? That is the place where God dwells. You can take that side of you and apply it to your entire life. Your life can run smoothly every day, but first you have to recognize how you unwittingly push your higher Self away. This is what we'll explore next.

How Our Society Avoids God

The terror of society, which is the basis of morals, the terror of God, which is the secret of religion—these are the two things that govern us.
~Oscar Wilde

Recently I stepped off a curb, stopped short, jumped back, and barely missed getting hit by a minivan peeling around the corner. It seemed like the woman saw me but didn't care. She was going to get where she was going, no matter what. Anger flashed through me. "Whoa, lady, what's your problem?" Then I quickly corrected myself, "Oh, yeah, that's right, I bless and forgive you." Maybe she was rushing to pick up her kid at day care. Anyway, I hurried to cross the street because the Don't Walk sign was already blinking, and waited at the next corner to cross. As I got the green light and my Walk sign began to flash, I had to wait while three extra cars ran the red light.

We are in such a hurry, and in our chaos we lose our center; we lose God within. We would all be wealthy if we had a dollar for every time we've thought, "Get out of my way!" "You're going too slow!" "You idiot, what's with you?" "You're ticking me off!"

Where are we trying to go? How many of us know how to sit still and enjoy life—on a daily basis? Not many. I used to live on a lake and had a beautiful deck. I read my book while on the deck, so I could enjoy the lake and feel productive at the same time. There were two elderly men on my block, and they just sat on their boat docks, gazing. I thought, "What's wrong with them? How can they just sit there and do nothing? They're wasting time!" Today I sit peacefully, just like they did.

We are the richest and most prosperous nation in history, yet we truly don't enjoy our abundance because we're too busy. We have lost our core, the spiritual connection that the founding fathers had. The American Revolution was fought for the inalienable right to pursue life, liberty, and happiness. Today, however, instead of remembering that contentment is a function of spiritual connectedness, we pursue pleasure in a better job, a bigger home, and incessant activity. We desperately try to control the details of our lives to make them perfect.

We get our ideas about how we should live from the media, yet much of the media projects a campaign of fear and consumption. News isn't "news" unless it's bad, which reinforces the idea that danger lurks around every corner. Advertisements tell us we aren't happy unless we have the latest sports car or fashions and an exciting life of dining, dancing, travel, and activity. If we aren't glamorous, we're missing the boat. If we're not rushing from our fast-paced job to our fast-paced sports, video games, or night clubs, we must not be having fun.

My client Dusty came to a session after her mother died. She lamented, "I don't know what I'm going to do with all my time." She had visited her mother in the nursing home several days a week for ten years and now felt empty and alone. I asked her what she did for fun and she said she didn't have any fun. She said she didn't go out much and thought she should go out more. I questioned what she did when she got home from work, and she said she spent time with her dogs. "I get a kick out of them! They are so much fun! And I just love having friends over for dinner." I pointed out that it seemed like she did indeed enjoy herself, and she replied, "I thought that because I wasn't going out on the town, there was something wrong with me."

Another client of mine worried that she was unable to meditate or relax. She has an anxiety disorder and tends to ruminate on problems. We explored the times when she feels the best, and she said it's when she's lying on the bed with her dog, looking out onto her tree-lined backyard. I told her that this is a form of relaxation and meditation, and that she doesn't have to sit in the lotus position for hours to get in touch with her true Self. She was already doing it, but she didn't even realize it.

It is by quieting our racing minds that we get in touch with our inner Self. Most of us stay active or attempt a perfectly controlled life to avoid our inner spirituality. Deep down *everyone* feels a vague sense of anxiety, an emptiness, a hole. This is the sense of separation from our Higher Self, God, our Source. To fill the void we run around frantically busy, distracting ourselves while striving for future dreams and goals. We sedate ourselves with addictions or compulsions, to avoid the pain and guilt of the past. We obsess and worry, planning every detail of our lives so we don't feel the underlying lack of control. People who believe in a positive afterlife squelch some of this anxiety, but many people who say that they believe in heaven still face death with tremendous fear. In addition, many people live in absolute dread of what's lurking around the corner, but they hide it well, even from themselves. As Henry David Thoreau observed, "The mass of men lead lives of quiet desperation."

Karl Marx said that religion is the opiate of the masses. For most of history, wealth and education belonged to the upper class, and the masses turned to religion, for that was all they had. Common people were unable to read and were not allowed to own land, as they were subject to the king or feudal lord. Without the ability to own their own possessions, they had no incentive to become self-sufficient. Without the ability to read, they could not develop their intelligence and form their own religious opinions. The church held great power and told people what to believe and what would happen to them if they didn't believe.

In America, each man is his own ruler. We are independent, intelligent, and can think for ourselves. Today only about 30 percent of our population attends church. Perhaps the other 70 percent have become disillusioned with dogmatic religious teachings. Our founding fathers shoved off religious oppression, and the independent American will not be told what to do or how to think. Our country was the first great experiment in religious and financial freedom for the masses. We have been blessed that the working and middle classes can improve their quality of life more easily than in the past. Therefore, restrictive spiritual teachings go against the grain of a free citizenry.

Today, instead of religion being the opiate of the masses, we have pharmacology, technology, and entertainment. The average American spends multiple hours in front of the television, allowing distraction from real life. The noise and fast-paced images make us forget our troubles. We have reality television shows because too many people feel dead and unfulfilled in their own lives. Advertisements tell us to ask our doctor about a purple pill, enticing us with scenes of carefree bliss. Numerous Americans are on some type of psychotropic drug, hoping that the magic pill will fill the emptiness in their lives.[1] Countless others distract and numb themselves with the latest technological gizmo, getting lost for hours in their machines.

Television, medication, and electronic technology are wonderful tools for pleasure and relief when used in a balanced manner. However, for many they have become addictions in their own right. They provide the sedating, mind-numbing fix to avoid the truth of our being, to avoid facing our fears and exploring life, to avoid becoming the wondrous people that we can be.

There is a simple, powerful way out of our collective misery that everyone can access. Jesus came two thousand years ago to teach us that we are one with God, that we are loved, forgiven, and have eternal life. He taught us to experience oneness with God *in our hearts* rather than from a set of rules. Ironically, religious rules have sprung up around Jesus' teachings and prevented many people from hearing his message. He broke the rules and was condemned to die for it. One of his most famous teachings contradicted the concept of "an eye for an eye," as he told us to "turn the other cheek." Jesus taught us to love and forgive everyone, not just the people who followed the rules. He hung out with the "scum" of society, the tax collectors and prostitutes. Yet he did not pity them; he saw them as equals. Jesus called God "Father" to let us know that we don't have to be afraid of God.

Jesus taught that we don't have to feel guilty, and that no matter what we've done, God loves us and we are forgiven. He did not create a church with guilt-inducing rules, yet the name Jesus frequently evokes images of preachers shouting that we are guilty sinners. Sadly, too many of us do not know the real Jesus, and do not realize that he taught that we could be as loving, serene, and powerful as he is.

Jesus came to teach us how to live life to the fullest, how to be supremely happy, how to recognize that we can tap into our inner spirit in the same way that he did. We do not have to believe in Jesus to understand that his teachings of love and forgiveness are the key to happiness.

There seems to be a resurgence of positive religion today, even though the masses don't participate. Many spirit-filled churches teach the love of Jesus, the positive-thinking, up-lifting, and happy message of Jesus. These churches are like loving, helpful, supportive extended families in an age when many families are no longer supportive to their members. These centers are joyful places, not places that evoke fear of hellfire. There is also a resurgence of spirituality outside the confines of organized religion. This book is about *A Course in Miracles*, which is one path for those who respect Jesus' teachings but do not feel beholden to church doctrine.

False Assumptions about God

> *There can be but little liberty on earth*
> *while men worship a tyrant in heaven.*
> ~Robert Ingersoll

Every society has its mores and standards that dictate what we're supposed to think, how we're supposed to feel, and how we're supposed to act. These messages are both overt and covert, yet we all know what they are. Most people in our society have adopted the Judeo-Christian concept of God without questioning it in depth. Even people who have never stepped foot in a church know the story of Adam and Eve and Jesus' crucifixion. These stories have overtones of an angry God who exacts certain demands or there will be hell to pay, literally.

Children are sometimes unwittingly and sometimes deliberately taught that God is a big, bad bogeyman. Therefore, many people develop superstitious beliefs that they can't fully shake in adulthood, because they're so ingrained in their emotional makeup. Children have what's called "magical thinking," in which they believe they are the cause of external events. For example, if Mommy comes home from work in a bad mood, little Susie believes she has done something wrong to make her angry. If a child is told that God is going to send him to hell for lying or stealing, the child is not mature enough to logically conclude that there really is no hell. Internally he stores this fear, which becomes a pervasive, underlying fear of God. Many people don't realize they have a fear of God until tragedy happens and they blame God for it.

Many who have come to believe in a loving God as adults still have trouble shaking the little voice that taunts, "You're going to hell!" One of my friends remembers giggling in church while his mother hushed him angrily, snapping, "God is going to strike you dead!" He says that *terrified* him! Another friend put medals of the saints under her grandparents' mattress because they did not attend church and she did not want them to go to hell. Yet another relates one of the most shaming moments of her life, when it occurred to her that Jesus must have had a penis. She laughs at it today, but says at the time it was terrifying, and in her mind of a child she was doomed. A client of mine blamed God throughout her childhood because her father abandoned her.

My partner Rod was raised in the Catholic Church. As he was a constant troublemaker, the nuns threatened that he would go to hell, where there was ripping of flesh and gnashing of teeth. He got temporary relief by going to confession, but he sinned so often by fighting and lusting after girls that he gave up and assumed he was damned. After he broke away from the church, it took almost twenty-five years before he felt comfortable at Easter. He was taught that if he did not go to confession during the year before each Easter that he would be excommunicated from the church, which meant eternal hellfire. He says that even though he didn't logically believe in hell anymore, the fear was still in his gut. This is how strongly these messages affect us!

When I was a small child, I worried that my parents were going to hell because they did not go to church. My mom was definitely going to hell because she smoked. I know now that God does not want anyone to feel fear or be afraid of Him, yet I learned that to be God-fearing was good.

Would we send our parent or child to burn and be tortured eternally? Of course not. The mother of a serial killer, while knowing he's done wrong, would not condemn her son to the electric chair. We have projected our fears onto God, which is why so many beliefs about God are completely illogical. This is not the sole domain of the Christian religion, for just about every theology contains strange elements. This is because, from our earthly perspective, we cannot conceive of pure Love and true reality. Thus, we make up stories to explain the concept of God, because our minds seek explanations. Unfortunately, the answers lose rationality when fear, rather than love, becomes the predominant focus.

Tragic Consequences of False Beliefs

There ain't no fans nor no rest and, brother,
there ain't no Cokes in hell.
~Anonymous North Carolina preacher

My client Terry was in therapy for about a year and a half for alcoholism. He was sober and trying hard to improve himself. One day he came in and began speaking in a shaky voice. "Lorri, I've got lung cancer. I'm going to die." A single constrained tear rolled down his face, followed by a stifled sob. "I know I'm going to hell because of all the people I killed and tortured in Vietnam." He then broke into unbridled tears. My heart ached to see him so terrified, and I tried to reassure him. "Terry, there is no such thing as the hell you were taught. That was just said to control and frighten us, just as you are frightened now." Unfortunately, Terry was not reassured. He left, stating that even though he and I were close, he would not be back because he would feel embarrassed and weak if I watched him die.

I never saw Terry again, but years later came across a thank-you card he had written to me, and it put a smile on my face. I loved Terry, and I only wish I could have helped him through his terrifying experience. I knew that he would eventually be okay, but probably not until his body died and he found out that there had been nothing to worry about after all.

The type of fear that Terry had is one I hope to dispel in this book. You are safe, there is no death in reality, and you are loved by a God who would never even think of sending you to a hell. God does not, and never has, seen us as sinful and separated from Him. Sadly, this is not what a lot of us are taught growing up. Many of us are instilled with the same type of fear, if not terror, that Terry experienced. While religions may mean well, the results of their teachings can be extremely harmful, as in Terry's case. Terry suffered needless terror and trauma when he could have had a loving and positive transition into the next realm.

My client Sharon was in psychotherapy to address her profound grief over her only child's death in a car accident. When she saw the wreckage wrapped around a tree, her first thought was, "Someone really wanted my daughter." Sharon anguished because she had only recently given her daughter permission to drive and was racked by guilt at her decision. During Sharon's therapy she spent session after session expressing her rage, grief, and hopelessness. How different it would have been if she knew that her daughter lived on and she could have continued contact with her. I sent Sharon to a psychic medium, and she received information that only she and her daughter had known. This helped her, but she still felt her daughter was far away and she wouldn't see her again until she died herself. Today I would teach Sharon how to have ongoing contact with her child herself, but at the time I did not know how to do this.

One day Sharon stated she had driven by a church and screamed in hatred at God, giving Him the finger. Notice the assumption she made, that God was the one who took her daughter away. Sharon was not particularly religious, yet she still ascribed control of the world's affairs to a God who would deprive her of the most precious thing in her life. She said that she used to wish that she was more loving like her daughter had been, and after her daughter's death she did become more compassionate. She wondered if God used this situation to help her learn this. Although this is a common explanation during grief, it is not the way God instructs us. God reaches out to us only in love, not through pain (chapters 4 and 5 explain this more fully).

A less intense though still damaging type of reaction to the threat of hellfire is the guilt and fear that many people feel when they think they've done something wrong. I had a young mother as a client, Jan, who was a sweet, intelligent woman with an angelic face. To look at her you would never suspect the shame she carried. Jan had a young child and was pregnant with her second. The year before she had had a brief affair and got pregnant by the other man. She had not been having sex with her husband, so she decided she must have an abortion to hide her affair. Jan was so racked with self-loathing and guilt that she was depressed, anxious, obsessive-compulsive, and hateful toward her husband. She was convinced that God would never forgive her and that she would go to hell for murdering her baby.

What if Jan was raised with the knowledge of a God that loved her no matter what she did? What if she knew that she was innocent by virtue of being a beloved child of God, one He would always embrace and never condemn? She would still have sorrow and guilt over the affair and the abortion, but they would be much less intense. When people believe that God himself hates them, they feel hopeless and despairing. There is no way out.

When I was about ten, my best friend's cousin Alice had twins, and one of them died at three months of sudden infant death syndrome. I felt so bad when I heard that Alice was wailing, screaming, and moaning. Insensitive people told her that she at least had the other baby and she shrieked, "I don't care! I want Emma back!" My friend's father was extremely angry and I cowered as he shouted, "If one more person tells me this is God's will, I'll punch his lights out!" I thought silently to myself that it was God's will, as that's what I'd been taught in church. I sure wasn't going to say it out loud, though.

A Course in Miracles offers a different way of thinking about traumas such as these. It definitively repudiates that God created the cruelty in this world. The *Course* says, **the world you see is the delusional system. . . . If this were the real world, God *would* be cruel (T-13.in.2:2; 3:1).** If Alice believed in the traditional idea of heaven, it likely gave her some small comfort of reuniting with her child. However, she has probably grieved for this child all these years. If Alice were to practice the ACIM Workbook lessons, she could learn to experience that she and her baby are one and that there is no separation in reality. We are capable of feeling our loved one's presence regardless of physical death. Heaven is a state of mind found right here and now. It is not some far-off place after we die. This is what Jesus meant in the Bible, when he said, "the kingdom of God is within you" (Luke 17:21). As we do the Workbook lessons, we become more peaceful by the day, despite whatever is happening in our lives.*

---

* Go to my website, http://www.lorricoburn.com, for a free e-mail newsletter that helps apply *Course* principles in daily life.

CHAPTER THREE

THE DREAM

Our birth is but a sleep and a forgetting.
~William Wordsworth

There is no world!
This is the central thought the Course
attempts to teach (W-p.I.132.6:2-3).

I was at a coffee shop with my sixteen-year-old niece Catherine. One of Catherine's friends died of cancer at age fifteen, and Catherine's reaction was, "I hate God!" Catherine suffers terribly from migraines, and she has had a constant headache for over a year. She has missed a lot of school, as she is unable to get up in the morning because of her excruciating pain. She was hospitalized for several weeks in a head pain clinic, but she still did not improve. She cannot understand why God allows her to suffer so. I explained the concept that this world is a dream, but that we still seem to suffer within the dream. She surprised me by saying that she and her boyfriend had just been discussing the dream idea. She said, "What if we just think we're living this life, but we're really only having a dream? Wouldn't that be weird?" I complimented her for thinking outside the box and told her that her inner wisdom was revealing the truth to her.

While the dream concept may seem foreign to many Westerners, the idea has been around a long time in the East. The Hindus call this world "Maya," which means "illusion." The Gnostics and many early Christians also believed that the world was a dream. Buddhism perceives this world as an illusion as well. When I first heard the idea that this world is an illusion, it was in a book about Hinduism. The author was asking God why people have to suffer, and God's answer was to not worry about it since it was only a dream. This author implied that God created this earth, and placed us here to experience the dream. This angered me. I hollered at God, "I don't care if it's simply a dream; I'm still here and I don't like where You put me!"

This issue of whether God created this world and sent us here is the question *A Course in Miracles* answers clearly. God neither created this earth, nor did He put us here. We are not really here; we are just *imagining* that we are. We are asleep, dreaming this world, but our *experience* is that it is real. In order to change the experience, we need to awaken from the dream. The first step in awakening is to *allow* the idea that this is a dream, and not resist this concept. We have a choice about whether to wake up, and we need to make a decision to do so for awakening to occur.

> ### *The world you see is an illusion of a world.*
> ### *God did not create it . . . (C-4.1:1-2).*

My client Gary is a passionate musician, full of life, emotional, and charismatic. Gary raises an objection to the term "illusion." He makes a good point that simply calling this life an illusion seems to invalidate our experiences. He recently met a woman who appears to be his soul mate. They met at a music festival far from their respective homes, and the energy, love, and acceptance between them is mesmerizing. How could this not be real? Gary's right—it is real. In fact, love is the only thing that is real and never dies. It is their separate physical bodies that aren't real. Physical bodies always decay and die, but the spiritual love between them remains. That's why this love feels so profound, so otherworldly, because it is a symbol of the oneness we have with God. It is the belief in separation, the belief that love can possibly die, that is the illusion.

> *You are at home in God,*
> *dreaming of exile but perfectly capable*
> *of awakening to reality. Is it your decision*
> *to do so? You recognize from your own*
> *experience that what you see in dreams you think*
> *is real while you are asleep. Yet the instant*
> *you waken you realize that everything*
> *that seemed to happen in the dream did not*
> *happen at all. You do not think this strange,*
> *even though all the laws of what you awaken to*
> *were violated while you slept. Is it not possible*
> *that you merely shifted from one dream to*
> *another, without really waking? (T-10.I.2:1-6)*

> *The choice is not between which dreams*
> *to keep, but only if you want to live in dreams*
> *or to awaken from them (T-29.IV.1:5).*

Notice the above comment that we do not think nighttime dreams are strange. This is because we see them as normal. Likewise, we see our so-called waking lives as normal, when in reality they are as ephemeral as our dreams at night. God made us with all the creative powers of Himself, and we have free will to do whatever we want with that creativity. Because our imaginations are so creative and powerful, we made this incredible world with its array of fascinating delights and horrors. If we want to keep dreaming of exile, we can do that. If we want to wake up and realize our true nature, we can do that as well.

The Perceived Separation

> *Every parting gives a foretaste of death;*
> *every coming together again a foretaste of the resurrection.*
> *~Arthur Schopenhauer*

*A sense of separation from God is the only
lack you really need correct (T-1.VI.2:1).*

We are not truly separate from God, yet we are dreaming that
we are. From this dream arise countless scenarios of loss and death
in which we feel frightened and alone. Conversely, there are an
equal amount of wonderful, delightful experiences that symbolize
our reunion with God. The terror of the separation and the joy
of the reunion are replayed symbolically over and over. Looking
at this world, we can think, "What a crazy imagination I must
have!" Indeed, how in the world did we imagine that we could
separate from God, and why would we even want to? The *Course*
states that God created us in his likeness, with all of His creative
powers. In our imagination we pondered the idea, "I wonder what
it would be like to be apart from God?" This is called **a tiny, mad
idea (T-19.IV.C.5:6)** because it's impossible that we could ever
separate from God's love. In that split second, this dream world
was made, in all its various forms.

The idea of the opposite of heaven brought gruesome scenarios
of death, disease, and destruction. The belief in separation has
caused an epidemic of depression and anxiety in our society. Never
have more people been on antidepressants and tranquilizers. We
have lost our center. **Depression is an inevitable consequence of
separation. So are anxiety, worry, a deep sense of helplessness,
misery, suffering, and intense fear of loss (W-p.I.41.1:2-3).**

Why would we even *want* to imagine being away from God if
heaven is so blissful? Because we are free to imagine anything we
choose, for that is the creativity God gave us. What we do with
it is our choice. One day when I was mad at God and taking him
to task, I complained, "God, why did you make me so I could
imagine such horrors? I would rather be ignorant and in bliss."
God's response led to an "aha" moment in which I emotionally
grasped the truth. "Would you rather be a puppet?" God replied.
"No, of course not," I thought. "I love my freedom." I compared
God's answer to how I want my daughter to be her own person.
Even though I think I know best what would make her happy, I
let her make her own decisions. Similarly, God loves us enough

to let us create our own lives. We are free to choose whatever we want to experience. No restrictions are placed on us, because love offers freedom.

> *Your other life has continued*
> *without interruption, and has been*
> *and always will be totally unaffected*
> *by your attempts to dissociate it (T-4.VI.1:7).*

Who among us hasn't awakened in a cold sweat from a nightmare and felt extremely relieved to realize it was just a dream? While we are dreaming we respond with the same physiological reactions as if the events were really happening. We don't remember that our bodies are safe in our beds. Thus it is in what we call our real life. We think the events are really happening and we respond accordingly. Sometimes our lives are happy dreams; other times they are nightmares. They are dreams all the same. When they are happy dreams we are attached to them and don't want them to end. We want to keep our happy family as it is, or never lose that current best friend. We want things to remain the same to ensure our happiness, but the one constant in life is change. When our lives are filled with sorrow or difficulties, then we want to change them and get rid of the pain as soon as possible. Death and loss pull the rug out from under us, and we are distressed until life is stable again. We can't wait for that part of the dream to end.

Regardless of what happens in our illusory life, regardless of what beautiful dream or ugly nightmare we are having or have had, our true life with God goes on uninterrupted. When we awaken we see that this has always been so. Have you ever gone through a particularly painful time in your life, then looked back and realized how much you contributed to the problem? I experienced this with one of the biggest traumas of my life, losing custody of my six-year-old daughter. This was very humiliating and I felt like the scourge of the earth, extremely ashamed. The stereotype of a mother who loses custody is that she is no good, a terrible person, a drug addict, or a whore. Why else would any mother lose custody of a young daughter? Yet I was none of these. We had three psychological evaluators in our case and all three judged both my former husband and me to be adequate parents, bonded well to our daughter. The final evaluator judged my daughter to be more emotionally connected with her father, so decided he should have custody of her.

However, my former husband, Donald, was moving 250 miles away. There was a clause in our divorce agreement that if either parent moved away, the one remaining in the original area would retain custody. Donald had insisted on this clause because he thought I might move away. The evaluator ignored this clause, Donald ignored this clause, and the court ignored it as well, going against its own previous ruling. One of the most prestigious lawyers in the state told me that 80 percent of case law indicated that I should have gotten custody. In spite of this, I appealed and lost. I was devastated and did not get over this for six years, experiencing rage, depression, injustice, despair, and suicidal feelings.

In hindsight, I can see how I drew this nightmare to myself. This was subconscious, of course, as consciously I'd never choose to hurt myself so drastically. I felt guilty around my mothering, so I was punishing myself. While I was a loving mother, I always questioned my worthiness and my daughter's need for me, and I felt that her father was a much better parent than I was. There were numerous court rulings that defied the law and defied logic. They defied law and logic because my dream mirrored my own self-image rather than logic. I made the dream up as I went, and I lost every step of the way because I thought I was a loser. I was enraged at the unjust court system, which also reflected my rage at the injustice of life in general.

Today I do not believe this critical loss would affect me as strongly, for my self-image has changed and I am learning that I don't need to create drama and trauma. I can clearly see many actions of mine during that court period that perpetuated the problem. At the time I thought I was just responding to outside events designed to harm me. I did not realize that my responses were always creating new scenarios. I know now to practice forgiveness, recognizing that this is all a dream. If the situation happened today I may or may not lose custody of my child, but I would accept the outcome more easily.

Our dreams appear very real to us. Losing my child felt all too real for me, but as I am awakening from the dream I feel relief and have even regained love for my ex-husband, who I now see was just playing his role in the dream. I see the whole situation now as something I conjured up to make real my fears of separation and loss. Today I mostly feel the love that was behind the whole situation all along, my love for my daughter, as well as my daughter's and her father's love for me. For the most part, I no longer blame my daughter's father, and the conflict between us has decreased dramatically. After all, I put him in my dream. Forgiveness is the main technique for awakening from the dream, and had I known how to forgive it would not have taken me six long years to recover and wake up. This process of forgiveness will be described in more detail later on.

Recognizing the dream can profoundly change all areas of our lives. Many of us get upset with our government and think life would be better if only the politicians would get their act together. Today I can no longer fault the president and Congress for making decisions that I disagree with, for that is the dream, too. All of us are figures in the dream, and it is up to me to see them and myself as actors in the dream and not get upset about them. This has not been easy, but when I have been able to do it, it has brought peace.

In the past I used to go on regular rants about all sorts of issues. The dents in my floors and walls are witnesses to them. Griping and complaining were some of my favorite sources of entertainment, and I would rage out loud during the entire morning drive to work about the complaint du jour. I can still throw tantrums if I choose, but they don't hold the power they used to. How can I be upset with a dream? The other day I was having a raging fit and right in the middle of it I burst out laughing! I watched myself getting mad and realized I was acting upset over something that wasn't real. Laughter erupts regularly these days, as I witness the crazy dream I've made and see how much importance I've placed on *nothing*! Now, rather than complain about the apparent problems in my life, I am changing my mind about them, and that automatically brings peace. I used to *try* to lighten up, as I didn't like feeling so serious, but *trying* to change didn't work. Seeing the truth did.

My friend Pat underwent a bone marrow transplant about ten years ago. She was in tremendous fear about the very real possibility that she could die. When she finally accepted that she could indeed die, she felt a deep peace come over her. What she did was let go of attachment to her personal identity and body. Only in the dream can "we" die. Our real Self knows It is never born and never dies. When Pat released the fear that was covering her true nature, the peaceful Self emerged.

The dream can be compared to living in a ten-story building. We live on the first floor here on earth, and we are unaware that there are ten floors to our universe. When catastrophes happen, we're thrown into the basement, where it's cold, damp, and dark. There, the negative effects of the dream are very real. We suffer and are in despair, and it's hard to see a way out of the misery. During tragedies, however, we have a chance to climb higher, as we access our love to help one another. When we act lovingly instead of fearfully, it's as if we're on the fifth floor. Life's a little nicer up here. As we step back from the dream even further and recognize the illusion, we are on the eighth floor. We see more because we're higher up. When we awaken fully and are released from the dream, we're on the tenth floor. We're home with God, and it's heaven.

I heard an Indian yoga teacher say that people in India, for all their poverty and disease, tend to be happier than we are in the United States, with all our wealth. He said they focus on the spiritual reality more than we do, and this decreases their suffering. When we are focused on the physical reality, even if it's the ongoing quest to improve our life circumstances, we can lose the higher perspective. We lose touch with our innate core, our real self, in which true happiness lies. This happiness is not dependent on external circumstances, but it is always present.

What would your life be like if you truly recognized that it's all a dream and that you are still safe at home with God? Would anything ever make you afraid again? Would you lighten up?

Would you start seeing the figures in your dream as extensions of your own imagination? Would you be afraid to die? Imagine the difference in your life if you could truly grasp the truth that this is all a dream. Nothing would be the same again!

In our nighttime dreams we can become aware that we are dreaming. Before going to sleep we can set the intention that we will be aware that we are dreaming. This is called "lucid dreaming." When we have lucid dreams, we can remind ourselves that we're dreaming, enter the dream, and change the outcome. Try this. If you've had a recurring dream that you don't like, tell yourself that the next time you have it you are going to change it. You can also apply this process to your daytime dreams.

There Is No Death

> *There is no death! What seems so is transition.*
> *This life of mortal breath*
> *Is but a suburb of the life elysian,*
> *Whose portal we call "Death."*
> *~Henry Wadsworth Longfellow*

> **Death is the central dream from**
> **which all illusions stem. Is it not madness**
> **to think of life as being born, aging,**
> **losing vitality, and dying in the end?**
> **Without the idea of death there is no world.**
> **All dreams will end with this one**
> **(M-27.1:1-2; 6:3-4).**

It is said that there are no atheists in foxholes. Certainly war provokes terror, as fear of death and bodily destruction are at their peak. Soldiers pray for safety and loved ones at home pray for their safe return. Impending death brings to many a sense of aloneness and panic. However, we can connect with a power of love greater than us, which allows us to find our way to peace. Feeling this connection has brought peace to many in the midst of war. There is a sense of gentle calm that things are okay no matter what happens.

One of my clients, John, found peace during the Vietnam War by carrying the Prayer of St. Joseph with him. He carries it with him to this day, grateful for how it helped him. John describes an intriguing incident when his buddy Dan was severely wounded by shrapnel in his leg. Dan went into shock and asked John if the bees were still around. Puzzled, John said, "Bees, what bees?" "The bees that stung my leg," Dan replied. John saw shrapnel holes, while Dan saw bee stings. John was awed by the power of the mind to trick itself. As he read *The Disappearance of the Universe*, he kept recalling Dan's illusory bee stings. This helped John understand how we fool ourselves by believing our dreams.

Whether the problem is war or something seemingly less serious, the answer is the same. When we remember our oneness with God, the problem will no longer be a problem. When we remember it is a dream, we can no longer be upset with it. The more we remember that we are at home in heaven *now*, the more we will experience serenity.

> *It must be so that either God is mad*
> *or is this world a place of madness.*
> *Not one Thought of His makes any sense at all within*
> *this world. And nothing that the world believes*
> *as true has any meaning in His Mind at all*
> *(T-25.VII.3:2-4).*

When I read the above statement, I feel relieved. Thank God that God did not make this place of madness! And I thank God that His thoughts are completely contrary to this world. This world of madness has so many traumas: war, illness, death, divorce, job loss, relationship conflict, political conflict, famine, natural disasters, and so on. All of these carry a sense of angst, a fear of loss. All of these losses are types of deaths. We fear losing whatever it is we are attached to, be it a person, a lifestyle, or an opinion.

These things give us security, comfort, safety, and familiarity. One of my friends jokes that her two husbands feared losing their possessions more than her. Her first husband was a scholar and worried that someone would break into their home and steal his books. Her second husband was devoted to his dogs, and worried they'd be kidnapped for animal research. We usually worry about what we're most attached to, and these things are substitutes for the safety of God.

My sister's mother-in-law, Omi, looked the epitome of a grandma. Her cherubic round face had a halo of fluffy silver hair, and her German accent topped it off. Omi was a gentle soul, one of the sweetest people I ever met, and one of my biggest spiritual teachers. About twenty-five years ago Omi and her husband, Opa, were robbed in their home on an isolated country road. They were elderly, wealthy, and easy prey for the hired hand that framed the robbery. One night a stranger knocked on their door, claiming she was stranded, and asked to use their phone. Gentle, unsuspecting souls that they were, they let her in, and were terrorized by the man who pushed in behind her. The intruders ransacked the house, knowing where to find the valuables, and hit Opa on the head. Opa died of a stroke three days later.

Omi's response to her husband's murder made a profound impact on me. I asked her how she could go on, and she gave me a clipping of a favorite quote from Catherine Marshall: "When someone you love is with God, he is not far away." This brought her peace. She lived it and knew it. The love was still there and could not be destroyed by death. Years later, Omi was in her nineties, physically deteriorating and wishing she would die. I had Omi's picture on my refrigerator, looked at it, and asked her, "I wonder when you are going to be set free from that body of yours?" I got a call from my sister the next day. Omi had passed into the arms of God right about the time I spoke to her picture.

Omi's experience with her husband's death is in stark contrast to the experience of my client Toni. Toni's husband was killed in a car accident in which she was a passenger. She gave him CPR, but he was pronounced dead upon the arrival of the ambulance. This trauma paralyzed Toni, leaving her emotionally numb and stricken for several years. Because her husband did not believe in life after death, she assumed that his spirit either no longer existed or went to hell. She was unsure about the ability to contact loved ones after death and was disappointed that she didn't feel his presence. They had had marital problems and she took the absence of his spirit to mean that he hadn't really loved her. Toni also carried a lot of guilt over not having done enough to save his life. This guilt and fear blocked the love and delayed her recovery process by years. As she began releasing her guilt and fear, she started coming out of her numb state.

How different it would have been for Toni if she could have embraced the truth that she was not separated from her husband in reality. Yes, his body was gone, but his spirit wasn't. I kept telling her that when she got over her fears and doubts, she would realize this, and that her guilt and fear were blocking the truth, much like a cloud blocks the sun. The sun is still behind the cloud, but if we think the sun is gone forever, we will panic. However, each time we allow for the smallest possibility of immortality, some sunshine warms us through the cloud.

Another client of mine, Dory, nursed her mother through cancer, and upon her death frequently sensed her mother's presence by smelling her perfume. Dory entered therapy for her alcoholism, feeling tremendous guilt over her alcohol-related behavior. She said she had not felt her mother's presence lately, and thought her mom must have disapproved of her. I told her that her mother did not disapprove of her; rather, it was her own guilt that was blocking her mom's love. We discussed the movie *Flatliners*, in which some medical students deliberately induce heart attacks and brain death to see what near-death experiences are like. Each student experiences a situation that reflects how guilty he feels about *himself*. When the self-image and guilt heals, so does the experience. Dory took that to heart, and reported in the next session that she once again smelled her mom's perfume. She felt relieved and reconnected, and all she did was release her guilt so she could receive her mom's love.

> *You think that death is of the body.*
> *Yet it is but an idea. . . . A thought is in the*
> *mind. Death is the thought that you are*
> *separate from your Creator (W-p.I.167.3:1-3; 4:1).*

Albert Einstein, one of the most creative geniuses of our time, had this to say about death: "Now he has departed from this strange world a little ahead of me. That means nothing. People like us, who believe in physics, know that the distinction between past, present, and future is only a stubbornly persistent illusion."

There is no death! Since this is a dream and dream figures are not real, then how can there be death? Yet we are attached to our dream figures and want them to be real. We love our children, our mates, our family and friends. The confusion lies in thinking that we are our bodies. We are not our bodies; we are not our personalities; we are not these lives. As Dorothy departed the Land of Oz, she was saddened to lose Scarecrow, Tin Man, and Lion. Yet she awoke to find them beside her in the form of her neighbors. We do not lose our loved ones; they simply change form.

How much more comforting it is when we can say, "He is not apart from me, he is *a part of* me!" This is the truth. Yet when our loved ones die we will feel sadness and grief, because our human form carries emotions. There is a difference between allowing the feeling of grief and judging the feeling of grief. Allowance is forgiveness, and forgiveness frees us.

One of my favorite stories is about a Buddhist teacher who was crying because a child had died. His students were dismayed and exclaimed, "But, teacher, we thought you said death was an illusion! Why are you crying?" "Ah," the teacher replied, "The death of a child is the biggest illusion of all!" This story speaks to the importance of not denying our feelings even when we know it's all an illusion. If we get mad at ourselves for feeling grief, anger, or other such emotions, that itself makes the illusion real and keeps us stuck in it. It's best just to feel what we're feeling and let it pass through without resisting it. At the same time, we can pray for help in recognizing and releasing the false thoughts that we are separated from our loved one. Embracing the truth itself transforms the grief.

This life is just too painful and our emotions are too strong to simply dismiss them with a cavalier, "Oh, that's just an illusion!" That's too harsh. A more positive response to life's pain is, "The only reality is God. God's love is the only thing that endures." My friend Laura used to avoid her feelings and act like her problems didn't exist. She is afraid that if she sees life as an illusion now she will resort to denying her pain and remain stuck. Laura is on the right track, as denying or pushing away our feelings just keeps them stuck to us longer. A common psychotherapy phrase is, "What we resist persists." However, we can keep the awareness that this is all a dream in the back of our minds, while still allowing grief, anger, and sadness. Experiencing the feelings allows us to move through them, and we need to be kind to ourselves and allow the process to take as long as it does without judging ourselves. Some issues can take years to get through, and that's okay. Realizing that life here is an illusion does not initially take away our pain, and processing the feelings is part of awakening. To fake being happy when we're not will actually thwart our progress. Eventually we see that feelings themselves are illusions, and then we are free.

My friend Lisa was in a rage toward her father for his denial that he sexually abused her. She is a *Course* student and stopped attending meetings for awhile because she felt the group members did not validate her anger. The *Course* states that on the level of truth no anger is justified, because this is a dream. However, we need to use our small "t" truth of emotions to get to our capital "T" truth of ultimate reality. Our emotions feel like our truth in the moment. Lisa allowed herself to be angry with her father and eventually forgave him. She couldn't have done it if she felt guilty for, or denied, being angry.

When I visited my niece Catherine in the hospital, her blood pressure dropped dramatically. I panicked, afraid she was going to die. In the back of my mind was the notion that this was just a dream, yet that did not stem my anxiety. While we are in the midst of overpowering emotions, sometimes the best we can do is pray for help, and we will eventually feel peace.

There is no death and the body is not real. If you think you are your body, then are you the body that you have when you are twenty-five, or are you the body that you have when you are sixty? If you say, "I am a nurse," and you change careers, then who are you? If you get cancer and your body wastes away, who are you then? Who are you after the body dies? If you are married and identify yourself as Mrs. Joe Smith, who are you when Joe Smith dies?

My ninety-four-year-old father went into assisted living six years ago. My dad was always extremely healthy and vibrant—this was a man who climbed a four-hundred-foot sand dune overlooking Lake Michigan when he was seventy-three years old. He was so organized (or obsessive-compulsive) that he recorded his gas mileage on every single tank for fifty years. Now he cannot figure out the difference between Poligrip and toothpaste, thinks it's ok to wash his hands in the toilet, and has completely reconstructed his past due to dementia. He proudly tells people who comment on his University of Michigan cane, hat and sweater that he played football for the legendary coach Bo Schembechler. He can make up a story on the spot, even though he never even met Bo.

It has been extremely painful to watch my dad decline, and I get frustrated more often than I wish. But when I accept that my dad is not his body and the essence of his love will always remain, I'm at peace. My dad has always demonstrated unconditional love toward me, and I have realized that his love is a symbol of God's love. Therefore, I cannot possibly lose it, even when his body breaks down and dies.

> *Only the eternal can be loved,*
> *for love does not die (T-10.V.9:1).*

Not only can I not lose my dad's love, but he cannot lose the love inside of himself. My dad is one of those people who radiates inner joy and love. He is everyone's favorite uncle and favorite neighbor. Thus, when he went into assisted living, even though it was a huge loss of independence, he carried with him his true Self, and he is as happy as ever. The people at the retirement home love him as much as all his friends and neighbors always have. They say, "Here comes Wally," because they hear him singing as he walks down the hall. This internal joy is everyone's true nature, yet few of us express it.

As with my dad, our outer lives, personalities, and bodies are constantly changing. However, what God created is changeless. It does not decay and die. What we really are is the Self, which is the extension of God's mind, created as pure joy, love, and peace. No external circumstance can change our one Self, the mind, in which there is only light. Everything that we are dreaming comes from this one mind, which is from the creative Source. Any possibility that can be imagined in the mind can become manifest in the material world. However, none of the events in this material world has ever happened in reality, because it's only been a dream in the mind.

When you begin waking up from the dream, you actually start experiencing this truth. In my years of spiritual study I had read this concept many times, and from many spiritual traditions. It only started becoming real in the past few years, however, with my practice of forgiveness through the *Course* Workbook lessons. The love, joy, and peace inside of us used to be just words to me. I understood them intellectually, but they felt empty. Now I *experience* them. They *do* come from inside of me, for I can feel them in circumstances that only made me feel anxious before. Seeing your life as a dream instead of something to get upset about changes your perspective.

It's Only A Movie!

All the world's a stage,
And all the men and women merely players.
~Shakespeare

During my custody situation there were many times I could hardly make it through the day without breaking down in tears. One day I struggled to keep my emotions in check and constantly used the affirmation, "It's only a movie. It's only a movie." If I didn't make it real, I wouldn't be in so much despair over what was happening. I couldn't bear the thought of what my little girl was going through, or the thought of losing her. That night when I got home there was a feature column in the newspaper. The headline was "It's only a movie!" The column was about the movie *Titanic*, and it commented on how the movie character could keep her gold earrings on through all the gushing water and perilous jumps. I laughed and thanked God for the reassurance.

We identify with movie characters and strive to be heroic, loving, and courageous, to triumph over life's trials. But we are not really these characters. We are mind, not body. The mind can be compared to a film projector in a movie theater. From the projector mind, scenes are projected out onto the screen, upon which appear the events of our lives. We are the actor, director, and producer of our movie, but since we don't know it's a movie, we make it real.

At the movies, the screen does not show real events, only images. However, we suspend our disbelief. We know they're not true, but to enjoy them fully we pretend that they are. We cry at the death scenes; we rejoice at the reunions. But if someone dies on the screen we do not jump out of our seats to save him. If there is a war scene we do not run for cover or join in the battle, for we know it's not really happening.

Movies, like "real life," have continual themes of separation and reunion. These are metaphors of our perceived separation from God and our return to Him. Many songs are all about lost love or love regained. What triggers our emotions more than this? The hero comes home from war; what a joyous reunion! The bride loses her husband in the war; what a tragic separation! Actually, we love the drama. We love the dream. It gets our juices flowing. It gives us meaning in this dream life. Overcoming personal tragedy with love brings a sense of connection to the community and family.

As testament to how much we love the drama, look at how we gawk at car accidents. Even if we don't look, we've got to admit there's the urge to. Then we go and tell all our friends about the horrible car accident we saw. Another example is television news. The more tragic, the better. We love bad news! It gives us something to talk about, something to get upset about, something to get excited about. How many times did we see replays of the Twin Towers falling? Thousands of times! What grabs people more than war scenes? Today we witness the war as it's happening, and this love of blood and gore is no different than that of the Roman gladiators. One of my clients was a Vietnam veteran and he guiltily admitted that when he was in a firefight it excited him. He related, "It was horrifying! Men were screaming in anguish, missiles were exploding, and fire engulfed us. But . . . I loved it!" He did not realize that his adrenaline rush was a common thrill during war.

There are racks of tabloids at the supermarket, and most of us glance at them to see which celebrity is getting divorced, is a drug addict, or has been caught in a sex scandal. The drama of Hollywood pulls many of us in. We love to hear the dirt. As much as we like to see celebrities soar, we love it even more when they fall. Yesterday's darling is today's goat. Television portrays the lives of the rich and famous and we are fascinated. Still, it is all a dream. Dreams of glory, dreams of defeat—we are captivated by our own dream.

> *Yet the Bible says that a deep sleep*
> *fell upon Adam, and nowhere is there reference*
> *to his waking up (T-2.I.3: 6).*

We are asleep, and we don't even know it. Just as dreams feel unreal, extreme crises and tragedies often create a sense of disbelief, a feeling of unreality. Try this exercise right now: imagine that you just got news that your loved one has been killed in a car accident. How would you feel? Would you wail and howl, panic, rage, or go numb from shock or denial? Imagine, then, that an hour later you get a call that it was all a mistake. It wasn't your loved one after all. Would you feel tremendous relief, happiness, and gratitude? Even though your loved one was never killed to begin with, you responded as if he or she were. You believed it was real, and therefore you had the corresponding emotions.

This is exactly what we are doing with our dream lives. We are reacting to them as if they are real, instead of remembering the truth that we are safe at home with God. In our extreme forgetfulness we experience untold amounts of grief. This may sound unbelievable, but when we practice the lessons in *A Course in Miracles* we actually start *experiencing* peace instead of grief.

Physics and the Illusion

The whole history of science has been the gradual realization that events do not happen in an arbitrary manner, but that they reflect a certain underlying order, which may or may not be divinely inspired.
~Stephen Hawking

Lest we think that the dreamlike nature of this world is a simple fantasy, we need look no further than science for possible evidence. Many things are invisible to the naked eye, such as ultraviolet light rays, cells, and germs. Look at your body and the chair you are sitting in right now. They seem solid, right? Wrong. Quantum physics has shown us that what we think is solid matter is really a mass of swirling atoms and that this universe is made up mostly of empty space. Since what we see with our eyes isn't what we think it is, can we consider that our perception of reality may be entirely different than *true reality*? Is it possible that this entire world that we think is real and solid is but an amorphous dream?

Scientists used to believe that matter was independent of us and responded to fixed laws. With the advent of quantum mechanics, however, scientists have changed their view of the nature of reality and are constantly revising it. Brian Greene, the Harvard-educated physicist and author of *The Fabric of the Cosmos*, states, "physicists such as myself are acutely aware that the reality we observe—matter evolving on the stage of space and time—may have little to do with the reality, if any, that's out there. . . . But during the last hundred years, discoveries in physics have suggested revisions to our everyday sense of reality that are as dramatic, as mind bending, and as paradigm-shaking as the most imaginative science fiction."[1] Notice that Greene says "if any" reality is out there. Perhaps there is no reality out there and it's all in our mind.

The *Course* states, as we shall see in chapter 4, that there is only one of us. Only one Son of God and we are all Him. How can this be when there are billions of separate bodies? Greene goes on to comment, "[There is] the current wild speculation that the universe we see may be nothing more than a cosmic hologram."[2] A hologram is a photograph or system in which each individual part contains within it the whole. For example, when a small piece of a holographic photograph is examined, that tiny piece shows all of the details of the larger picture. Hence, if the theory about the holographic nature of the universe is true, then each one of us contains within us everyone else. Einstein said, "The tragedy of human nature is the illusion of separation." These statements from noted physicists lend support to the idea that we are indeed *one*. The *Course* says, **there is no difference between the part and whole (T-8.VIII.1:15).**

Bell's theorem, a basic physics principle, posits that all things are interconnected. Say a photon is split into two halves, and one particle is in New York and the other is in Los Angeles. This theorem shows that when the particle in New York shifts, the one in Los Angeles has an immediate, corresponding shift—simultaneously. It doesn't matter that they appear to be thousands of miles apart; they are still connected. The *Course* speaks to this by saying **minds are joined (W-p.I.19.2:1).** Ultimately, there is only one Mind, the Mind of God, and we are all connected within it. It is everywhere present, and there is no separation, even though space and time *appear* to make us separate.

Most of us have heard the phrase from the dispute "a particle or a wave." Quantum physics has shown that a photon of light can appear as either a particle or a wave, but it can't be both. When we look at it, it becomes a particle; when we're not looking, it is a wave potential. The viewpoint of the observer determines what it becomes, and until this point, the outcome is pure potentiality. Therefore, matter does not act independently of us, rather it responds to our interaction with it. Thoughts are energy or matter; thus, we are constantly creating our lives with our thoughts. What our mind projector focuses on determines what shows up on our screen. As we will see in chapter 4, we are constantly making choices between love and fear, between God and this illusory world. We have approximately sixty thousand thoughts a day, and the thoughts we focus on determine our reality. When we choose thoughts of love, we eventually awaken from the dream. Just as the photon can be either a particle or a wave, we can choose the reality of God or the illusion of this world, but we can't have both.

The world arises from our mind, the projector, and is projected outward onto the screen of our lives. The mind is *outside* of space and time as we know it. The mind, which is the only thing that is real, projects the *appearance* of solid bodies living on earth for a period of time, but time is an illusion. Once again, what we perceive with our five senses is not reality. The brilliant physicist Stephen Hawking states, "The laws of science do not distinguish between the past and the future." As mentioned previously, Einstein also said that the distinction between past, present, and future is an illusion. The *Course* says, **past, present, and future are not continuous, unless you force continuity on them (T-13. VI.4:2).**

The theory of relativity proves that the space-time continuum is relative; that is, it is not a fixed measurement. For example, say a person travels into outer space close to the speed of light and is gone for several years. Depending on the speed he is traveling, fifty years can pass on earth, yet he will only have aged a few years. He returns to earth to find he is still in his twenties, while his friends are in their seventies or have died. Thus, time is not what it appears to be. ACIM states that in the brief instant in which we feared separation from God, this universe and every event in it *seemed* to appear. However, they did not really happen because time does not really exist. The only reality is the light and love of God. When time dissolves we experience true reality, which is beyond this world.

People who have had near-death experiences report being surrounded by a shining light and feeling profound peace unlike anything they've ever felt. These lucky people have experienced a moment of enlightenment beyond the veil of this illusion, beyond time. Many live changed lives in which they no longer fear death, for they know the timeless love behind it all.

In timelessness we coexist with God (T-2.V.17:7).

Yet what is done in dreams has not been really done. It is impossible to convince the dreamer that this is so, for dreams are what they are because of their illusion of reality. Only in waking is the full release from them . . . (T-17.I.1:5-7).

In *The Wizard of Oz*, Dorothy cannot be convinced that her dream isn't real. Auntie Em tries to reassure her that she simply had a bad dream, but Dorothy insists that Oz was an actual place. Dorothy's dream, like our lives, feels very real, but only has the *illusion* of reality. In the movie *The Matrix*, Morpheus encourages Neo to awaken by reminding him that he has often felt that something is not quite right with this world. Neo makes the courageous decision and chooses to awaken from his dream. He is thus liberated and becomes his Christ Self, which is the path we are all meant to take. We'll explore this path further in chapter 4.

Problems with the Illusion

Doubt is an incentive to search for truth,
and patient inquiry leads the way to it.
~Gamaliel Bailey

As I discuss the dream concept, I often hear, "I just can't wrap my mind around the idea that all of this isn't real. It doesn't make sense to me. Does this mean my life doesn't have any meaning, and the people I love aren't really there?" These are good questions and one reason why the *Course* says it is not the right path for everyone.

I have friends who practice Wicca and Native American paths, and they find their connection with God through nature. My friend who is a Native American shaman gets very angry at these lines in ACIM: **[This] is a required *Course*. Only the time you take it is voluntary (T-in.1:2-3).** He interprets that *A Course in Miracles* claims that we have to take *its* instruction alone. It really means that the *Course* we must learn is that we are one with God. There are many ways to do this, because we are all different.

I often feel the vastness of God as I stand by a roaring ocean or ski down a majestic mountain. The bliss, enthusiasm, and tranquillity come not from the ocean and the mountain, however, but from the mind that made them. Nature in all its beauty is part of the illusion, but the love we experience through nature is real. Separate bodies are also illusory, but the love we have for our family and friends also comes from the one Mind. The love behind the illusion is what is real and indestructible. Our mind is so powerful that we can make anything we want. The forms of the mountains, the sea, and our loved ones appear as long as we need them. The *Course* reassures us that we can't lose beauty and love. **All your past except its beauty is gone. . . . I have saved all your kindnesses and every loving thought you ever had (T-5.IV.8:2-3).**

We do not have to understand or believe in the idea of the dream to benefit from *A Course in Miracles*. The goal of the *Course* is inner peace while we appear to be living in the illusion. The *Course* teaches that forgiveness is the primary practice we should undertake if we are to be happy. Learning to forgive regularly provides such phenomenal benefits that it alone is worth doing the *Course*.

The Workbook acknowledges that many people will not be able to accept the dream idea, and that's okay. **There is no world! This is the central thought the *Course* attempts to teach. Not everyone is ready to accept it (W-p.I.132.6:2-4).** If you can't accept the dream concept and don't want to, that's okay. If you can't understand it but want to, pray for help. You will be given just the right concepts for you to help expand your awareness. One day understanding will come like the proverbial light bulb turning on, and you will be thrilled.

There was a study done on kittens raised in empty rooms with either vertical or horizontal stripes on the wall. The kittens were then placed in a room with a table and chairs. The kittens raised with horizontal stripes kept bumping into the chair and table legs, but were able to jump on and off the table and chairs. The ones raised with vertical stripes had no problem walking around the legs, but were unable to jump on or off the table. This illustrates how we become accustomed to certain environments, and this becomes our reality. Whatever stripes the kittens were raised with became their "reality," and they couldn't see anything else.

It can be hard to recognize or understand things that are different from our experience. I have a friend who is a scientist and there was a ghost in his house. He said he never would have believed it unless it had happened to him, because as a scientist he was trained to only trust what he can see. Likewise, all of our senses tell us that this earth is real. We don't have any paradigm otherwise. Therefore, it takes expansion of our thinking to accept this new idea that this life is an illusion.

Well, if we understand that this is all an illusion, do we stop enjoying life? No! We actually are freed to engage more fully in life because we live in the present moment and are not in fear. We feel a mystical sense of oneness with nature and thoroughly enjoy dancing, sports, and the arts. We take life less seriously, enjoying the moment, appreciating the physicality, but letting go of attachment to particular forms. We know love will show up again in an equally beautiful and engaging form, so we have less fear of loss.

Waking Up

Dreams are true while they last, and do we not live in dreams?
~Lord Tennyson

Since we are just dreaming, how come God doesn't just wake us up? Actually, God has been calling to us since the beginning of time, but we have been too dense to hear our wake-up calls. We can wake up gradually by doing the Workbook lessons. We are so engulfed in the dream that a sudden awakening could cause us great distress and disorientation.

> *Only after the deep sleep fell upon Adam could he experience nightmares. If a light is suddenly turned on while someone is dreaming a fearful dream, he may initially interpret the light itself as part of his dream and be afraid of it. However, when he awakens, the light is correctly perceived as the release from the dream (T-2.I.4:5-7).*

This idea that we are dreaming our lives scares many of us at first. If it's true, then what do our lives mean? If it's true, then how are we going to relate to life anymore? If it's true, then everything we've believed so far is false, and we don't know how to handle that. I have found that a lot of people don't like to hear that this life is a dream. They are attached to the dream or simply can't comprehend the idea. Even people who attend *A Course in Miracles* study groups sometimes don't want to focus on waking up from the dream, preferring to make the dream happier. This is what our whole society is questing after, the pursuit of happiness, making our lives as rich and fulfilled as possible.

We are one of the most prosperous cultures in history, and while we have been wonderfully blessed, the abundance has kept us focused on external pursuits instead of inner truth. There are so many great things to do, places to see, and dreams to achieve! We keep thinking that we'll find heaven on earth when we have the right job, the perfect family, the beautiful home, or lots of money. But we have been looking in all the wrong places! There is nothing wrong with wanting to be happy, but happiness will *never* be found within the dream. Oh, we may be happy for awhile, when we've accomplished or attained something, but that happiness soon turns to the quest for the next thing. All along, we do not realize that true happiness is found inside of ourselves, when we wake up and recognize the truth. **There are no satisfactions in the world (W-p.I.133.2:5).**

> *You are the Kingdom of Heaven, but you have*
> *let the belief in darkness enter your mind*
> *and so you need a new light (T-5.II.4:1).*

All the peace, love, and joy you have been looking for in your hobbies, accomplishments, and relationships are actually a part of your very Being. We eventually feel empty, in spite of achieving goals, because what we're really looking for is our true Self. We are compelled to pursue happiness because we are compelled to seek the true nature of our Being. We are compelled to find our true home, our Source, the reason we exist. People who meditate experience an inner calm when the outer world is shut out. The true Self is allowed to surface when the dream, the outside world, is ignored. Peace, love, and joy are inherent qualities of our Being, but they get lost in the busyness of our lives.

If you truly knew that everything you could possibly want was already inside of you, how would that change your behavior? Would you take it easy? Would you relax and enjoy the peace that is present wherever you are, whether it's a city highway or a country lake? We think peace is only found when we have the perfect setting, but it is available at all times, everywhere. It is when we awaken that we understand the childhood tune, "Row, row, row your boat, gently down the stream, merrily, merrily, merrily, merrily, life is but a dream."*

The Miracle

> *What a surprise to find you could shift the contents in your head*
> *like rearranging furniture in a room.*
> *~Lisa Alther*

> *Reality is never frightening.*
> *It is impossible that it could upset me.*
> *Reality brings only perfect peace.*

---

* Go to my website, http://www.lorricoburn.com, for a free PDF download, "Ten Tips to Awaken from the Dream."

When I am upset, it is always because
I have replaced reality with illusions I made up
(W-p.I.52.1:2-5).

It is from this savage fantasy that you want to escape.
Is it not joyous news to hear that it is not real? Is it
not a happy discovery to find that you can escape?
All that you fear does not exist (W-p.I.22.2:1-3; 5).

This world is not the true reality. Only love, only God, is real. The world of God can never frighten us as this world does. As the comment above notes, it *is* joyous news to find out that all the pain and suffering are not real and that escape is possible. My escape from this prison began with accepting the idea that this life is just a dream. At first, I too couldn't comprehend that this world was a dream, but as I turned my thinking over to the true Self within, my thoughts were changed for me. We are so entrenched in this dream world that we cannot do this by ourselves. After all, we don't even know we're dreaming to begin with! We think we know what reality is, but we are seeing an illusion. We have to be willing to have our thinking changed, indeed, to have our normal way of processing turned upside down. **To learn this *Course* requires willingness to question every value that you hold (T-24.in.2:1).** The changes in thought are certainly radical, but the benefits are definitely worth it!

A miracle is a correction. It does not create,
nor really change at all. It merely looks on devastation,
and reminds the mind that what it sees is false
(W-p.II.13.1:1-3).

The miracle is the change in thinking, the awareness that this life is false. The miracle does not necessarily change outer circumstances; rather, it changes how we view them. ACIM is unlike some thought systems that hold that external situations will definitely change if only we change our inner feelings and thoughts. Before I learned what ACIM teaches, I thought that my miracle was getting custody of my daughter. I did all the affirmations, visualizations, and prayers that I was told would help me win. Yet I still lost and felt that somehow I must have failed in my efforts, not doing them perfectly enough. Now I realize I was given an even greater miracle: to see the love behind all the apparent ugliness and loss. **The real miracle is the love that inspires them (T-1.I.3:2).** I would rather have the love and forgiveness I feel today than to have my daughter and remain hateful and judgmental. I would rather know that it was all an illusion that I dreamed up than to have won in court. I would rather my inner experience be changed than the outer condition. The peace I have today, which I feel within me as my true, natural state of being, is the real miracle, and I am grateful.*

There is no way I could have forgiven this excruciating loss on my own. As it was, my ego's engagement in the situation kept me in hell for six years. We all have this ego voice that condemns us and makes us feel guilty, and it is the biggest block to awareness of God's love. The good news is that we also have the Holy Spirit's voice that leads us to peace. We will explore these two voices in the next chapter.

---

*   Go to my website, http://www.lorricoburn.com, to download the audio *Opening to Receive Miracles*, for a detailed explanation of how you can create miracles in your life.

CHAPTER FOUR

THE SELF AND THE EGO

We all carry within us our ravages, our crimes, our places of exile.
~Albert Camus

The ego's purpose is fear ... (T-5.V.1:3).

During my last marriage, I spent a good deal of my emotional life hating my husband's ex-wife, Sandra. We had a lot of contact with her because my husband had shared custody of their daughter. I obsessed about Sandra and recounted her faults over and over. I thought she was arrogant, materialistic, controlling, and bitchy. I believed I was so much more loving and better for my husband than she had been, and I therefore felt superior to her. I couldn't stand when she would call our house, and I would close the blinds when she came to pick up her daughter. I knew I was acting immature and jealous, but it felt like I couldn't stop. It controlled me and I hated being that way. I tried to think of Sandra's good points and felt kindly for moments, but never for very long. One day I was coming home from church and I was singing a chant to try to think positively about her. The verse went, "It's a joy to get to know you, it's a joy to get to know you, and I really am liking to be in your world." I was feeling all warm and fuzzy and proud of myself for being a kind person, when I turned the corner and there was her car in my driveway. I immediately went "Aaargh!!! That bitch is here!" So much for being a loving, spiritual soul!

This is one example of what *A Course in Miracles* calls the "ego." In this dream world, we seem to have two parts to us, our higher Self, which is designated with a capital "S," and our ego, which is the false self. The ego's role is "Edging God Out." The ego is a myth, a story, to explain why we're afraid and think we're separated from God. It is not real. It is similar to the nastiness of the biblical figure of Satan, but with some crucial differences. In the Bible Satan is a real entity with power who is at war with God. In ACIM, the ego is *not* real, and therefore has no true power. Since God is all there is in ultimate reality, there is no one else to wage war with. When we recognize this, all the power we gave to the ego will vanish.

The part of us that *is* real and never dies is one with God. This is the higher Self, also called the "One Self," the "Christ Self," or the "Holy Spirit." There is only one Self, and we are all part of it, as if we are all rays emanating from the sun or waves arising from the ocean. The ultimate truth of our Being is that we *are* love, for that is how God created us. The Christ Self does not judge and sees everyone as innocent. We dreamed up the ego, which comprises every emotion, thought, and behavior that is not love. It is angry, depressed, guilty, afraid, lusty, and proud. It lives on fear, misery, and conflict. **The ego always seeks to divide and separate. The Holy Spirit always seeks to unify and heal (T-7.IV.5:2-3).** The ego thinks it is separate and different from everyone else, just as I thought of myself as distinct and unlike Sandra in order to hate her.

There is only one mind, and that is the mind of God.[1] We were created with the same mind as God, but when we mistakenly thought we separated, this mind appeared to split into what we call the right mind and the wrong mind. The right mind retains its memory of its true Self and its voice is the Holy Spirit. The wrong mind is the voice of the ego, which always leads us astray. What is commonly called "sin" is really only error, the error of forgetting who we really are. We forget that we are the one Self, and in our forgetting, we make negative decisions from our ego self. The ego is invested in sin, because it wants to judge others and remain separate from them. Seeing someone as sinful rather than innocent is the ego's way of ensuring separation. When we view others from our right mind, we see them as innocent, even when their choices are erroneous. The goal of *A Course in Miracles* is twofold: first, to teach us to think with the right mind, which enables us to awaken from the dream and return to God; second, to minimize the effects of the ego while we are still in the dream, because the ego makes us unhappy.

God created only one Son; therefore, God did not make the ego, we did. We made the ego to handle the guilt we feel for "leaving" God. Of course, we did not leave God, but we all have deep subconscious guilt from thinking that we did. This guilt goes far deeper than conscious guilt for things we think we've done wrong. Hence, it explains why we constantly try to hurt ourselves. We all have the ego side that hates ourselves. That sounds like a strong statement, yet when we truly examine our thoughts and behaviors, we begin to see just how often we sabotage our happiness. Because the guilt is *sub*-conscious, below the level of our awareness, we usually don't see it. The self-destructive side is right on the surface in drug addicts and criminals, but "normal" people are self destructive, too.

The *Course* states that in addition to our guilt, we fear that God is mad at us for separating from Him. When I first read the *Course*, I couldn't relate to this. It wasn't until I sabotaged myself in a ridiculously harmful way that I saw what it was saying. When I looked back, I couldn't believe how hurtful I had been to myself, and I thought God must have thought I was an idiot. I thought all the pain I brought on myself was deserved, and that God was disappointed in me. Most of us don't like to look at this side of ourselves, as we prefer to focus on the healthy, loving side. Yet if we don't examine the deep guilt and shame, we can't heal it. We usually know what our negative traits are, but often we don't see this very dark side of ourselves until we do something extreme. Most of us eventually sabotage ourselves viciously, and in hindsight are amazed at how blind and self-destructive we were.

My client Lyn is a good example of how we avoid deep subconscious ego guilt. Lyn did excellent work in therapy and succeeded in leaving her verbally abusive husband. Once she settled in her new home, I suggested she work on her weight, as she carries an extra one hundred pounds. Lyn had avoided this issue in therapy every time I'd brought it up. When she began talking about it, I was surprised to hear her say, "I'm despicable!" In all the time we'd worked together, I knew she didn't like being overweight, but I had not realized that she felt that bad about it. With this deep shame, I saw why she'd pushed it away. Our egos hate ourselves, and hate is not too strong a word. The ego shouts and screams for our death, much as the gladiator fights in ancient Rome. For Lyn, obesity is the ego's gladiator arena, the one in which she destroys herself violently, though at a slower pace than the gladiators' fight to the death. It is death all the same; and again, though this is a powerful statement, we need to look at how most of us are killing ourselves in one way or another. If it's not acknowledged, it can't be healed. At Alcoholics Anonymous meetings people introduce themselves, "Hi, I'm Bill and I'm an alcoholic." It puts it right out on the table to bypass the denial of the ego. As long as Lyn denies and avoids her self-destructive eating, she cannot heal. The promise, however, is that when we expose the ego for the illusion it is, we become whole.

This chapter explores the ego in many of its ugly forms. As long as we are thinking with the ego mind instead of our right mind, we remain trapped in the illusory dream. We will then discuss how to substitute the Holy Spirit's voice for the ego's, which leads us to remember our true Self and wake up from this dream world.

Basic Ego Masks

There is nothing that gives us more assurance than a mask.
~Colette

Our egos are essentially the personalities we identify with. In truth, we are Spirit, and our identity is Love. The personality traits we hold dear are the illusory masks we put on for the dream world. They are not who we are; they are who we *think* we are.

When we don't need the masks any more, we're set free from the prison of our false self.

We define ourselves by our masks. We're proud when we wear our masks well, and ashamed when we think we've failed to live up to our masks. Pride and shame are two opposite sides of the same mask, much like the comedy and tragedy masks. Our egos compare our masks with those of others and we usually think our masks are better.

There are six basic masks, and most of us have one dominant and one secondary. The categories also overlap. The more diverse our personality is, the more traits we have across the spectrum. The healthier we are, the less we get into the extreme behaviors of our particular styles. The six basic styles are: pleaser, worker, valuer, fun-lover, thrill seeker, and handler. We'll go over the six ego masks in general, and then give a vignette on how they interact.

Sheila is a *pleaser*. She likes to make sure everyone is taken care of and she is a peacemaker. Sheila tends to have a hard time saying no and puts her own needs second. Sheila is proud of herself when she makes you happy. She is ashamed of herself when people get mad at her or don't seem to like her. She also feels she's failed if those around her can't get along—she feels she hasn't done her job as nurturer and peacemaker. When Sheila gets into extreme ego behavior she acts needy and feels rejected. She may go overboard buying you gifts to get you to like her, or she may get clingy. When she is in her loving Christ Self, she gives without expectation of return, and without trying to make peace or get your approval. If your loved one is a pleaser and is in a funk, bring her a gift, tell her she looks nice, or tell her you appreciate her being around. This will pick up her spirits.

Martina is a *worker*. She prides herself on being efficient, responsible, organized, and on time. She tends to want tasks done a certain way and gets mad at herself if she doesn't do a good job. While Sheila the pleaser would rather have you tell her she's a nice person, Martina would rather be respected for her competent work. Martina would feel mortified if she were ever reprimanded on the job or fired. Her extreme ego behavior tends to be workaholism, compulsive cleaning, and irritability when others are irresponsible. The work of others often doesn't measure up to her standards. Her Christ Self comes through when she does a job for the joy of work itself, without judging whether it's perfect. When Martina is in a bad mood, you can support her by cleaning up the house or getting your work done on time. You can let her know you appreciate the hard work she's put in.

Bill is a *valuer*. Bill holds values and opinions dear and has high standards for himself and others. Bill is detail oriented and thorough, so he makes a good accountant, research scientist, or opinionated talk show host. If you need directions to Bill's office, he'll tell you something like this: "Take Main Street six blocks to Bridge Street. You'll pass a McDonald's on your right, an Arby's on your left, and you'll see an auto repair shop and a hair salon. Turn right onto Bridge and go three-tenths of a mile; the street will curve slightly to the left and there'll be a brown brick office building on the left and a white limestone building on the right. The name on the building is "The Johnson Building." Take the first set of elevators, not the second set, and go to the fourth floor. You'll pass the third floor where the lawyers are, but mine is the fourth floor; turn right off the elevator, go past the bathroom two doors and I'm in Suite 406." More details than most people need!

Bill is proud of a job done to minute perfection, and also feels pride in knowing there is a right and wrong way to do everything. However, Bill's children often feel they can't do anything right, because he tries to teach them the right way to do things and corrects them frequently. When he gets into extreme negative behavior he will insist your way is wrong and can demand his way or the highway. He may get obsessive-compulsive about details. His loving Christ Self shows up in his dedication and loyalty and his desire to do right by others in his work. If he is down and you want to lift his spirits, tell him you respect his opinions and thoughtful attention to the particulars of a situation.

Sue is a *fun-lover*. She's the one who loves a party and will drop everything on the spur of the moment for a good time. She likes to joke, live in the moment, and can get bogged down by overly responsible people. Sue thinks others fret about details too much, and feels there's no point to life if it's all work and no play. She can do a great job when she sets her mind to it, but she does best when she makes the work fun or follows it with playtime. She's the one whose office has cute things like a Tigger stuffed animal and a wind-up toy. Sue is proud of her ability to hang loose, but she gets ashamed when others see her carefree absent-mindedness as irresponsible. She can get easily distracted and miss deadlines. Her higher Self shows up with her joyful, in-the-moment attitude. Her motto is "Life is good!" When Sue gets down, start telling her jokes or goof around. Watch a sitcom with her. Make the project you're working on more fun.

Stan is a *thrill seeker.* He tends to be charming and sociable, but his gregariousness can be a cover for avoiding deep connections. Stan wants to be where the action is and prides himself on taking risks and charging full-speed into adventure. Stan gets restless and bored when things aren't exciting, and rather than recognize that he's feeling bad about himself, he tends to pick fights with others. Extreme behavior might be cocaine use or taking undue risks with dangerous sports. His loving Self comes through as he spearheads an exceptional charity project, one that others would have thought impossible to achieve. If your loved one is a thrill seeker and seems depressed, encourage him to create a challenge or engage in some extreme sport. But leave him alone as he does it.

Bob is the *handler.* He will handle things on his own, thank you very much. He prides himself on his ability to manage things himself, and feels weak if he can't get a tough job, especially a physically challenging one, done right. He is reserved with his feelings, even though they run deep. He is loyal, and once given clear directions, will handle a job without asking the boss a lot of questions. He doesn't need a lot of praise, but appreciates an occasional nod. His extreme behavior is refusing to receive physical or emotional support, and being out of touch with his feelings. His Christ Self comes through when he comes to your aid and doesn't expect anything in return. His reward is the act of doing for another. If he's in a bad mood, leave him alone and trust that he can manage things himself. If he's extremely depressed or physically ailing, however, he will need to be coaxed to get help.

Let's spend a day at the beach with each ego type. Sheila, the pleaser, brings you an iced tea, makes sure you have sunscreen, and offers to put it on your back. If you run out of sunscreen, she gives you hers, and says, "That's okay, I'll just put my blouse over my shoulders. I didn't want to get sun on them anyway."

Worker Martina has a certain amount of time allotted to the beach, before she has to get back to her tasks. She lies in the sun for the same amount of time on each side, and while lying there, she plans her next project. She brings her laptop to the beach, to kill two birds with one stone. She feels good about lying in the sun if she gets a nice tan, but is upset if she didn't, because then she wasted her time.

Bill, the valuer, suggests that you put your sunscreen on thirty minutes before you go out in the sun and tells you the latest statistics on skin cancer. He encourages you to stay out of the sun between the hottest hours of 10 a.m. and 3 p.m. Bill tells the lifeguard he's doing a fine job and is pleased to see the bathers obeying the rules. He enjoys taking his family to the beach because it's what you do because you love them. He appreciates the state park system and gladly contributes because their services are important.

Fun-lover Sue splashes in the waves when she's sixty years old and builds sand castles with her grandchildren. She puts on sunscreen, but if she forgets to reapply it and burns, she says, "It was worth it." She tosses beach balls at you and tries to engage you in the fun.

Stan, the thrill seeker, is on his surfboard, catching the biggest waves. He comes in for a beer with the gang before he goes to the beach party at night. If he trusts you, you can come along, but if he thinks you're boring or a dimwit, you won't be included.

Handler Bob walks down the beach alone or sits far away from the crowd. You can walk or sit with him, but just don't ruin it by talking. He ponders a problem by the sea or gathers strength from the pounding waves. He feels the steadiness of the tide's rhythm, and it balances him.

These are the normal everyday masks we wear, but they're still not who we really are. We think nothing of someone's negative behavior, because it's "normal." "Oh, that's just Jill being Jill." Beyond these daily masks, however, we all have frightening masks of terror and insanity. We usually try to keep these hidden from others, because we can't stand them ourselves. How many times have you thought, "Boy, if people *really* knew how I felt inside, they wouldn't like me?" We *all* feel this way and we all have dark shadows. The next section points out the insanity of our egos. It's not fun to look at, but until we admit that part of us is absolutely crazy, we can't fix it.

The Insanity of the Ego

When we remember that we are all mad,
the mysteries disappear and life stands explained.
~Mark Twain

God has but one Son,
knowing them all as one (T-9.VI.3:5).

The body is the central figure in the dreaming of the
world. There is no dream without it (T-27.VIII.1:1-2).

When we erroneously decided that we were separate from God, the illusory ego arose. Life is now like an amusement park fun house. We see the bizarre, distorted shapes in the mirrors, and we believe those reflections are actually what we are. It's as if we have really bad eyes and need strong glasses, yet we think our eyesight is fine. We are not our bodies, nor are we separate personalities, but we think we are. We identify with our personalities as evidenced by our responses to the question, "Who are you?" "I'm Bob and I'm the president of the bank. I have a wife and three kids." We identify ourselves by our unique stories, those incidents that shaped our lives. "I'm Julie, and when I was ten I was in a house fire that killed my mother." "I'm Tom, and I was the captain of my high school football team." "I'm Sue and I was the baby of the family." "I'm Joe, and my parents divorced when I was ten and my stepfather abused me." "I'm Jenny, and I overcame breast cancer when I was thirty-five." None of these stories is who we really are. They are part of our ego-based identities and they keep us feeling separate and different from others.

It is as if our spirits are concealed in earth suits. When the suits are unzipped, only the shining light of Spirit remains. However, the appearance of separate bodies with individual earth suits is what allows the dream world to seem real. In fact, there would be no dream at all if there weren't bodies. How could we be separate from one another if there didn't seem to be individual bodies? How could we wage hatred or war if we knew our neighbors were part of our Self? Oneness sees no enemies. The ego, on the other hand, needs an enemy to exist. It is one big attack and counterattack. If we pay attention, we see that there is nary a group that does not have an enemy. Families usually have at least one member who is the scapegoat or black sheep. Every classroom has at least one nerd. The scapegoat carries the shame for the group, and this keeps the other members from looking at their own deep subconscious guilt, because his dysfunction is so obviously bad that theirs looks mild in comparison.

> *Never forget that the ego is not sane (T-5.V.3:8).*
> *This is why the ego is insane; it teaches you*
> *that you are not what you are (T-7.III.2:6).*

> *The ego uses the body for attack, for pleasure*
> *and for pride (T-6.V.A.5:3). Sometimes it dreams it is a*
> *conqueror of bodies weaker than itself (T-27.VIII.2:6).*
> *Its safety is its main concern. Its comfort is*
> *its guiding rule. It tries to look for pleasure, and avoid*
> *the things that would be hurtful (T-27.VIII.1:5-7).*

The *Course* clearly states that when we are identifying with the ego rather than our true Self, we are insane. Who chooses anger and hatred when he can choose love and peace? Who chooses to see himself as frightened and separate from God when he can feel safe at home? Who chooses death over life? Yet this is what the insane ego does. Violence and righteous fury are the junk food of emotions and are some of the more obvious crazy aspects of the ego. These venomous feelings get our blood flowing, get us aroused, and provide justification for war.

My partner Rod was quite violent when he was young. He is Hispanic and his crowd hated and vehemently fought the African Americans. Both cultures had a macho code of conduct, which could as well be called an ego code of conduct. This macho code convinced Rod that terror and assault would actually *solve* problems. Rod was in jail several times and injured people to the point of hospitalization. He recalls the exhilarating feeling as his hand splintered while he beat someone's head. Rod describes, "Ripped muscles, the gushing blood, meant *victory*! That's why you were elated! You felt powerful! But that is sort of the clean part. The ugly part is if you do it in front of a crowd, in front of guys, then you go kick him in the head. That cements the 'he's bad!' routine. You carry whatever it is to the extreme."

Rod felt good about being a "real man" according to his culture, but he says he now realizes he was glorifying the insane ego and building a fortress to shield himself from the Holy Spirit. The ego loves having an enemy, for it cannot exist without feeling separate. It makes itself superior to others, thus justifying attack. Being in ego *always* eventually makes us feel bad, even if we are not aware of it. Rod reports being vaguely aware that his violence did not feel good, yet the ego convinced him he was doing the right thing. On the surface he felt good, but deep down the truth quietly haunted him.

Rod remembers the movie *The Blackboard Jungle* with Burt Lancaster, in which some teenagers killed a man for no good reason. One of the teens saw a psychiatrist, who interpreted that he murdered the man out of fear. The teen reacted vehemently to this interpretation and threatened the psychiatrist: "I'll show you who's afraid now. I'll kill you next!" He could not tolerate feeling afraid, and he had to deny it and project it onto the doctor. Now the doctor would be the one afraid, certainly not the teen. Rod was an adolescent at the time and strongly identified with the teen killer, as that's how Rod had learned to deal with his fear. He denied it existed and made someone else afraid of him. That made Rod feel temporarily safe and strong.

In one of our spiritual meetings, Rod explained how he acted tough to cover his fear. Another member of the group, Ed, was the nerdy kid who always got beaten up by the bullies like Rod. As Rod and Ed each expressed their sadness and vulnerability, with tears in their eyes, a miracle occurred. They discovered that their outward personas, completely opposite from each other, were both illusions. They were both coming from fear instead of love. Rod and Ed joined in their hearts, dropped the false views they held of themselves, and opened to their oneness.

While Rod physically assaulted and severely injured others, I "only" attacked my husband's ex-wife, Sandra, mentally. I used to think that my negative thoughts about Sandra made me more pure than Rod. After all, I never dreamed of physical violence or said nasty things to her face. However, any thought or action that is not love is from the ego. When I mentally attacked Sandra, I thought I was making myself feel better. Actually, I still felt queasy in the pit of my stomach and my chest and jaw were tight. *A Course in Miracles* makes no distinction among attacks, mental or physical, seeing them *all* as unjustified and equally erroneous. Only bodies and personalities can attack, and we can only attack someone if we feel he is an enemy. If we were all shimmering golden spirits, why would we attack one another? Since bodies are not real, there is *never* justification for attack. The one Self does not divide and turn against itself; therefore, any time we attack we are identifying with the ego.

The ego's insanity is seen when powerful and famous figures self-destruct. It's as if they punish themselves to strip away what they have attained. The ego wants us to feel lousy about ourselves, so success frequently comes with an equally hard fall unless we have solid, loving self-esteem. Bill Clinton almost destroyed his presidency with his sex addiction. If that's not insane, what is? He's not the first and won't be the last to do so. Lest we judge, we *all* have those parts of our selves that are absolutely self-destructive. Addictions come in many forms, including sex, drugs, alcohol, tobacco, caffeine, food, gambling, sports, relationships, work, hobbies, TV, and more. I used to pride myself that my addictions and flaws weren't as bad as others'. What a joke! My arrogance caught up with me and knocked me down hard. The ego then made me feel guilty for being arrogant and falling down, even though arrogance and failure are part of the ego itself. I am grateful today that I can see my own and everyone's innocence instead.

The ego's hold on us is like a trap that poachers use to catch monkeys. The trap is simple: the monkey reaches into a container to get a banana and when it tries to pull the banana out it can't, because the hole is only big enough for its hand. The monkey can get free if it drops the banana, but it holds on to its prize for dear life—literally, its hold costs the monkey its life. Such are we, as we hold dear to the addictions that destroy us.

My friend Margo struggles with drug addiction, was in prison for five years, lost custody of her child, and was homeless, sleeping in city parks. Margo relates a powerful epiphany at ten years old. She felt the presence of God, the thunder and lightening type of presence, but in a profound loving sense. She knew her oneness with that power. She relates, "By age eleven I was a drug addict. I think I've been running all my life from that power. It's like, 'Oh, my God! That's too big! That can't be who I am!' " Margo's biggest fear, which is the same fear we all have, is owning that she indeed is the Christ. Her ego wants her to think she's a hopeless, hapless drug addict, a nothing, a nobody. The ego *always* feels guilty, *always* tells her she's a piece of crap, and *always* hates her. That won't change, for that's the very nature of the ego. What she needs to remember is that her epiphany is true. She is her higher Self; she is *not* her ego. Today, she gets glimpses of her true Self when she is sober and doing her inner work. As she practices the *Course* she experiences miracles often, and I am thrilled to see her thinking change. Margo has chronic pancreatitis from her alcoholism and is in constant pain. She knows that if she takes another drink she will die. Yet God has given her a miracle in which she blesses her pain and sees it as her teacher. She sees it as the thing that is keeping her alive and she is grateful for it. She says that this change in her perception has stopped her suffering.

She still feels the pain, but it is much less than it used to be and she does not suffer because she doesn't struggle with it. She doesn't judge the pain as bad, nor is she afraid of it, which is what her ego would have her do.

Margo's drug addiction appears on the surface to be different and worse than other people's problems, but that too is an ego device to make us feel separate. **Everyone in this world seems to have his own special problems. Yet they are all the same . . . (W-p.I.79.2:1-2)**. Society's judgmental ego says Margo is scum, but Margo is as precious as Mother Teresa. In her illumined moments, perhaps Margo has experienced more truth than most of us. Society often judges people who march to a different drummer as foolish, as is sung in the Beatles song "The Fool on the Hill." The fool sits back and knows others are calling him a fool, but he knows that in their ignorance, they're the fools. Often the "fools" know more than we do.

Projection

Comparisons are odorous.
~Shakespeare

The ego cannot survive without judgment,
and is laid aside accordingly
(T-4.II.10:3).

My client Paula was a college student, and like many coeds, obsessed about being fat, even though she carried only ten extra pounds. Paula was on campus with a group of friends and a young man approached them, looked straight at her, and said, "Why are you so fat?" What she feared showed up in her life, and the man simply reflected what she was thinking about herself. We all are projecting our opinions and fears onto the world, but we are unaware of it. We think things happen *to* us, that the world presents itself *to* us, when it's really our projection.

Dory, the woman who smelled her mom's perfume, was worried that her teenaged sons were mad at her. Her second husband, who was not her sons' father, got a job in another state. Dory moved with her new husband and their child, and her other sons chose to remain behind and live with their father. Dory felt guilty, feeling she'd abandoned her sons, thinking she should have talked her husband out of taking the job. When she spoke to her sons by phone she felt they were holding back their anger and pretending things were okay. As she let go of her guilt, she learned they'd naturally assumed she'd follow her husband and were never mad to begin with. She realized she'd projected her guilt onto them, that it was her issue, not theirs.

My friend's son is a teenager, and uses the typical adolescent tactics to get to his mom. He attacked her by saying she was a horrible parent. She calmly suggested he go live with someone he thinks would be a better parent. He responded, "I would, but *you* couldn't handle it!" Being a proud teen, he couldn't possibly admit that *he* couldn't handle it, so he projected it onto his mom.

Rich, thirty-six, came to therapy to address his marital separation, alcoholism, and trauma from Vietnam. One day he asked me out to the parking lot to see his new car. It was a white Cadillac with red leather interior, and Rich beamed. "I've wanted one of these my whole life, and I figured you never know when you're gonna die, so why wait?" A week later Rich missed his appointment so I called his mother's home, where he was living. I asked for Rich and his mother said, coldly, "He's dead." I sputtered, "Oh, I meant your son, Rich Jr., not your husband." She replied, even more hostile, "I *heard* what you said. *My son is dead!*" He had had a heart attack.

This grief-stricken mother displaced her anger and pain onto me by being rude. If I was insecure, I could have heaped guilt upon myself for upsetting her. Instead, I saw her pain and did not take it personally.

The ego is constantly projecting guilt and judgment. Our perception of events and people depends on what we project onto them, because we do not see them as *they* are, but rather as *we* are. In projection we blame someone or something else for our own guilt, as with the alcoholic who says he only drinks because his wife is a nag. Projection also shows up when another person reflects what we are thinking inside, such as when the stranger asked Paula why she was fat. We project feelings onto other people or situations, so we don't have to look at them in ourselves. That way we don't have to feel guilty because the other person is the guilty one. For example, I felt jealous of Sandra's ability to make lots of money. Rather than acknowledging my own guilt over not having more money, I projected the guilt onto her and judged her as materialistic. I also saw her as arrogant, as if she thought she was better than I am, when that's exactly what I felt about her. It's always so much easier to see the faults of others than our own, and I am often embarrassed when I realize that what I think is awful about another person is really about me. Rod felt inferior as a Hispanic, but he projected his guilt onto African Americans. *They* were the inferiors, not him. Beating them up proved to his ego that he was better than they were. The winner of a fight gets to feel superior while the loser feels inferior. However, inferiority and superiority are both ego attitudes and are two sides of the same coin.

This dream world is a place of duality where there are two facets to everything, two sides to every coin. On earth there is nothing positive that does not have its negative counterpart. Up and down, left and right, in and out, sun and moon, male and female, light and dark, pain and pleasure, peace and war, here and there, and on and on. Atoms, the building blocks of all matter, have positively charged protons and negatively charged electrons. We cannot get away from duality, yet we are constantly trying to. Our human nature is to move toward pleasure and away from pain. Therefore, we judge things as good or bad, depending on what we want to show up in our lives. It is the ego that judges, for the true Self judges nothing, knowing that this world is literally nothing. The Christ Self sees only oneness and unity, while the ego constantly passes judgments about every single thing it encounters; indeed, *every single thing*. A healthy body is good, while illness is bad. Life is good; death is bad. Pleasure is good; sadness is bad. Friendliness is good, but being reclusive is bad, and so on.

Prior to my study of the *Course*, I got very angry at how everything in life had a downside. I couldn't understand why we had to have Democrats and Republicans—why couldn't we just meet in the middle instead of polarizing? I got upset with God for making men and women so attracted to each other, yet so different in their needs. What a setup for failure! Once I understood that the ego, not God, created the duality, it began to make sense and I was no longer mad. As my split mind began to heal, I chose love and ignored the ego setup.

> *Projection means anger, anger fosters assault, and assault promotes fear. Assault can ultimately be made only on the body (T-6.I.3:3; 4:1).*

> *The ego literally lives by comparisons (T-4.II.7:1).*

The ego thrives on comparisons and bitterness, for this is what duality fosters. Gary Renard, author of *The Disappearance of the Universe*, says that judgments are junk food for the ego. Take away judgments and the ego will starve to death. Comparisons, which are judgments, always lead to either vanity or resentment. For example, if a woman feels ugly she will constantly compare her looks to every woman she sees. The very first thing my friend asked about my husband's former wife, Sandra, was, "Is she pretty?" Ego has to immediately size up and gauge the level of threat. If a man feels weak, he will judge himself better or worse than other men based on their financial or physical power. If someone feels like a failure in his career, he will compare his success to others'. The person who hates himself, feels ashamed and feels like a failure is in ego as much as the person who feels lofty. Both are fear based, denying the true Self. Attacking oneself is no different than attacking someone else, for we are all one. Again, if there were no comparisons, the ego could not survive, for the love and oneness of the Self might be recognized.

There seems to be an epidemic of blame in our litigious society. Many of us remember the lawsuit in which the woman who spilled McDonald's coffee on herself was awarded an incredible amount of money. I heard an interview with her lawyer and he was so skillful that I found myself agreeing with him. I caught myself and said,

"Whoa! Look at how he just hooked you! Everyone knows coffee is hot, and if you spill it it's your responsibility!" Yet if there's somewhere to place blame other than on ourselves, the ego will do it. Recently three teenage girls were returning to school from lunch and were killed when they made a left turn onto a busy highway. It was the inexperienced student who pulled into traffic, yet the community screamed about the other driver's bad record. He was the loser; she was the nice, good student. It wasn't her mistake; the loser should have seen it coming. The pain of facing our own responsibility seems too hard, so we project it onto someone else. He's the guilty one, not us.

The ego is like a monster lurking inside us, poised to attack and judge. The minute we attack, we are in mental hell. We have constant judgments about others, and we are continually judging ourselves. During a typical day, notice your thoughts about yourself. If we're not attacking someone or something else, the ego runs a chronic monologue on how well we are doing, and we usually end up short. "I need to get this project done; I'm stalling." "I need to lose weight." "I need to save more money." "I need to make more money." "I'm running late." "I don't think I'm good enough at this." "I should exercise more." "I should've planned this better." "I didn't get very much done today." "I don't look very good today." "I'm not a very good parent." "I should've done something about this a long time ago." "I don't want to be doing this right now." "I should have gone to bed earlier last night." "I acted like an idiot at that party." "I wouldn't be in this mess I'm in now if I hadn't screwed up by doing _____." (Fill in the blank with the thing you did years ago that you still beat yourself up over.) The attack thoughts are endless, and they are often about fear of the future or guilt from the past.

Most of us are judging *all the time!* If you don't think that you are judging most of the time, take note of your thoughts about other people while in public. "She looks mean." "She looks friendly." "Look at those ugly clothes she's wearing." "Boy, he's fat!" "He's a toothpick; what a wimp." "He looks like he thinks he's God's gift to women." "That mother should get her kid under control." "That store clerk was unfriendly." "That person doesn't even bother to smile back at me." "He's being pushy." "She's prettier than I am." "I'm prettier than she is." "Look at his teeth!" "I bet I could whip that guy." "I'd better stay clear of that guy—he could take me down in a heartbeat." "I bet he makes more money than me." "He looks like a nerd." "What a loser." "I bet he thinks he's too good driving that Mercedes." "What the heck is wrong with you? Where'd you learn to drive?" "Why don't they paint their house?" Notice that all these thoughts are about *bodies and personalities*. We don't judge who they really are, for who they really are is the Son of God. We project our own self-loathing onto others, but when we learn to love ourselves, we stop attacking others.

There is a difference between judgment and discernment, however. To say someone is one hundred pounds overweight is discernment. To think she must be lazy, slovenly, and lack willpower is a judgment. To observe that someone is an alcoholic is discernment; to notice it with even a hint of disdain is judgment. To note that a father is smoking around his child and that secondhand smoke may harm the child is a fact. Adding, "What a selfish father!" introduces judgment.

> *What you project you disown, and therefore do not believe is yours. Since you have also judged against what you project, you continue to attack it because you continue to keep it separated. By doing this unconsciously, you try to keep the fact that you attacked yourself out of awareness, and thus imagine that you have made yourself safe. Yet projection will always hurt you (T-6.II.2:1; 3-4; 3:1).*

Alcoholics and other addicts are masters of projection. Addiction fosters such enormous amounts of guilt that the addict projects it onto other people or things, so she doesn't have to feel it. When I worked in a chemical dependency treatment center, I had a lot of clients who had been arrested for drunk driving. For about the first year I asked them what happened to cause their arrests. After that I wised up and quit asking, because invariably it wasn't their fault. They weren't driving erratically, they just had a taillight out. It was raining and they couldn't see. A squirrel darted out, so he ran off the road. The car in front stopped suddenly so she rear-ended her; it had nothing to do with being drunk.

I have a teenage client Kim, whose father is alcoholic. Kim's dad regularly comes home drunk from work and starts yelling. They got in an argument and he hollered that he wouldn't drink if she and her brother wouldn't fight so much. They didn't appreciate how hard he worked and left the house messy, and those were more reasons he drank. Being a typical outspoken teenager, Kim told her father, "No one puts that drink in your mouth but you! Don't blame me for your problems! Maybe I should clean up more around the house, but it's not my fault you drink!"

One of the saddest substance abuse cases I had involved two separate, unrelated clients. Dirk was an emergency medical volunteer who attended a car accident caused by a drunken mother. Her three children were in the car and two of them were okay, but one little girl looked dazed and limp. Dirk said when he sees children kicking and screaming he knows they're alright, but the stunned ones he worries about. The little girl died, and it really shook him up. Shortly thereafter another client told me about her girlfriend, who happened to be that same mother from the fatal accident. She said her friend's response was, "You think maybe I should cut back on my drinking a little?" This mother's guilt had to be so incredibly profound that she denied the extent of her drinking problem. This is an extreme example, but is testament to the insanity of the ego mind. However, the power of the Holy Spirit to heal our minds is even greater than this guilt, as we will see later in the chapter. While the death of a child appears harder to heal than an attack thought, the Holy Spirit removes one as easily as the other. The *Course* states, **there is no order of difficulty in miracles. One is not "harder" or "bigger" than another. They are all the same. All expressions of love are maximal (T-1.I.1:1-4).**

Impacting Our Own Dream

I've had thousands of problems in my life,
most of which never actually happened.
~Mark Twain

Whatever I see reflects my thoughts.
The fact that I see a world in which there is
suffering and loss and death shows me that I am seeing
only the representation of my insane thoughts,
and am not allowing my real thoughts to cast their
beneficent light on what I see (W-p.I.53.5:2; 4).

Most of us react to events as if they are happening *to* us, and are completely unaware that we play some role in attracting the events. Often our first reaction to this statement is, "There's no way I would have wanted *this* trauma in my life. No way!" Of course we wouldn't! But the ego would! That is why we have to become aware of the ego part of our mind, so we can make choices with the right mind. However, once we know that we are the designers of our dream, the ego uses that against us, too. Sadly, some experience guilt when they are unable to overcome serious illnesses or other difficult life patterns. They blame themselves for attracting negativity, for not being spiritual enough, for not thinking correctly, or for not visualizing their way to success

This blame is unfounded, as *all* blame is unfounded. Many of the decisions of the mind were made on another level, in a different dimension of the mind. The mind is outside of space and time, and things that happen to us, "good" and "bad," have been set into motion by decisions that we are unaware of. There is a universal law of attraction, in which like attracts like. When the mind makes decisions, whether in this realm or on a different plane, certain events happen as a result. When a choice is made from the loving, right mind, love is attracted. When a choice is made from the wrong, ego mind, negativity results.

While we are often not consciously in control of what events show up, what we can do is ask for the Holy Spirit's vision of the illness, problem, or trauma. This will change our mind about the meaning of the problem and bring us peace, but the outer situation may not necessarily change. The real problem is not the circumstance, but our belief that we are separated from God. Someone can be dying of cancer in the most blissful state of peace if he knows the truth of his oneness with life and God. My friend

Linda has breast cancer and has defied all the doctors' predictions. She was supposed to be dead four years ago, yet her face and eyes shine with love most of the time. She knows she is not her body and is using her cancer as her spiritual path. She chooses to go headlong into her body's pain, in order to see the illusion of it. She has had many breakthroughs and is far closer to the light of God than she was before her cancer. She is not afraid of dying, and uses every moment as a choice to awaken to truth.

*I am responsible for what I see.
I choose the feelings I experience,
and I decide upon the goal I would achieve. And
everything that seems to happen to me I ask for,
and receive as I have asked. Deceive yourself no longer
that you are helpless in the face of what is done to
you. Acknowledge but that you have been mistaken,
and all the effects of your mistakes will disappear.
No accident nor chance is possible within the universe
as God created it, outside of which is nothing.
Suffer, and you decided sin was your goal. Be happy,
and you gave the power of decision to Him
Who must decide for God for you (T-21.II.2:3-7; 3:4-6).*

We do not create trauma in our lives on a conscious level. No one deliberately asks for pain and suffering. When the *Course* points out that we are choosing our feelings and experiences, it means that we are, and have been, in the grip of the ego mind since time began, and it is our choice, and only ours, to choose differently. The *Course* is uncompromising in its insistence that if we are to be free of the traps of the ego mind, we must accept total responsibility for belief in the ego mind. We must turn our thoughts over to the right mind, to the Holy Spirit. A very helpful *Course* Workbook lesson to practice and affirm is: **I am not the victim of the world I see (W-p.I.31.h).**

The mind is extremely powerful; after all, we were created with the mind of God. I read about a homosexual man whose lover died of AIDS. This man received an HIV test that was negative, but was mistakenly told it was positive. He proceeded to develop the symptoms of AIDS one by one, in the same order as his lover had. As he was deteriorating, he received the news that he was not, in fact, HIV positive. This startled and shocked him, and he was astounded at the power of his thoughts. He began healing with this new information. Likewise, one of the founders of Unity Church, Myrtle Fillmore, contracted tuberculosis, as she had a long family history of the disease. Myrtle was transformed by the epiphany that her true identity was not her earthly family. She was a child of God; therefore, she could not inherit disease. This true thought from her right mind healed her body, and she dedicated her life to teaching this principle.

Since we are all one, there is only one mind from which all thoughts come. There is one Self and one dream; however, our subjective experience is that we are living separate lives and dreaming separate dreams. In our seeming separateness, we appear to have individual life situations, and usually there are particular themes that keep recurring. For example, my client Sammy swore that everywhere he went someone would pick a fight with him. Sammy was a very angry man, but that anger was a cover for fear. One day Sammy was minding his own business while sitting in a park, and from across the way a man came over and began to harass him, seemingly out of the blue. What Sammy did not realize is that he sent out angry thoughts that drew the fights to him. Yes, the fights would seem to happen when he was doing nothing that would draw them, but *in his mind on a subconscious level* he was constantly fighting, and this is what showed up in his world. Instead of choosing peaceful, forgiving thoughts he became a weightlifter to toughen up and presented an imposing figure. Eventually this choice brought about Sammy's murder in a drug deal, as he drew to himself the violence that was ever present in his mind. I received a call from his probation officer asking if his chart had a phone number for next of kin, as Sammy had been found shot dead in a hotel room.

Fortunately, most of us have life themes that are not as violent as Sammy's. Yet, we all have recurring issues that show up in areas where we have not forgiven others or ourselves. This is clearly seen when we attract love relationships that turn out to be almost exactly like the previous one. Problems show up in infinite varieties, such as money, relationship, health, or job concerns. What have been your ongoing problem areas, the ones that feel like an albatross around your neck? These are the areas in which we need to do forgiveness work, and we will describe how to do that in chapter 5. Any issue that is not healed is an issue that has not been forgiven.

Sammy's anger led to the death of his body, yet the real Self never dies. We think our anger is about the things that are happening outside of us or to us, but it's really a projection of our own wrong mind. The book *Angry All the Time*, by Ron Potter Efron, indicates that we think we're angry because of the headline we read this morning, because of the traffic jam, because of our boss, or because of the crazy politicians. Efron corrects this misperception by pointing out that anger addicts are angry *because* they're angry. Just like an alcoholic drinks because he's alcoholic, not because the Yankees won or because the Yankees lost. *Everything* is a projection of our own inner state of mind.

> *Projection makes perception.*
> *The world you see is what you gave it,*
> *nothing more than that. But though it is no more than*
> *that, it is not less. Therefore, to you it is important.*
> *It is the witness to your state of mind,*
> *the outside picture of an inward condition.*
> *As a man thinketh, so does he perceive.*
> *Therefore, seek not to change the world, but choose to*
> *change your mind about the world (T-21.in.1:1-7).*

This entire world is one big projection, one big delusion stemming from our wrong mind. That's why we act stupid so often. I used to have a boyfriend, Richard, who insisted that I "had a thing" for black men. He was afraid I would leave him for a black man. He attacked me for enjoying Eddie Murphy's comedy videos, which shocked me, as I simply thought they were hilarious. I liked Robin Williams just as much, but that didn't count. Richard's accusations seemed strange because I had never had a black boyfriend and had no intention of leaving him for a black man or anyone else, for that matter. We were on vacation in Key West and a bizarre incident occurred. Strolling along the street, we came upon a tourist trolley. The tour operator began his spiel, "Hi, I'm Eddie and I'll be your tour operator for today. We'll be heading past Ernest Hemingway's home...Well, Helloooo!!" He stopped abruptly in the midst of his announcement to flirt with me, and, you guessed it, he was a black man. I was stunned and laughed. Richard was outraged, berating me for laughing instead of telling the man off. This incident was too weird to be coincidental. It was obviously a projection. Our egos subconsciously conjured up an event in our dream in which we could justify our fears. When the event appeared to happen, we both could have chosen with the Holy Spirit and laughed at its bizarre nature. Instead, we both believed the ego lies; Richard gained "proof" that I liked black men and I got "proof" that Richard was nuts.

I had a client, Donna, who felt like a victim all her life. She'd been abused as a child, and like most of us, had recreated the same patterns in her adult life. We keep reliving the same old scenarios in different forms, just like in the movie *Groundhog Day*, until we learn to love ourselves and others. Donna came to therapy to address trauma around an attack in a department store. She was shopping and minding her own business, when a stranger hauled off and punched her in the face. This sounds a lot like Sammy. During therapy, it happened again. In a local discount store a stranger assaulted her. What are the chances of being attacked in a store, much less twice? Unfortunately, Donna could not see how she was drawing this to herself, and her therapy was unsuccessful. The sad thing is that she will keep drawing assaults to herself in various ways until she stops believing that she needs to be punished. Very few of us consciously think we need to be punished, and we would deny it if someone told us that's what we're doing. Yet every negative thing that we think "happens *to* us" is really from our own ego. It is being projected onto the screen of our lives from the wrong mind that thinks it's guilty. The ego mind actually wants us to feel guilty. **Whenever you respond to your ego you will experience guilt, and you will fear punishment (T-5.V.3:6).**

We think we're keeping ourselves safe and guilt-free by projecting, but our safety lies only in our innocence. Spirit has shown me painful lessons about my own projections. These were hard to face, and I still feel chagrined thinking about them. While on vacation in Chicago with my daughter and niece, I took a wrong turn and ended up in a bad neighborhood at night. I started swearing like a sailor as the girls cowered in the back seat. I realized I was out of control, but I felt justified because I was mad and scared. At a stoplight in the ghetto, a street person came up to the window and banged on it, asking for a Kleenex. No way was I going to roll down the window! He said I was selfish and that I should help him out because his cousin was Frank Sinatra. As I continued to refuse to look his way, he blew his nose on his sleeve and wiped it on the hood of the car! The girls exclaimed, "Oh, gross!!!" The strangeness of the incident made me feel it happened for a reason, but I was confused. I prayed and said, "Okay, what was that all about?" I got an image that when I was ranting and raving about being lost, that I was just as ugly as the street person was. I responded, "No way, God! I wasn't as ugly as that!" Humiliated, I saw the truth in it and apologized to the girls.

Another humbling incident occurred at my niece's wedding. Because I wasn't studying the *Course* at the time, this one took a few years for me to understand. One of my pet peeves was smoking in restaurants, and this was before smoking became prohibited in public. I had been particularly judgmental about cigars, and I felt that anyone who smoked them in public was extremely rude. At the wedding reception the men at the table next to us were smoking cigars, of all things! I was very upset and went over to their table to ask them to stop. They were arrogant and refused to stop smoking, and I left with a glare of disdain. Shortly thereafter, one of the men came over to our table and snapped a picture of me, the bitch. I was appalled at this! I thought, "Those bastards! Who do they think they are? *I'm* the bride's aunt. Furthermore, *I'm pregnant* and it shows the height of their rudeness to smoke around a pregnant woman!"

Looking back on that situation, I see how I projected my own arrogance and rudeness onto the smokers. I did not ask them to stop smoking with an air of kindness and equality. I thought I was better than they were and they felt my attacking attitude. Thus, they mirrored back to me my own arrogance and attack. I thought they were bastards and they responded by labeling me a bitch. I attacked with words and they attacked with behavior by taking my picture and continuing to smoke. I identified with my pregnant body and felt they were attacking me with their smoking. In reality, those men were my brothers, one with me in God. We attacked one another on this level because we thought we were separate, but the attack was only an illusion.

Ego Disguises

> Man has always sacrificed truth to his
> vanity, comfort and advantage.
> He lives not by truth but by make-believe.
> ~W. Somerset Maugham

**The whole purpose of this course is
to teach you that the ego is unbelievable and
will forever be unbelievable (T-7.VIII.7:1).**

The ego does not just show up as negativity. It can be hidden in seemingly altruistic acts. I used to do volunteer work for the church and visited people who were homebound. I didn't like doing it, but I did it because I thought I should. What a kind, helpful person I thought I was, another reason to feel proud. My service appeared loving on the surface, but it was really coming from guilt, which is from the ego. Today I find plenty of ways to be helpful that I enjoy, and I do not participate in things strictly from guilt. We only extend our true Self through love and joy, so although I was helping in some manner, I was also unhelpful because my presence had negativity and guilt attached. Upon realizing that I wasn't as helpful as I could have been, I felt guilty. The ego is so tricky that once we become aware of it, it finds back doors to enter without being caught. It loves to make us feel guilty for not being aware of it sooner. The ego gets us coming and going, the typical "damned if you do, damned if you don't" scenario.

One of my favorite people is a client named Beth. Beth is one of those sweet, friendly people who is always giving gifts and taking care of other people's needs. Part of this is from Beth's genuine loving nature, as she's a natural giver. However, the other part comes from her ego, the side of her that feels unlovable and wants people to like her. When she ran a business she never made any money because she constantly gave away samples and added free items to the sale. She was the type to shy away when someone was pushy, always taking a back seat. The ego told Beth that she was just being generous, helpful, and peacemaking, when really she was attacking herself by not honoring her own needs. She also was unable to receive compliments and fooled herself into thinking she was being humble. This false humility is another way the ego demeans us, for Spirit knows that everyone is equally beautiful and deserves compliments.

Beth has grown quite a bit in the past few years, fortunately. She has eliminated the people in her life who were taking advantage of her, and no longer lets herself be abused. She also has stopped loaning money to people who don't pay it back and no longer is compelled to give gifts all the time. Beth understands that she makes up her own dream, as she has experienced attracting things into her life with her thinking. When she was broke as a single mother, she didn't have the money to buy a bathroom rug. She really wanted a blue rug and without her saying anything, a neighbor offered, "Hey, I've got this blue rug that I don't need. Do you want it?" Now in her sessions we refer to incidents in her life as "blue rug-ish."

Beth's ego disguised itself as helpful, yet the ego's outcome will always be negative. For example, my client Sheryl has a dream of becoming a tattoo artist. She absolutely loves tattoos and sees her body as a piece of artwork. However, she has financial troubles and works long hours, then feels too exhausted to practice her tattooing. Her ego tells her she has to work three jobs to pay her bills, or she's not being responsible. Yet Sheryl knows the Holy Spirit is telling her to slow down and develop her artistry, for then she will be able to make far more than what she's making now. She continues to drive herself, however, and keeps getting sick and is unable to work because of it. She's had several hand surgeries due to osteoarthritis, which represents the ego's attempt to shake her belief in her dream. After all, how can she tattoo when her hand is crippled? However, I have seen physical illnesses disappear when guilt has been released. Another friend of mine had chronic neck and back pain for ten years, and when she resolved emotional issues the pain disappeared and has not returned for five years.

Punishing ourselves physically and mentally is common, and is one of the ego's responses to guilt. Another client of mine, Lynn, loves skiing; it is her passion and she has always wanted to move to Colorado and work on ski patrol. She wears a necklace with a skier on it, and her checks have a skier logo. Lynn recently got divorced, but she still does her former husband's laundry and cooks his dinners. Throughout their marriage they fought because she wanted to move out west and he didn't. Now she says she can't move and leave him alone, even though they live in separate homes. She is miserable here and deceives herself into thinking she's helping her former husband, when she is in fact denying her true Self. When married, her ego blamed him to perpetuate her bitterness. Now that she is free, she still finds a way to stay miserable, which is exactly what the ego wants. It tricks her by reversing her prior blame, now suggesting she's "helping" him. When we are in a cycle of recurring problems, we can be sure it's the ego perpetuating it, for Spirit *always* offers a way out of difficulty. Spirit guides us step by step, one day at a time, to happiness. *Always.*

Yet another ego disguise is tribalism, used to instill pride, which we value in our culture. We are proud of our particular school, our sports team, our state, our country, our political party. We esteem pride, not recognizing that it often reinforces separation. We think we're the coolest for belonging to our particular tribe, certainly cooler than people in other tribes. Bumper stickers and car decals let us know what people feel proud of, and I recently saw an interesting one: "My German Shepherd is smarter than your honor student!"

Loving and honoring our tribe is positive when it activates our inherent loving nature through generosity and sharing with other tribes. However, it is divisive when it suggests superiority and separateness, and in the extreme when it leads to war. War is the ultimate renunciation of our oneness, as we are actually murdering those we consider different from us. Rather than questioning the insanity of war, however, the front page of the paper shows a photo of a grieving widow next to a flag-draped coffin, which evokes empathy and sadness. How can we question the war when this hero just gave his life? This is a trick of the ego, to glorify war and instill pride rather than foster peace and oneness.

Glorifying war is similar to how we eroticize self-destruction. Picture that familiar painting, often hanging in diners, of Marilyn Monroe, Elvis Presley, James Dean, and Humphrey Bogart. The caption reads "Boulevard of Broken Dreams." These sex symbols all experienced tragic deaths. Shouldn't idolizing death be seen as insane? Yet, being fooled by the ego, we don't even see through it.

Tom Wolfe, in *The Bonfire of the Vanities*, depicts the egocentricity of his characters with stunning acumen. Each character idolizes himself as the most cool, most clever, and most qualified person. His personal experience makes him more savvy, more smart, and more sensible than the next guy. The Wall Street millionaire, the ghetto kid, and the tabloid journalist all have the same internal vanity, while their exterior lives look vastly different. This again is how the ego tricks us into thinking we're separate and unique.

A further example of the slippery nature of the ego is the recurring theme of lost loves in movies and songs. Movies are always more poignant when someone dies. We romanticize death and loss; for men it's usually portrayed in war stories and for women it's in romance. However, romantic "love" often isn't love at all; rather, it's possession and unhealthy attachment. We frequently equate the depth of our love by the amount of jealousy or loss we feel. I felt pleased when one of my boyfriends wanted to beat the crap out of another guy who won me over, yet this wasn't coming from his love, but his insecurity. I erroneously thought it showed how much he loved me. Likewise, my deep, intense longing for an old flame was evidence not of love, but of fear of loss and separation. When I stopped longing for him, I loved him just as much and felt that he was still with me in spirit. True love knows that love can never die and there is no such thing as separation from a loved one. The ego doesn't want us to know this, and so it romanticizes lost loves, glorifies war, and eroticizes self-destruction. Pretty tricky!

Choosing with the Holy Spirit

Closer is He than breathing, and nearer than hands and feet.
~Lord Tennyson

You can speak from the spirit or from the ego,
as you choose (T-4.in.2:1). I have said you have
but two emotions, love and fear (T-13.V.1:1).

The Holy Spirit can use every single thing the ego makes and turn it into an opportunity to awaken. However, we have to ask for this. We have free will, and Spirit will not step in without our permission. We make about sixty thousand decisions a day, and every single decision we make is between love and fear, between the Holy Spirit and the ego. We have to choose between one or the other, because we can't hear both at the same time. Every time we choose with the Holy Spirit, the ego's voice becomes weaker.

For some of us it may appear that we can feel both loving and fearful at the same time. However, if we are feeling fear of any kind, we can be sure that we are choosing the ego's script, as the Holy Spirit's decision brings us only peace. If we think we are feeling both, it could be that we are jumping back and forth between the two scripts, moment to moment. It could also be that the ego is telling us that we are feeling love when it's really fear. For example, if someone we love is dying, we may be holding great feelings of love for him while fearing his death. However, this is primarily fear disguised as love. Love knows no separation. It knows there is no death and that the body is not real. Love is a state of being inside of us that knows no lack or loss. Therefore, what passes as love often is actually fear. This is explained more in the next chapter under "Special Relationships."

When we choose the Holy Spirit our lives become smoother and happier. It doesn't mean everything goes perfectly, but things don't bother us like they used to. We don't have to control how things show up anymore. Spirit wants to give us total joy and love, but we constantly refuse it. Sometimes gifts are material things, and other times they are simply love, peace, and joy without external items. I often joke with my clients about how they sabotage good things. Sometimes Spirit offers us a palace, but we respond, "Oh, I'd rather live in the sewer." God hands us a silver platter with scrumptious treats, and we say, "I'll only take a tiny piece," or, "No, thanks, God, I'll eat my cold hot dog."

Making life choices is what psychotherapy is all about, but in the space of the ego, choices can become chains. As a psychotherapist, I used to pride myself on my analytical abilities, but the problem was I'd analyze to death. I drove myself crazy figuring out every possible causative angle and every consequence of proposed solutions. In Alcoholics Anonymous they call this "analysis paralysis." I learned the Sedona Method® technique for releasing feelings and one of the questions is "Can you let go of trying to figure it out?"

My first reaction was panic! Where would I be without my control? The ego made me think I was in control, when I was actually out of control and preventing a solution through obsessive thinking. I feel embarrassed to realize that all my overanalyzing was but the ego at work. **The ego cannot know anything (T-6. IV.3:1)**, but answers come easily and effortlessly when we are in the relaxed, silent space of knowing, where our true Self abides.

Worry is fear, and therefore is of the ego. Many of us make a second occupation of worrying. We worry about our children, our jobs, our health, our status, our finances. Imagining catastrophes becomes a pastime, previewing what could wreck our lives in the future. In the back of our minds we know we're supposed to trust that everything will be okay, but very few of us are able to do this. This, again, is the ego's doing. The higher Self is not afraid of *anything*.

In addition to worry, our society has a constant obsession with being busy. Many people don't feel worthwhile if they're not working long, hard hours. Many of us plan every detail of our schedules and are so busy that we don't have time for spontaneous pleasures. I was a workaholic for many years, and when not working I scheduled many recreational activities. If I slowed down, I felt intense anxiety. For years I longed to go to the bookstore and read in the café. Every time I'd go, however, I got a headache and found a reason why I had to get home and work. I simply didn't allow myself to do my favorite thing, which is reading. On weekends I was so exhausted from the day's recreational activities or cleaning that I would read only one page before I fell asleep. If I did try to read at home during the day, I saw dust on the end table and got up to clean it. If friends dropped in unannounced, I did dishes so I wouldn't waste time sitting and talking. The ego was a driving, relentless force that would not let me relax. As I read I go into a reverie and feel God's presence, so the ego kept me from that. The more I read, the better I feel, and the more my true nature is expressed. Today I read often without feeling guilty and unproductive. I feel like I'm in heaven, and I am, for as I express my peaceful nature, I am right back home with God.

Some of my worst anxiety comes when I have an entire day off. I look forward to it, only to be filled with angst and guilt when it's here. I feel guilty about not being at work and making money. I start ruminating on someone I'm jealous of. I remember someone that angered me. I do one project only to feel guilty that I'm not tackling a different one. I work in my garden and get upset about the heat, the cold, the bugs. I feel guilty that I just planted beautiful flowers without enjoying them at all. I get a headache from all the obsessive pressure to get everything done. And on and on. The ego doesn't want us to revel in our freedom, to enjoy today. The ego pulls us into the past with guilt and regret, or into the future with hopes or fears. It obsesses on what it can't have or do, as that is its nature. Spirit is found only in the present moment, and the ego cannot exist in the pure awareness of the now. God is eternal, beyond time and space; therefore, there is no past or future. It is always *now*. Thankfully, I'm gradually getting better at enjoying the now moment.

What is it that *you* love to do but don't allow yourself to do it? What is it *you* keep telling yourself that you'll do someday when you have more time or money? Start doing it now! The ego will make you feel guilty, but you can choose not to listen. You may feel anxious as you step into new, uncomfortable behaviors, but know that that's just the ego trying to hold you back, and forge ahead anyway.

Have you ever felt happy and noticed that, out of the blue, you're ruminating on some problem from the past or some fear of the future? Have you noticed that your mind is complaining much of the time, even if you're doing something you love? My client succinctly describes it, "The world is one big complaint! I used to think it was just the corporation I work for, but now I see it everywhere." The ego doesn't want to die, so it claws and struggles to keep us miserable and in its grip. We are trapped by the ego much like a fly struggling in a spider's web. Often, severe anxiety will arise when the ego senses that we are close to breaking free. If we aren't attacking and complaining, we feel empty and alone. This is what psychology calls "existential anxiety." It is the vague recognition that something's wrong in this world, that our true home is not here.

A Miss Universe, upon being crowned, simultaneously thought how wonderful it was and also, "Is this all there is?" She realized the difference between joy and pleasure. Joy is a state of mind; it comes from within regardless of outer circumstances. We can experience loss and difficulties and still feel joy. Joy, peace, and love are the gifts of our true Self and cannot be lost. Pleasure, on the other hand, is temporary. New possessions, going places, sex, doing different things, and so on, can offer pleasure, but they come with a price. Pain is pleasure's opposite in the world of duality; thus, pain is inherent whenever we feel pleasure. If we enjoy painting but don't have time to paint or our hand gets injured we will feel a loss. The minute we love another person the loss of his body is inevitable, through death or the severing of the relationship. If we revel in sports we feel exuberant when our team wins but blue when it loses. The *Course* says, **You do not ask too much of life, but far too little. When you let your mind be drawn to bodily concerns, to things you buy, to eminence as valued by the world, you ask for sorrow, not for happiness. This course does not attempt to take from you the little that you have. It does not substitute utopian ideas for satisfactions which the world contains. There are no satisfactions in the world (W-p.I.133.2:1-5)**. This is not saying we can't enjoy the things of the world, but that we have to realize they are not where true joy lies. Nothing on this level is perfect, yet the ego keeps us questing for the perfect love, perfect family, perfect job, perfect life. But the ego's quest is a dead-end street. Have you ever noticed a sense of emptiness when you've attained a long-held goal? That's because nothing in this world can ever ultimately satisfy you. Only our return home to God brings lasting peace.

Are you aware that when you're happy, little irritations don't bother you as much as when you're stressed? When you're happy you're closer to your internal joy. I had some bug bites recently and noticed that when I was upset, they started itching. I hardly noticed them when I was mellow.

The ego doesn't want us to feel mellow, so it exaggerates external pleasures. It always wants new and more exciting things, always looks to what's next. It fears boredom, equating it with emptiness. In our society there seems to be a trend toward increasing thrills and intensity. Our sex-crazed culture keeps the focus on the illusory body instead of the inner self. The violent and sexual content in the media is more graphic, while greed on Wall Street seems at an all-time high. My sister was at an amusement park where each year a bigger, faster, more thrilling attraction is introduced. She commented that the old roller coasters seem boring and aren't fun anymore. Slowing down in our culture is a no-no, so the ego's got us exactly where it wants us. The ego knows that when we slow down we remember the Christ Self within. Within ourselves we are never bored, anxious, or empty.

Remembering the Christ Self is a choice. Choice is emphasized repeatedly in ACIM. We choose which voice to heed, the ego's or the Holy Spirit's. We choose between love and fear. We choose whether to believe in the dream or not. The amount of peace we experience and whether or not we awaken from the dream depends on *our* choice. No one else makes it for us. However, our choice determines what we experience on this level. **Would you be hostage to the ego or host to God (T-11.II.7:1)?** Since the ego always tries to guilt-trip us, *Course* teacher Dr. Michael Mirdad suggests we respond with, "Why should I listen to you? You always say that!"[2] The ego's voice is like Dorothy's chant, "Lions and tigers and bears! Oh, my!" There's always something to be afraid of. As long as we appear to inhabit bodies the ego voice will be present, but we can ignore it.

Remember, the Holy Spirit is just the voice of our own right mind. (See chapter 7 for a more detailed explanation of listening to the Holy Spirit's voice.) We do not give our power away to anyone else; we reclaim our *own* power. How do we choose the Holy Spirit's voice? We take a breath, get as quiet as we can, and listen for the peaceful, loving voice inside. It is like a whisper; it is our intuition. It takes some practice, but we eventually learn to discern the ego's voice from the Holy Spirit's.

The two voices speak for different interpretations of the same thing simultaneously; or almost simultaneously, for the ego always speaks first (T-5.VI.3:5).

Since the ego always speaks first, we have to pause and get silent. This prayer is an easy way to ask the Holy Spirit for guidance:

What would You have me do?
Where would You have me go?
What would You have me say, and to whom?
(W-p.I.71.9:3-5)

My friend gets irritated about asking for the Holy Spirit's help. Frustrated, he says, "I'm smart enough to figure this out! Why do I need to ask for help?" Only the ego would say this, for it does not accept the freedom and ease that come with surrender to the Holy Spirit's guidance. **Your ego cannot accept this freedom, and will oppose it at every possible moment and in every possible way (T-5. VI.2:9).** This is not an exaggeration. Once we recognize the ego we see it *everywhere*. The good news is that we can also recognize it as an illusion and refuse to give it power.

> *Do not be afraid of the ego.*
> *It depends on your mind, and as you made it*
> *by believing in it, so you can dispel it*
> *by withdrawing belief from it. When you are willing*
> *to accept sole responsibility for the ego's existence*
> *you will have laid aside all anger and all attack*
> *(T-7.VIII.5:1-2;4).*

The ego is not real; therefore, it has no power, except what we award it. All of our fears about our own unworthiness are just that—fears. God sees us as completely worthy and sinless. The ego desires that you see yourself as wretched, inferior, unloving, hateful, incompetent, ugly, and created in original sin. The truth is that you are the one Self, the one that God created as perfect, whole, and loving. When we love ourselves, we remember this truth.

Guilt always calls for punishment, but the Holy Spirit reminds us of our innocence. **The ego believes that by punishing itself it will mitigate the punishment of God (T-5.V.5:6).** Perhaps this is why criminals often return to the scene of a crime, secretly hoping to get caught. In what ways do you punish yourself? Do you berate yourself for things you've done? Do you deny yourself pleasures? Do you push away those who love you? Do you keep yourself so busy that you can't relax? Do you subdue your emotions with addictions? Do you allow friends in your life that are no good for you? The Holy Spirit within you will show you how to love yourself. I had a client, Ron, who was newly sober and in Alcoholics Anonymous. The main focus of his therapy was learning to treat himself with love. He had an AA sponsor who seemed stuck in ego. His sponsor disagreed with me, chiding Ron, "No! You've got to be hard on yourself! You can't let up on yourself or you'll slip!" Ron explained that he could learn to avoid relapses by loving himself, but his sponsor wouldn't buy it. So, Ron let that sponsor go. I ran into Ron recently and he's doing great. He's been sober ten years, is happy, and is loving his life.

Being Our True Self

We are not human beings having a spiritual experience.
We are spiritual beings having a human experience.
~Teilhard de Chardin

> ***You are one Self, united and secure***
> ***in light and joy and peace. You are one Self,***
> ***complete and healed and whole...***
> ***You are one Self, in perfect harmony with***
> ***all there is...You are one Self, the holy Son of***
> ***God, united with your brothers in that Self...***
> ***This is your Self, the Son of God Himself,***
> ***sinless as Its Creator, with His strength within you and***
> ***His Love forever yours (W-p.I.95.12:1; 3; 13:1-2; 4).***

There are no conditions imposed by God, no judgments, and no tests to pass. Because you have never left God, you have never done anything wrong. What is the meaning of sin in a dream? Nothing, for a dream is nothing. The negative behaviors and thoughts that are called "sin" are merely ego delusions, a lack of love, the faulty belief in separation from God and our fellow humans. We attack others and we attack ourselves because we have forgotten who we really are. Since we are still our Christ Self, in spite of appearances, all the attacks are simply errors. When we recognize our oneness with God by removing old thought patterns, we will wake up. We will see that *we* made up the dream, *we* made up the ego, and *we* have the power to choose what we will believe in.

There is one problem and one solution (W-p.I.90.1:4). The problem is separation and the solution is to recognize we are already home with God. In *The Disappearance of the Universe,*

Gary Renard commented that all his life he had been trying to *improve* the dream, and now he was being asked to *wake up* from the dream. This struck me and dramatically altered the way I approach my clients' and my own goals.

My psychotherapy practice has been successful, and I have been blessed to witness many clients grow in self-love and enjoyment of life. However, I have recently realized that I was going about change the hard way. Psychotherapy focuses on increasing one's self-love and self-esteem. The problem is, we can improve our self-esteem all we want and we are still left with the wrong ego mind that stirs up chaos. We are trapped in an endless cycle of attaining perfection, whether it's in our life circumstances or in ourselves. We attain one goal only to soon feel dissatisfied, then we're on relentlessly to the next goal. **No one could solve all the problems the world appears to hold. Some spring up unexpectedly, just as you think you have resolved the previous ones. Others remain unsolved under a cloud of denial, and rise to haunt you from time to time, only to be hidden again but still unsolved (W-p.I.79.5:1;4-5).** This endless array of problems keeps us trapped in the illusion of improving the dream. We feel content when we meet our goals, and lousy when we don't. Until reading the *Course* I never understood why old problems kept coming up in spite of all the work I'd done on myself and all the goals I'd achieved. Out of the shadows that coiled snake would strike, sneering that I was a fool, a fake, or a failure. "What a fool you are! You actually believed this could work!" "You're just a fake; you don't even know what you're talking about!" "What a failure! You're right back at square one!" Examining our feelings and motives in psychotherapy allows us to understand and manage our lives better, but since the ego always comes up with another angle to thwart us, true, permanent change is kept at bay.

We don't *improve* the ego, we *remove* the ego. This is the only way to truly change deep down, for it's the only way to heal the endless storehouse of ego guilt. Most guilt is subconscious. The problems and guilt that we are aware of are like the tip of the iceberg; we only see a little of it, while three-fourths lie underneath. We often don't recognize the extent of this self-hatred until we fall flat on our face with self-sabotage. We see it when we wreck our relationships, get addicted, and stay stuck in our careers. Self-improvement methods and psychotherapy take us only so far, because they get to some, but not all, of the subconscious ego guilt. Positive thinking, while it works in the short term, is still part of this level of duality; therefore, its opposite polarity of negative thinking will eventually show up. The only true healing is recognizing that the entire ego is not real and releasing the illusion. But first we have to acknowledge the full extent of ego hatred, so we can choose with the Holy Spirit instead.

Ego thoughts resemble weeds in a garden. If the garden is untended, weeds spring out of control and choke the flowers, just as the ego chokes our Spirit. As we pull out the weeds we leave more room for Spirit to blossom. The difference between the teachings of *A Course in Miracles* and most self-improvement paths is that the *Course* teaches us to pull the weeds out by their roots, rather than simply shearing off the tops for them to grow back. Taking out the ego's roots means realizing that the ego really has no roots at all, that it is not real.

Today I teach my clients to tap into the higher Self, the Holy Spirit. I like to imagine my higher Self as a radiant and serene being. I try to become her, to think and feel as she does, and to make decisions from that space. The more I visualize myself as her, the more peaceful I feel and act. A friend of mine accesses her higher Self by imagining a dialogue with an old, wise woman, rocking patiently on a porch. One client sees herself as a graceful birch tree, while another identifies herself as a happy, carefree sunflower.

Babies embody their higher selves more than adults, and that's why most of us love looking deep into their eyes. There is no fear that the baby is thinking we're ugly or stupid or not good enough. A happy baby simply extends the love and joy inherent in its nature, because it hasn't yet learned to squelch them. Likewise, Mother Teresa, Mahatma Ghandi, and Jesus were people who so identified with the love of God that they radiated light. They were humble, yet powerful, embodying the Christ Self. They were able to *receive* God's love, and therefore they were able to *give* it. However, they had to come to terms with the ego as well. Mother Teresa is known to have said, "[I am] 60 percent Attila the Hun"— 60 percent monster, yet the power of love prevailed, as it is destined to do with every one of us. Mother Teresa also stated that she would march *for* peace, but not *against* war. She recognized that being against something was an ego attack, so she expressed her love instead.

So, what does the ego want to do with pure love? Kill it! Jesus and Ghandi were both murdered by the collective mass ego. Others who have proclaimed oneness and equality among mankind have also been assassinated—Lincoln, Kennedy, and Martin Luther King. As we have witnessed with all of these heroes, the body can be killed but the message of love cannot die. These models of the nature of the true Self stay with us.

The Hero's Journey

There was never a place for her in the ranks of the terrible, slow army of the cautious. She ran ahead, where there were no paths.
~Dorothy Parker

There are glimpses of the true Self all over, and we often find them in movies. Forrest Gump is a good example of someone who is without an ego. He does not plan and analyze, but he simply acts from love. He is connected to his higher Self and accomplishes amazing things because he does not perceive limits. He wins the world Ping-Pong championship, runs across the entire country, and is a war hero and football star because he doesn't have an ego telling him he can't be these things. The extremely popular movie *The Matrix* is a metaphor for the transformation of the ego self into the Christ Self, using numerous biblical references within its science fiction context. *Star Wars, The Wizard of Oz*, and many other classics take us on the archetypal hero's journey. Mythologist Joseph Campbell detailed the hero's journey, noting that every culture contains myths and stories about the transformation of the self. During the journey the hero fails and loses his sense of self, and after many trials, comes to remember his true identity.

It is basically the triumph of the higher Self over the ego self. We resonate with these movies because we know in our depth that they reveal our own journey back to God. The powerful phrase "May the Force be with you," inspires us as it speaks to the truth in our Being.

The movie *The Lion King* provides a perfect metaphor for the hero's journey back to his true Self. Mufasa, the father lion, represents God; Simba, the son, represents the Self; Scar, the hateful, jealous brother, is the ego; and Rafiki, the baboon prophet, speaks for the Holy Spirit. Simba is slated to rule the kingdom when his father dies, but Scar cleverly tries to kill him, setting up a stampede to trample the unsuspecting cub. Mufasa attempts to rescue Simba and gets caught on a cliff. Scar, in a position to save Mufasa, cackles as he lets go of his hand, and Mufasa dies. (We are meant to have all of our Father's power, but the ego tries to keep us from it. God is always reaching out to us, but the ego wants God out of the way.)

Scar tells Simba it's his fault his father died, because Mufasa was only trying to rescue Simba. Simba, ashamed, exiles himself from the kingdom. Scar becomes king, deceiving his subjects that Simba also died in the stampede. (We feel guilty thinking we've angered God, and we believe we are exiled from heaven. The ego is ruler of the illusory world and says there is no God.)

Simba takes up with friends who live the life of leisure, while he tries to forget his pain. One day his girlfriend, Nala, unexpectedly finds him and tells him he must take responsibility and assume his throne for Scar (the ego) has destroyed the kingdom. Simba agonizes over this, feeling unworthy of being king. Simba, looking heavenward, cries out in pain that his father has abandoned him, when he had promised to always be there. Simba thinks this is because he killed his father. (The ego distracts us from our true nature with external pleasures, but the Son of God needs to claim ownership of his identity. We pray for help, but in our guilt erroneously think God wants nothing to do with us. This is exactly how the ego wants us to feel.)

The prophet Rafiki appears and challenges that Simba doesn't even know who he himself is. Rafiki tells him he's Mufasa's son.

Simba is startled and asks if Rafiki knew his father, and Rafiki responds that he *knows* his father, in the present tense. (God is alive and available.) Rafiki says he will show Simba his father and leads him to a pool of water, telling him to look into the water. Simba is disappointed, bemoaning that he sees only his own reflection. Rafiki tells him to look closer and he will see that his father lives within him. (The Holy Spirit's voice always responds to our cries for help. Every problem stems from forgetting who we really are—the Son of God. We feel separated from God, but we are made in His image and He lives inside us. We have simply forgotten.)

An image of Mufasa appears in the clouds. In a powerful, thundering voice, Mufasa declares that Simba has forgotten him. Simba denies this, to which Mufasa responds that Simba has forgotten Mufasa because he has forgotten that he is the son of a king. Mufasa's image fades as he admonishes Simba to remember who he is. **To forget me (Jesus) is to forget yourself and Him Who created you (T-7.V.10:2).** Simba receives his father's message, claims his true identity, and returns home. (He remembers he's the Son of God and returns home to heaven. It was waiting for him all along, but he did not feel worthy.)

Once home, Scar attempts to make Simba feel guilty for his father's death, but finally admits that he killed Mufasa. (The ego makes us feel guilty when we're innocent. The ego's motive is to kill our awareness of God and our Self. Unlike Scar, however, the ego will never tell us this.) Simba, becoming wise to Scar's tactics, proclaims that he will no longer listen to him because he always lies. Simba then banishes Scar, who puts up a fight to the death. Scar dies and the kingdom is restored to peace and beauty. (When we declare we will no longer listen to the ego, it fights for survival. When the ego is absent our lives are lovely and peaceful.)

Simba's hero's journey is the path my client Harry has taken in real life. Harry's ego battle has been a thirty-year history of alcoholism. Harry has a powerful presence about him, and he had it even when he was drinking. He is a foreman and his workers respect and admire him. This is because he radiates the presence of God, even though others don't recognize that's what it is. Harry has heard God's voice since childhood, and it was what helped him through life in this world. His mother was in a mental institution several times and was too narcissistic to love her children. He felt completely alone in the family, but he felt God's comforting presence and guidance. As Harry began to get sober, he spoke of how he was aware all along that he was running from God. He drank to drown out the Holy Spirit's voice, as that was the only way he could get away from the Voice and making the choice for it. He'd stare at the bottle, wrestling with himself, then drink anyway, feeling tremendous guilt that the alcohol would anesthetize only temporarily. He realizes now that God wasn't mad at him, as he thought He was. He states, "I didn't even know I was being loved." Today Harry finds that when he asks the Holy Spirit what to do, and does it rather than resist, life is easy. He has been sober for three years, solved conflicts at work and with his wife, and has calmed down his obsessive-compulsive behavior by listening to the Holy Spirit's voice instead of the ego's. Our sessions became like broken records. He'd present a problem and I'd say the same thing every time. "Have you prayed about it?" Now he simply comes in and tells me that he prayed, what the Holy Spirit told him to do, and how it solved the problem. Recently Harry had severe financial problems and his answer to his prayer was, "You'll be in church next week." Harry calls our sessions "church" because we both feel God's presence emanating as we talk. Harry had to cancel his appointment the week before, and when he rescheduled, it was right after I'd attended an abundance seminar. I raved about the program and encouraged him to attend, and he was convinced he'd gotten his answer to his money problems in "church."

Harry is so connected to God that loving behavior predominates in his life. He has never read much spiritual literature and was raised in Catholic schools. Much of his spiritual growth consisted of getting rid of the ego guilt that was pounded into him by his church, which he jokingly refers to as "Our Lady of Perpetual Guilt." When Harry starts talking, words flow as if they were from the mouth of God Himself. He makes statements about the love of God and the nature of this dream world that he never learned in church. He just allows his innate knowledge to surface.

Harry is no different than you and me. He simply steps out of the way and lets God come through. He doesn't need me anymore, because the Holy Spirit is the best therapist around. The more we practice honoring the still, small inner voice that speaks of love, the more we will be like Harry.

This is a course in cause and not effect (T-21. VII.7:8). Therefore, seek not to change the world, but choose to change your mind about the world (T-21.in.1:7).

A Course in Miracles is not concerned with changing the outer conditions of our lives, although they often do improve when we change our minds. ACIM does not encourage us to visualize our way to success or affirm our goals or work to achieve our aspirations. It does not judge these activities, it simply sees them as choices within the dream. Seemingly positive outcomes are what ACIM calls **the happy dream (T-18.V.h)**. Truly, however, it does not matter what we accomplish in the dream, for the dream is not real. It does not matter if you are a drug addict, a wealthy benefactor, a construction worker, a prostitute, a banker, a lawyer, or a criminal. It is all equally meaningless. The ego reacts to these statements with horror! Of course it matters! Getting what you want out of life is the name of the game. Contributing to societal good is worthier than being a no-count. The hero is certainly better than the skid-row bum, right?

Not in God's eyes. These are nothing but ego comparisons and believing them keeps us hooked into this world. We need to change our mind about the meaning of this world. *The only use this world has is to lead us to wake up from the dream that we are separate from God.* Nothing else. Achieving our goals will score us no more brownie points with God than watching TV, for in God's eyes we are already perfect. The only thing that matters is recognizing that this is all a dream and that we are home with God right now.

We then see this world without fear, and the resulting love for all people and things is the miracle. As we wake up, we can still work to solve world problems, such as hunger, war, and pollution, if we feel led to do so. However, we act from a place of nonattachment and awareness that this is just a dream. Furthermore, just because it is a dream does not give us license to kill or steal. If we murder and thieve on this level, we will experience consequences, such as going to jail. We act from a place of love within the dream as much as we are able. Not only does loving action propel us to spiritual awareness, it gives us a much happier dream.

My client asks a good question, "Since it's a dream and you're not really hurting anyone, how do you convince people to not join gangs or the Mafia and steal or kill whenever they want?" The answer is *what you do to others you are doing to yourself.* There is only one Self; therefore, if you attack another, you attack yourself. If you love another, you love yourself. If you forgive another, you forgive yourself. Another good question is since it's a dream that's never happened, why bother to do anything at all? Why do we need to choose the Holy Spirit's voice, why do we need to forgive, why not just wait until we die, since we're still at home with God? The reason we do anything is that we will not experience being home with God until we forgive everything within the dream. This process is what enables us to be aware of the illusion.

> *Now try to reach the Son of God in you.*
> *This is the Self that never sinned, nor made*
> *an image to replace reality. This is the Self that never*
> *left Its home in God to walk the world uncertainly.*
> *This is the Self that knows no fear, nor could conceive*
> *of loss or suffering or death (W-p.I.94.3:5-8).*

As I was writing this book, one of my friends died suddenly. Jim was a vibrant middle-aged man, and this came as a shock. He had what appeared to be a severe cold, and as his wife Mary drove him to the emergency room he slumped over, dead of a heart attack. What a horrifying thing for Mary! I automatically knew that Jim was okay, that his spirit went home and that he was probably experiencing the most joy he had ever felt. My concern was for Mary. I began worrying about her, then remembered that *A Course in Miracles* teaches that it is not helpful to hold anything less than the truth about someone. **Do not side with sickness (illusions) in the presence of a Son of God even if he believes in it.... Your recognition of him as part of God reminds him of the truth about himself (T-10.III.3:4-5).** So, I sent Mary light and prayers, affirming that she knows that she is the Christ, whole, complete, and safe in the arms of God. That the essence of her true nature is peace and love, and that no apparent traumas can take this away.

In this situation, the ego would have Mary believe that all is lost, that she is separated from Jim and will never see him again. The ego actually *wants* her to suffer, as this is what it thrives on. It is so easy to fall into these feelings, particularly with such a seemingly devastating episode. However, this is when the choice to hear the Holy Spirit's voice is crucial, to minimize despair and overwhelming grief. When Mary prays and asks, "Holy Spirit, let me see your vision of this," she will be given strength and peace. She may need to remind herself of this repeatedly, for the urge to slip into the ego's way of thinking will be compelling. However, when grief subsides, she can use this situation as an opportunity to express her true Self, the one that is not afraid and knows there is no death or loss in reality. During her grief we would never want to say, "But, Mary, it's just a dream!" That would be an insensitive insult to Mary's experience. People have to open to this concept in their own time.

Grief is the perfect venue for the ego's foothold, yet any time we are not at peace we are thinking with the ego. The remedy for overcoming the ego is always the same: choose the Holy Spirit's voice. Take a deep breath, close your eyes, and go within in silence. Ask Spirit a question, and wait quietly for an answer. *Then do what it says!* Practicing this over and over will eventually become a habit, and the peace will come more quickly. You can memorize the prayer below and repeat it as often as you need to. The lessons in the *Course* Workbook also act as affirmations to help us see things from God's perspective and reverse our conditioned thinking.

I must have decided wrongly, because I am not at peace. I made the decision myself, but I can also decide otherwise. I want to decide otherwise, because I want to be at peace. I do not feel guilty, because the Holy Spirit will undo all the consequences of my wrong decision if I will let Him. I choose to let Him, by allowing Him to decide for God for me (T-5.VII.6:7-11).

We need to commit to refuse to listen to the ego's negativity and choose the Holy Spirit's voice instead. For years I vacillated, acting from my real Self when I felt like it and griping and complaining whenever I was too lazy to choose with my right mind. I felt entitled to grouse when anything made me mad. But this only made me swing erratically from ego to Spirit and back and forth again. It was like a roller coaster. I was joyous one minute and hateful the next. I finally realized that unbridled anger was keeping me down, and I've resolved not to allow it anymore. I am committed to acting from Spirit *all the time;* it is not always easy, and at times can feel downright impossible. However, as the *Course* says, **It is essential that you realize your thinking will be erratic until a firm commitment to one or the other is made (T-3.II.1:5).**

In the next chapter we learn to see the Holy Spirit's vision with the people and circumstances that push our buttons the most, the ones we need to forgive.

CHAPTER FIVE

TRUE FORGIVENESS

Love looks not with eyes, but with the mind.
~Shakespeare

God is our goal; forgiveness is the means
by which our minds return to Him at last (W.pII.256.1:9).

Shelley came to therapy to address her depression and alcoholism. She was already sober and attending Alcoholics Anonymous but found that she cried all the time, couldn't sleep, was irritable and angry, and felt like dying. She had thought that when she quit drinking her problems would go away, but she realized that all the problems she drank to cover up were still there. Shelley developed a sarcastic personality to cover her deep pain and ridiculed the idea of a loving God. Her family history could have been material for a soap opera, and most of her family members were violent alcoholics. In his drunkenness, her father repeatedly raped Shelley's older sister. This had been going on since she was a little girl. So, as a teen, her sister eventually took matters into her own hands. She waited in the garage for her father to arrive home from work, and as he got out of his car, she shot him dead. The courts let her off on grounds of self-defense. Shelley's good friend, in a drunken frenzy, poured gasoline on herself, struck a match to set herself on fire, and died in agonizing screams. Shelley's twelve-year-old sister was playing with a handgun and shot and killed herself. Shelley agonized over whether this was an accident or suicide, hoping it was just an accident. She felt tremendous guilt that she had not been able to save her sister.

Shelley was not only living a dream, she was living a nightmare of epic proportions. How do we forgive a situation like this? How in the world do we see all these horrible things as just a dream? Perhaps a better question is how do we live with something like this *without* seeing it as a dream and forgiving it? These types of traumas are just too big to deal with without some form of understanding. Prior to studying *A Course in Miracles* I approached God with anger: "God, I don't care if you gave us free will! Why did you make us capable of such barbaric atrocities? Couldn't you have just made us with only the capacity for kindness?" The pain I felt over incidents such as these was overwhelming. It sometimes swept me under with grief and despair, even if the troubles did not directly happen to me.

Today I constantly remind myself, "It's only a dream. Everyone is safe. Don't make it real." *A Course in Miracles* is emphatic that all things in physical form be seen as illusions. Until we consistently see things as a dream we will be trapped in the fear, bitterness, and sorrow of this false world. While it may seem impossible to forgive the horrors that Shelley's family experienced, ACIM states that the *process* of forgiveness is the same, be it a murder or a snide remark. This seems ludicrous at first, but since *everything* is a dream, *everything* is equally illusory. However, because we are engaged in the illusion and see it as real, a murder, suicide, or any death is likely to take longer to forgive than things we judge as minor in comparison. But in truth, a murder seen as a falsehood is as forgivable as any other deception.

I witnessed this process in action with a friend of mine whose sister was murdered. He was devoted to his spiritual path and knew that it was only the body that was killed, and that his sister's spirit lived on. He knew that life is a dream, and he seemed able to find peace much more quickly than someone who did not have this framework. At the time I was amazed, thinking, "This stuff actually works!" Today I have seen so many miracles that I am no longer amazed, simply grateful.

This chapter addresses what the definition of true forgiveness is, and how true forgiveness varies from the ego's version of forgiveness. We will learn how to forgive and develop the awareness that forgiveness is the main tool we use for awakening from the dream. Relationships are the primary venue for forgiveness, and we explore what the *Course* defines as "special relationships," and their valuable role in healing.

The Definition of Forgiveness

> *Even doubtful accusations leave a stain behind them.*
> *~Thomas Fuller*

> **God does not forgive because He has never condemned. And there must be condemnation before forgiveness is necessary. Forgiveness is the great need of this world, but that is because it is a world of illusions. Those who forgive are thus releasing themselves from illusions, while those who withhold forgiveness are binding themselves to them. As you condemn only yourself, so do you forgive only yourself (W-p.I.46.1:1-5).**

> **The ego, too, has a plan of forgiveness. . . .**
> **The ego's plan, of course, makes no sense and will not work. The ego's plan is to have you see error clearly first, and then overlook it. Yet how can you overlook what you have made real (T-9.IV.4:1-2; 4-5)?**

Since the topic of forgiveness tends to immediately bring up the ego's resistance, we need to start with what forgiveness is *not*. (If you are uncomfortable with the word "forgiveness," substitute a different word. It is the concept of unconditional love that is important, not the semantics. Other possibilities are "acceptance," "letting go," "transcendence," "release," and "nonjudgment.")

Forgiveness is *not* allowing someone to abuse us, forgiveness is *not* condoning abusive behavior, and forgiveness is *not* for the other person. Forgiveness does not mean we let someone steal from us, or physically or emotionally abuse us. It does not mean we think this behavior is acceptable, for people still need to take responsibility for their actions. Forgiveness means that we address the behavior with appropriate consequences, but we don't condemn the person who did it. We still recognize that in spite of appearances, that person has the Christ Self within him, and in truth is beautiful, perfect, and beloved by God, as we all are.

Forgiveness is not for the other person so much as it is for us. We cannot enter the kingdom of heaven within us if we are holding even one person out of our hearts. As we learned, there are two thought systems, that of the ego and that of God. We can only be in one or the other at any given time. If we are judging, we are in the ego's thought system and we have shut ourselves off from the fullness of God.

The world's definition of forgiveness, which is that of the ego, is to magnanimously forgive someone who has harmed us. "He did me wrong, but I'll be the bigger person and forgive him." This is making sin real, and then overlooking it. Yet *A Course in Miracles* is clear, direct, and uncompromising in its definition. In a dream, there is no sin. We are all innocent and no one has done anything wrong in truth. This is so contrary to what we are taught, and what we experience, that there is no way we can change our thinking without the Holy Spirit's help. "She slept with my husband! What do you mean she didn't do anything wrong!" "He murdered someone! How can he be innocent and how can murder not be wrong?" Indeed, on this level, there are things that appear right and wrong and extremely vicious and hurtful. However, to be healed, we have to be *willing* to have our entire worldview changed by the Holy Spirit. Only in undoing the ego's false belief system will we understand what the *Course* calls "true forgiveness." *True forgiveness is that this world does not exist; therefore, the events never truly happened!*

Since this is impossible for most of us in our present state of mind, we do not have to *understand* this concept in order to forgive.

Our job is to be *willing* to have our minds healed. The Holy Spirit will change our minds for us. We don't even have to believe that this world is a dream in order to be healed, for when we are healed, we will automatically wake up to the truth. So don't worry about "getting it." The process of healing is explained more later in this chapter under "Three Simple Steps."

Since this is only a dream and nothing happened, why do we have to forgive? The answer is that true forgiveness is the central method, the major practice, by which we return our minds back to God. Therefore, the people who frustrate us are our helpers, because they are giving us opportunities to practice forgiveness. We will stay stuck in the illusion of misery and suffering until we *completely* forgive all of our brothers, ourselves, and the dream of this world. Even forgiveness itself is an illusion, because there is nothing to forgive. However, since we are mired in the dream world, we need a tool to get us unstuck. Forgiveness is this tool, and it needs to be seen as the most essential tool in the toolbox. It is the right tool for the job. Lacking forgiveness would be like not having a hammer or screwdriver in our toolbox. We wouldn't get a whole lot done.

Another reason we should forgive is our mental and physical health. When we don't forgive we harbor angry feelings, which lead to the release of cortisol, a stress hormone. Prolonged release of cortisol causes colitis, heart attacks, strokes, and immune disorders. We become more anxious and depressed. Respected author Carolyn Myss claims that lack of forgiveness is the underlying cause for every single unhealed illness. *Every single one.*

One of my favorite *Course* teachers is Reverend Jon Mundy. Jon was in at the ground floor of the *Course*'s inception, as he knew Helen Schucman and Bill Thetford, the scribe and transcriber. Jon states that ACIM is simple, but it is hardly easy. "The *Course* isn't easy because we are easily addicted to our emotions, our anger, our hurts and pains, our attack thoughts and grievances. We think they are real and we hold on to them for dear death (not life). This is why only forgiveness (which requires a reversal in thinking) can really set us free."[1]

My friend Mark was in prison because he almost killed his wife when he discovered her affair. His life theme has been to self-destruct in dramatic ways such as substance abuse, but he is not normally violent. Mark has a deeply spiritual nature in which he has sought God since childhood, and even felt called to a ministry. He realizes that his substance abuse and problems with his wife happened when he denied his connection with God and looked for God within the ego's world. When rage blinded him to Spirit he jumped headlong into the insanity of the ego. His out-of character homicidal behavior was so serious that, if not fully addressed, it could happen again in a fit of rage. When Mark first went into prison, he blamed his wife for withholding information that may have kept him out of prison. As his parole board review came up I said to him, "You know, on a spiritual level, *you* put *yourself* in here so that you wouldn't end up killing your wife. What the parole board decides is not going to be about *their* judgment of you, rather *your* judgment of yourself and your ability to stay sane if you are released." Mark saw this, because both he and his wife had been trying to forgive each other. The more he practiced forgiveness, the saner his thinking became, and he could take total responsibility for his behavior rather than blame her.

At his parole hearing, Mark's change must have been apparent, because he was released. While the parole board appears to have set Mark free, it was really Mark's forgiveness that set him free. All of us are prisoners in our minds until we forgive *everything* in this world. As testament to this, the Dharma Prison Network gives a book to prisoners titled *We're All Doing Time*, by Bo Lozoff. Freedom, whether in actual prison or mental prison, comes only from healing our minds.

Taking responsibility for what we have created is a crucial step in forgiveness. The *Course* states, **It is impossible the Son of God be merely driven by events outside of him. It is impossible that happenings that come to him were not his choice. His power of decision is the determiner of every situation in which he seems to find himself by chance or accident. No accident nor chance is possible within the universe as God created it, outside of which is nothing. Suffer, and you decided sin was your goal. Be happy, and**

you gave the power of decision to Him Who must decide for God for you (T-21.II.3:1-6). This can be a very hard pill to swallow. Our first reaction is usually, "No way did I ask for this!" And in one sense that is true, because the mind made the decisions on another level. Therefore, we should not heap ego guilt on top of ego decisions that we weren't conscious of. When we choose to redecide with the Holy Spirit, sometimes the external problems go away and sometimes they don't, but our mind *does* change, and this brings more peace. The thing to do is to realize that somewhere we decided wrongly and ask the Holy Spirit to correct our error. As ACIM says, **I do not feel guilty because the Holy Spirit will undo all the consequences of my wrong decision if I will let Him (T-5. VII.6:10).** This is one of my favorite verses. It releases us from guilt and fixes the problem at the same time. We need do nothing except choose the Holy Spirit's healing.

While the *Course* does not waver in its insistence on total forgiveness, we need to give ourselves time to forgive. We are often deeply hurt and angry, and emotions take time to cool down. The recognition that the perceived injury never happened is usually too big of a leap for us to take initially, because it did appear to happen on this level. Our rational mind cannot wrap itself around this idea unless our hearts are changed by the Holy Spirit. Therefore, we start where we are, practicing forgiveness in whatever manner we can, asking for the Holy Spirit's help as we go. Mark needed to first forgive his wife for what he perceived she did, for having an affair and not telling the whole truth. Then he needed to forgive himself for what he perceived he did, assaulting her and landing in prison. As he practices forgiveness, the Holy Spirit is correcting his thinking to see the ultimate truth that it never happened and was only the dream that his ego identity, Mark, made up. Mark is learning that his true identity is the Christ Self.

Similarly, we have to forgive ourselves when it's hard to forgive. Recently I was furious with a friend of mine, Marie. I made what I thought was an innocuous comment, which she took as an attack. My comment went through her ego filter and she thought I called her stupid. She attacked me with, "You think you know everything and you always have to be right!" She didn't listen to my explanation, so I attacked back, in my mind, not directly to her. I decided our friendship needed to change, and that I would never let her attack me again. I wanted her to admit that she blew things out of proportion. I obsessed and felt out of control with my thoughts, but I remembered the rule of thumb to wait until calmed down before we address problems. Otherwise the ego is sure to jump in.

In the past I would have called a friend to complain about Marie, and get her to side with me that Marie was wrong and I was right. I have a friend who says, "Your friends are the ones who hate the people that you do." I used to love that, and my ego still does. However, this time the Holy Spirit nudged me to call my friend Kate, who is always great at reminding me of *Course* principles. Kate suggested I say, "I'm sorry if what I said sounded attacking. I'm not attacking you. Please don't attack me." I resisted what Kate advised, because I wanted Marie to apologize first and take responsibility for dumping her issues on me. Then the little voice of the Holy Spirit kicked in and reminded me, **Do you prefer that you be right or happy (T-29.VII.1:9)?** So, I called Marie and told her I was sorry and didn't mean to sound attacking. I completely forgot the loving request that she not attack me, and turned it into, "And you attacked me horribly! Why'd you do that?" That just led Marie into more "attack back" and we got into another argument. Marie said I had a negative tone in my voice, which initially I denied. As she pressed, I said I didn't think she needed to react so strongly to a small tone and that she shouldn't be so sensitive. She said she couldn't help being sensitive; she was working on it but it still flared up easily and it's my fault for not working around it. I realized that even a small tone is an attack and apologized. She then apologized for reacting, and we remain friends. The ego is insidious. Even when I thought I was apologizing, I was continuing to deny my role in the conflict. Marie was a mirror for me, as my goal is to never attack at all. The ego twists that into, "Well, little attacks don't count." But they do, for the minute I attack Marie I'm attacking myself and our oneness. We cannot enter the kingdom of heaven if we are excluding *anyone*.

> *There is nothing to forgive.*
> *No one can hurt the Son of God.*
> *His guilt is wholly without cause, and being*
> *without cause, cannot exist (T-14.III.7:5-7).*

As I prepared to write this chapter, the ego kicked in and began a barrage of attacks on my qualifications to teach forgiveness. "Who are you to write about this? You haven't forgiven some major players in your own life, and some of the stuff happened almost fifteen years ago!" This pulled me into fear, and believing what the ego said, I got a massive migraine. There was too much ego pressure in my head, in my thinking, and I bought right into the illusion that I am guilty and too flawed to write this. As proof of my "guilt," my partner pointed out to me that I had not yet forgiven my friend Carly, who, in my mind, betrayed me fifteen years ago. Carly and I were best friends during childhood, and my favorite memories are riding our bikes together, taking the secret path along the creek to the candy store, and creating songs and plays to perform for our parents. Carly was my maid of honor and I stood up for her wedding as well. During the process of my divorce, she gave testimony in court that contributed to the downward spiral in which I eventually lost custody of my daughter. My ex-husband misled her, and I was angry that she did not consult me before testifying. She told a mutual friend that she did not realize what the testimony was going to entail, and said, "Lorri's going to hate me!" When I confronted her, however, she said that she only did what anyone else would do. She feels that she gave honest testimony and that was the right thing to do. I was in a rage and complained vehemently to everyone who would listen. After a few years I thought I had forgiven Carly, for I made small talk with her at a party and wasn't tempted to make a scene.

The ego always searches for a way to keep the emotions boiling, so it brings to mind all the excuses we need to not forgive. I resented Carly because she never apologized to me. In fact, this is the area that the ego hooks me on with everyone I haven't forgiven. Once someone apologizes I can let anything go, but if she hasn't apologized, forget it. The ego deludes me into thinking I am the bigger person because at least *I'll* admit when I do something wrong. Getting an apology would mean I'm right and Carly's wrong. I get to be the bigger per son by forgiving from my lofty position of righteousness. As I pondered this, a voice spoke to me, "How about seeing each of you as blame-less?" I gasped! "Oh, no!" I wanted *someone* to blame, even if it was me. This was how I knew it was the Holy Spirit's voice, not the ego's, as I certainly would never come up with that idea.

Love holds no grievances (W-p.I.68.h) and I clearly held a grievance against Carly. I asked the Holy Spirit for help, because my pain and judgment overwhelmed me. With all my forgiveness issues, I pray, "Holy Spirit, help me forgive because I just can't do this by myself. Help me to stop blaming and see what I need to see about *myself.*" The task of forgiveness feels too large, but we don't do it by ourselves. **Truth will correct all errors in my mind (W-p.I.107.h).** Sometimes it takes awhile before we see the results, but we need to trust that the Holy Spirit will make good on our intentions.

Yet no one can forgive a sin that he believes is real.
(T-27.II.2:4) You who want peace can find it
only by complete forgiveness (T-1.VI.1:1).

Guilt is the feeling that arises when we are attacking another's or our own innocence. I was still making Carly guilty, still making what she did real. For months while writing this, my lack of forgiveness was apparent because when Carly came to mind my first thought was, "She's a nice person, but I don't like what she did."

I could somewhat grasp the unreal, dreamlike nature of the incident, the hazy, strange scenario of my best friend going to court against me, verifying what a horrible person I am. I felt horrible about myself at the time, and my friend's action reflected what was in my own mind. Outer events are *always* a reflection of our own thoughts, and that's why ACIM says we need to change our *mind* about the world, rather than change the world itself. Finally I was ready to see the Holy Spirit's vision of Carly, and when I thought of her a smile came to my face as I remembered our childhood joy. I finally embraced her as a friend and teacher on my spiritual path. Through my reaction to her I saw how I denied truth, and saw that indeed she never did anything wrong. What "happened" now feels like a hazy dream, which is all it was in the first place.

The conflict with Carly brought up the ego's hatred of certain personality traits I have. We all hate ourselves to some degree or another, and while there are many personality traits of this body called "Lorri" that I like, there are just as many that I don't like. As I have been doing the ACIM Workbook lessons, it has become clearer to me that I am not this body or personality. Now when I see these ugly traits I use mindfulness meditation and reflect, "There's Lorri acting from the ego again," or, "There's Lorri thinking she's bad again," or "Lorri's forgotten her Christ Self." My issue with Carly was really my own lack of forgiveness toward myself. **Those who have accepted their innocence see nothing to forgive. Yet forgiveness is the means by which I will recognize my innocence (W-p.I.60.1:3-4)**. I thought I was trying to forgive Carly, but the process of forgiving her is what will ultimately help me accept my own innocence.

Special Relationships

Heaven has no rage like love to hatred turned,
Nor hell a fury like a woman scorned.
~William Congreve

To believe that special relationships, with special love, can offer you salvation is the belief that separation is salvation (T-15.V.3:3).

A Course in Miracles calls special relationships **the ego's chief weapon for keeping you from Heaven (T-16.V.2:3)**. A special relationship is defined as any relationship in which we are trying to get our ego needs met, rather than give love simply for the sake of loving, with no expectation of return. My relationship with

Carly was a special love relationship that turned into a special hate relationship, a common phenomenon when the ego is in charge. I adored Carly—she was my best friend, until she betrayed me, at least in my mind. She took away the love I thought I'd found in her. In this type of special love, the ego thinks it can get love by joining with someone who appears to be outside of us, in a separate body. Bodies are not the source of real love, as **there is no love but God's (W-p.I.127.h).** However, we can experience love *through* bodies. Real love, however, has nothing to do with our bodies, for love is what we *are*. Once I forgave Carly, it became a holy relationship, as I recognized the love that is still there, the love that was always present, in spite of my ego feeling burned.

A special relationship can be with a spouse, a child, friend, coworker, acquaintance, enemy, or anyone. Since very few of us feel complete and whole, we attempt to feel better by *getting* love from someone else. The *Course* teacher Dr. Michael Mirdad is a dynamic speaker and if you ever get a chance to hear him, do. I love his description of holy versus special relationships:

> *A Course in Miracles* makes it clear that there are only two forms of relationships: "holy (healthy, interdependent) relationships" and "special (unhealthy, codependent) relationships." The first, holy relationships, are relations that have become temples of healing, wherein a decision has been made to make healing, forgiveness, and unconditional love a top priority. Such relations have essentially been given to God to guide thoughts, words, and deeds. Special relations, on the other hand, are divided into two categories that share the same exact purpose. These are "special love" and "special hate" relations. In either case, the relationship has a common, "special" function—assigned by your ego—which is to distract you from noticing that whatever void you feel within and whatever love you seek from another person can only be filled with God and real, unconditional love. In a special love relationship you might seem to feel

love for someone or a least feel like you like them and get along with them as a friend, family member, partner or whatever. But in the deep recesses of your mind, you are saying, "You know, I feel separated from God, which makes me feel pretty low inside, but if you're nice to me, I'm going to feel good and forget about that. So I like you and appreciate you for your special function." Special love relationships may look like real love, but they are not the same in that these are only loving relations as long as we get our way and these people love and support us in the way we need them to.

Special hate relationships might look totally different from special love, but they are in fact the same in their ultimate goal—to distract you from life's real problems and the only true solution—that you feel separate from God and divine love, and only God can fill you. As anyone might guess, special hate relationships are pretty obvious, as these are with people you think you don't like. But beneath all the seemingly justifiable reasons for disliking a person (or group of people), is one simple, special statement. "I would be happier, healthier, and more complete if it weren't for that other person or organization." In other words, instead of crediting another person for you feeling good (as in a special love relationship), you are blaming them for you feeling bad. But again, notice the common thread that in both cases, you are projecting your power and well-being onto another.[2]

Most of our "loving" relationships are special love relationships. It appears that our relationships have elements of unconditional, holy love, as well as ego demands. However, the *Course* says that unless we consciously dedicate our relationships to serving *only* unconditional love, *only* the purpose for which the Holy Spirit would use them, then they continue to be special relationships.

If we're honest with ourselves, we admit that we often withdraw approval or contact when someone angers us or doesn't live up to our expectations. If we're self-aware and devoted to love, we feel guilty when this occurs, but we don't want to stay in the guilt, since that's just the ego at work again. We can simply ask the Holy Spirit to make this a holy relationship, to let the relationship be whatever it is supposed to be for the higher purpose of healing.

The beauty of this is that our special love or special hate partner actually becomes what the *Course* calls our "savior." It is in forgiving this person that we find our way back to God, and thus this person, whether we think we love him or hate him, is our beloved. This is where the *Course*'s approach to our return to God is somewhat different than other spiritual paths. The Eastern philosophies encourage meditation as the primary means to letting go of the individual self and recognizing the oneness of all. ACIM uses the approach of *consciously choosing forgiveness* as the means to realize oneness.

Love songs usually carry one of two themes, either "Now that I've found my one true love, I'll never be lonely again," or "Now that I've lost you, I'll never love again." If the special love switches to special hate, we hear, "You done me wrong" songs. A couple I know jokingly says, "I trade you very much," instead of "I love you very much." They admit that what passes for love in our culture is often an exchange, and when one partner quits his part, all of a sudden the "love" is gone. How is it that love we thought would last forever turns into revulsion and hatred? My partner Rod's student was enchanted with his girlfriend who had a "cute little space between her teeth." This imperfection endeared her to him. When they broke up, she suddenly became "that gap-toothed bitch." We can tell if love was real in the first place if we continue to love the person no matter what he's done to us, even when we no longer need anything from him. This is not to be confused with continuing to allow someone to abuse us in the name of "love." That is just the ego calling it love to keep us from true love.

> *The search for the special relationship*
> *is the sign that you equate yourself with the ego and*
> *not with God. To the ego, unless a relationship*
> *has special value it has no meaning, for it perceives*
> *all love as special. The special relationship is totally*
> *meaningless without a body (T-16.VI.1:1; 3; 4:1).*

Special relationships could not occur without bodies. Marriage would not be special if we didn't pledge our bodies solely to our spouses. This special love is contrary to the love of God, which does not value bodies and extends love equally to all. **You see the flesh or recognize the spirit. There is no compromise between the two. If one is real, the other must be false . . . (T-31.VI.1:1-3).** This doesn't mean we can't love our spouses or value fidelity in marriage. It does mean that as we love our mates, we need to remember that it's their spirit we love, not their bodies; for bodies are temporary, illusory vehicles. If we think we can only love that one special person and no one else, we are coming from the ego and setting ourselves up for pain.

Would our children be as special to us if they did not come from our wombs or seeds? A Chinese proverb highlights the ego sense of pride we have around our children: "There is one pretty child in the world, and every mother has it." However, those who adopt children show unconditional love, perhaps sensing that all little ones are equally precious. Our spirit within loves all little children and all people equally, but our ego holds to specialness as a way to separate, make different, and cordon off our love.

Any conflict with *anyone* means we have entered into a special hate relationship with him, even if it's just a negative thought. Thoughts are things, so we are sending negative energy to that person if we judge him. Every interaction and every thought is an opportunity to bring that moment to the light. Our brothers are our saviors, for they help us learn true forgiveness. We cannot be in heaven unless we see *everyone* as innocent. As the Workbook states, **My unloving thoughts about _____ are keeping me in hell (W-p.I.39.8:3).**

Special relationships pull us in, especially abusive ones. My client Tina is married to a verbally abusive man, Tom. Tina has tried everything to get him to be kind. She has refused to respond to his abuse, pointed it out, responded kindly to his attacks, and been mean back. Nothing has worked. The thing Tina has been unable to do is stop judging Tom. She rails about him to all her friends, justifying her case that he's mean and she's nice. True, he is the abusive one on the surface, but what Tina doesn't see is that every time she speaks or thinks ill of Tom she's attacking him. As we saw in chapter 4, an attack is an attack, whether it's directly at the person, in our heads, or spoken in gossip. Tina's unloving thoughts about Tom are keeping her in hell, but she thinks it's Tom that's keeping her there. She is not seeing Tom's innocence, but his guilt, and this keeps her stuck in her own guilt. She can dislike his behavior while still seeing his Christ Self. The solution is not to change Tom but to stop judging him. Then, if he's still abusive, she can leave, but with love rather than hate. Tina's natural ego reaction to being attacked is to attack back; thus she needs to request her higher Self's help to stop.

Often when we fall in love, we feel as if we've met our "soul mate," the one and only true love of our life. We are usually at our best and happiest when we fall in love, as the loving Self comes out. The sky is bluer and the grass is greener, but we mistakenly think this is because we've found the soul mate we've searched for all our life. Rather, it is awakening in us the love that has always been inside of us and *is* our true Self. The love we have for the other person mirrors the Love that we are. When we are in touch with our higher Self, the sky is bluer regardless of whether we're in a relationship. The intense attraction of the soul mate represents the subconscious recognition of one with whom we will do our forgiveness lessons. This person will bring us to our senses, and wake us up to the truth of God. These relationships are crucial, for **there are no accidents in salvation. Those who are to meet will meet, because together they have the potential for a holy relationship. They are ready for each other (M-3.1:6-8).** This means that their relationship will bring forth all their ego ugliness to be healed.

Relationships are how we get back to God, regardless of

whether they're romantic. However, the intensity of starry-eyed relationships can propel our growth rapidly, because the pain of loss is so acute, and the compulsion to work them through feels like it owns us. Romance is the prime venue to expose our hidden guilt and self-hatred, and everything we judge about ourselves will surface. In the best scenarios, couples work through the ego issues while remembering and retaining their love for each other. They develop a holy relationship, in which their love is unconditional, giving, and kind. If they lose sight of each other's perfection they can become enemies, dropping into the special hate that arises when our expectations are disappointed.

The most important thing to keep in mind is to turn the partnership over to the Holy Spirit. We need to ask for Its vision of the relationship, which may be different than ours. For example, we usually want the love to last forever because it feels incredible and ecstatic. But the relationship may only be meant to last for a short time, until the forgiveness lesson is learned. However, the length does not matter, for time is not real. True love never dies, in spite of physical separation. What matters is that every relationship is dedicated to holiness.

My client Gerald had a series of special romantic relationships. Gerald was married twice and had one child with each of his wives. He also had two other serious liaisons. His mates were attracted to his charisma, intensity, and uncanny ability to zero in on the heart of any matter. He was a dynamic musician, with unusual sensitivity and soulfulness. He tended to attract women musicians who had been sexually abused, who vacillated between intense warmth and cool distance, and were independent and organized. His ability to love openly and freely made these women feel safe, and their caretaking and structure balanced his freewheeling, disorganized lifestyle.

The special relationships started out with the spark of genuine love between Gerald and his partners. They saw the best in each other, saw their Christ Selves, appreciated the goodness and looked past the negativity. They reveled in their complimentary strengths and weaknesses. After awhile, however, their hidden ego guilt surfaced with a vengeance. This *always* happens in relationships and this is why relationships are so valuable for growth. Whatever is unloving will arise to be healed. Gerald's partners tired of the down side of his personality, his moodiness, anger, and neediness. He felt controlled by them, pushed away by their fear of intimacy. His core issue was feeling unappreciated and unloved. They obliged him and focused on his faults, making him the scapegoat. When he got totally frustrated with the relationships, he turned to substance abuse, which made him the perfect target for his partners' blame. Substance abusers like Gerald almost always take on the scapegoat role, as their self-destructive behavior is so obvious. However, this serves as a smokescreen for their partners to avoid looking at their own self-hatred, which in Gerald's case was their fear of being open and exposed. They were attracted to his capacity for vulnerability, which is rare in a man. Since he modeled vulnerability, they had the opportunity to feel safe and loved without ego defenses. The *Course* points out that **in my defenselessness my safety lies (W-p.I.153.h)**. To become vulnerable, however, his partners would have had to look at their sexual abuse scars, and they chose instead to point out Gerald's problems. Likewise, Gerald blamed them for not appreciating him, instead of recognizing that he pushed them away with outlandish behavior.

Gerald now takes responsibility for drawing rejection into his life, and is learning to love himself. His partners' rejection of him was just a mirror for his own self-hatred, and as he has forgiven them, he has forgiven himself. He recognizes that he is the one who has to appreciate and love himself, and he recently attracted a relationship in which the woman respects and listens to him.

The Process of Forgiveness

The weak can never forgive. Forgiveness is the attribute of the strong.
~Ghandi

We learned in chapter 3 that we have a choice about which voice we listen to, the ego's or the Holy Spirit's. Likewise, forgiveness is a choice. **I never see my brother as he is . . . what I see in him is**

merely what I wish to see (W-p.II.335.1:2-3). Do we choose to see our brother as a total *innocent* or a total *idiot*? The choice to forgive is crucial, for we cannot judge our brother and feel God's presence within us at the same time. It's one or the other.

When I was in counseling after I lost custody of my daughter, the therapist asked me, "Are you ready to forgive your ex-husband?" I got offended and said, "No way!" The therapist repeated, "Are you ready to forgive your ex-husband?" Angrier, I said, "Absolutely not! He deserves to die in a fiery car crash and burn in hell!" Gently, the therapist repeated again, "Are you ready to forgive your ex-husband?" "NO! He doesn't *deserve* forgiveness! He's a hateful bastard!" Our session time was up and I left the office completely disgusted with my therapist. He obviously didn't understand what I'd been through or he wouldn't have been so obtuse. How could he expect me to forgive someone who had done something so awful to me?

I was shaken, and the therapist's words bothered me. It had never crossed my mind to forgive Donald. (This was before I got back into the *Course*.) I prayed and said, "Okay, if I'm supposed to forgive him, You've got to do it for me. I don't want to and I can't, but I'm willing if You'll help." That started the process. The Holy Spirit took over and I started getting better. My depression began to lift and I stopped feeling suicidal. My unloving thoughts about Donald were truly keeping me in hell. It took several years, and unforgiveness still crops up once in a while today, but the peace is far greater than before. I still haven't totally forgiven, though, as the *Course* emphasizes that forgiveness is total or not at all. If even a smidgen of judgment remains, we are still stuck in the dream. It also says, however, that the miracle is that we recognize the dream, and this provides relief even while we're still in it. Thus, on this level forgiveness is a process that takes time, but in ultimate truth, we are either awake and recognize there was never anything to forgive, or we're asleep, trapped in the dream.

Some people seem able to forgive a lot easier than I did, such as the Dalai Lama. He provides us with a precious example of forgiveness, and he exhibits the traits of love, peace, and joy that are hallmarks of enlightened beings. He has frequent bouts of giggling and a twinkle in his eyes. When we awaken from the dream we just naturally laugh at the silliness of it all. The Dalai Lama was exiled from his home when China waged war on Tibet, massacring monks and other citizens. He expresses compassion for the self-hatred the Chinese must have in order to commit such horrific acts. He sees them as wounded and fearful, which is a helpful reminder to aid in forgiveness. Martin Luther King Jr. also chose to see those who oppressed him as weak and hurt. When we feel people are attacking us, it's hard not to hate them back. In psychotherapy we speak of the wounded inner child who learned to attack in self-protection. If we focus on someone's wounds, sadness, and fear, our hearts are softened. The *Course* states that anytime someone attacks us he is in fear, and **fear is a call for love (T-12.I.8:13).**

If we want to awaken, we must remember that holding anyone out of our hearts will keep us from our Christ Self. This goes for political figures we love to hate, as well as anyone we think is a jerk. As the *Course* says, **exempt no one from your love, or you will be hiding a dark place in your mind where the Holy Spirit is not welcome (T-13.III.9:2).** Sometimes Spirit will arrange opportunities for us to forgive. One of my friends had an affair and years later his wife called a store to order something. The clerk just happened to be the woman her husband had the affair with! This gave the women a chance to talk things out, apologize, and let it go. Another friend of mine, Gil, has had a feud with his cousin since their grandma died. Gil resents that his cousin is withholding some sentimental trinkets that he'd given his grandma as gifts. The cousin lives out of state and when he came to town he visited his grandma's grave. It just so happened that Gil, who visits his grandma's grave twice a year, was at the grave when his cousin drove up. On a separate visit when his cousin was in town, Gil was visiting his father, and who happened to stop by? His cousin, who had not visited Gil's father in years! Unfortunately, as of this writing, Gil and his cousin have not availed themselves of their serendipitous opportunities to heal, and the feud continues.

When I was a teenager, my next-door neighbor was a man whom all the kids jeered. Joe peered out the tiny window in his door, always afraid that we would step on his perfect lawn. We saw him spying and deliberately touched our toe on the corner of his grass, so he would come out and yell, providing us with cheap entertainment. As I learned Christian values at church, I realized that Joe was probably hurting and thought people disliked him. I made a decision to befriend him and began to say "Hi, Mr. A!" every time I saw him. At first he did not even respond, then he hesitantly said "hello" back. Soon Joe said "hi" to me first, and he was actually smiling! We stayed friends until he moved, but the lesson in love he taught me has stayed with me forever. When our hearts are softened, we become open to the love and forgiveness that is our true nature.

Think of someone in your life that you need to forgive. What are you afraid of? Are you afraid this person will leave you? Are you afraid he won't leave you? Are you afraid he won't like you? Are you afraid he will take something from you, such as money, time, possessions, or even your life? Sometimes the person we hold a grievance against has no idea we're upset, while we've stewed long and hard, perhaps for years. The way to get over our fear is by forgiving him. Forgiveness is for us, not him. **Those you do not forgive you fear. And no one reaches love with fear beside him (T-19.IV.D.11:6-7).**

A beautiful example of forgiveness comes from my friend Joy, who hosts one of the ACIM study groups I attend. Joy's spirit is true to her name—she bubbles over with love, joy, and enthusiasm. A few years ago Joy's daughter Ann had a baby girl and Joy was thrilled. Shortly after the birth, however, Ann started being hateful to her husband and to Joy. She got a divorce and cut off contact with Joy. She would not tell Joy what was wrong, just that she couldn't stand her and wanted nothing to do with her. This dumbfounded Joy, but with information from Ann's husband, Joy began to piece together that Ann's father had sexually abused her. Joy surmised that Ann might be blaming her for not stopping it, so told Ann that she'd never been aware of it. Ann rejected the information that Joy had no knowledge of the abuse and chose to harden her heart and keep the separation. Joy was traumatized, both with the cutoff from Ann and her granddaughter, as well as the discovery of what her daughter had gone through and what her husband had done. I watched Joy cry and express her pain and disbelief over the tragic circumstances. Joy tried to reach out to Ann by sending gifts to the baby, and Ann responded through her brother with the message, "Tell Joy (not 'Mom') that I *never* want anything to do with her ever again!" That was nine years ago, and Joy has had no contact with Ann or her granddaughter since.

Joy felt numb and dazed upon receiving this message. She was walking to catch the bus to work and kept hearing the words from the *Course*, **Nothing real can be threatened. Nothing unreal exists. Herein lies the peace of God (T-in.2:2-4).** She says she didn't even know what these words really meant, but she had heard that you didn't have to know what they mean to have the Holy Spirit give you their truth. Suddenly she felt an incredible peace come over her, as if she were held in the arms of God. She felt so grateful, being lifted up from her loss and despair, given a gift of love and peace she never knew possible. Even though Joy has not seen her daughter or granddaughter for years, she has blossomed. She does not even feel it necessary to ever see her daughter again, if that's the way Ann wants it, because she knows in her heart that the love between them cannot be lost or threatened. She also knows that Ann's hateful behavior is not real, and she sees only the love that her daughter *is*. Joy has lived the *Course* principles and while external events have not seemingly improved, Joy has experienced the miracle of a change in her thinking. As a result, she is as happy and peaceful as if her daughter had never cut her off. She does not even feel sad about it, which most people would. Instead of clinging to a special relationship with her granddaughter, Joy treats the children in our church as her own grandchildren, knowing that in truth we are all one in love.

Joy and I discussed this at church, and she once again inspired me with her loving attitude. She told me her sister had called her excitedly the day before as she had seen Ann on the local cable TV channel. Ann looked really good and was involved in a community recycling project. Joy said she realized that Ann could do well without her, and perhaps did not choose to have a mother in her life. It was a lesson in letting go of Joy's ego identity as "mother," and accepting that roles imply separation and only oneness exists in truth. Later that morning I moseyed over to the church bookstore, where new and donated books are sold. I happened upon the book *One*, by Richard Bach, which Rod and I had just discussed a few days prior. I wanted to reread it so I was pleased to find it. The story is in line with ACIM principles that we are all one and the sense of separation is an illusion. Bach is the author of the classic *Jonathon Livingston Seagull*, and he also wrote *Illusions: The Adventures of a Reluctant Messiah*. As I glanced through *One* I was dumbstruck. There in the front cover was a dedication from Ann to Joy, dated Christmas, 1988. Ann wrote that she was proud of her mother, saw her as a wonderful role model, and admired how Joy was coming into her own as a full, loving person. I ran over to show Joy, who read it, and we both started crying. What an affirming gift from Spirit, to discover this *true* message from Ann, right when we had been talking about oneness!

Major forgiveness lessons often come from family members. My friend Diane had a difficult relationship with her alcoholic mother, whom Diane felt was narcissistic, critical, and emotionally unavailable. As her mother aged, Diane took her mother into her home and was worried about properly caring for her, as she saw her mother's health declining. Diane and her mother often exchanged sharp remarks and were generally tense and uncomfortable with each other. One day Diane found her mother slumped on the floor from a stroke. Diane blurted out, "You Bitch! I just *knew* you were going to do one more thing to screw things up!" Diane immediately felt horribly guilty, having just screamed at a stroke victim lying helpless on the floor. In the ensuing months, Diane got her mother nursing home care, and her mother died shortly thereafter. After her mother's death, Diane felt anxious and unsettled, and she beat herself up mentally. One day it occurred to her that she needed to forgive herself. She needed to let herself off the hook. She had been loving and compassionate most of the time, and it was human to not act perfectly loving all the time. Once Diane began forgiving herself, she felt the peacefulness that forgiveness provides. Forgiveness often starts with ourselves, but we find ourselves the hardest to forgive.

Forgiveness often occurs after a loved one has died, as in my client Joan's case. Joan's father sexually abused her from the age of five until he died when she was eleven. Bedtime was terrifying, as she wondered if he would slip into her room at night and force her to play the "game" of "ride the horsy." Her father was a mean drunk and she and her siblings ran for their rooms when he got home from work, trying to not make a peep for fear of his rage. Before his arrival they raced to clean up the house, in hopes he wouldn't find a misplaced shoe or toy to scream about. Joan remembers consciously deciding not to eat as a child, for she felt that was the only thing she could control. She developed anorexia, and later bulimia, regurgitating her meals regularly. She became depressed and had to take medication, was obsessive-compulsive, and chose a job as a strip dancer. As a dancer, Joan felt she regained power over men, tantalizing them with her body while they were forbidden to touch her. Joan married a man whom she met at the strip bar and quit dancing, hoping to get a job in which she could use her master's degree. However, she was still in a retail sales position, overqualified and underpaid. In their couples' counseling sessions her husband said, "Joan will never go anywhere in her career," and wanted her to resume stripping. By this time Joan was horrified at the thought of dancing again, as she'd gained self-respect and saw why she chose to repeat the pattern of being a sexual object.

Joan divorced her husband because he was a compulsive gambler and had an affair. She got an excellent job within her field and has been moving up the ladder. She is now in a loving, healthy relationship, after many attempts to sabotage it. Joan frequently broke up with her new boyfriend at the slightest fight, convinced that it was going to end eventually anyway, so she might as well do it now. That way it wouldn't be him leaving her. I kept reigning Joan in and pointed out that she was throwing away a good man because love felt unfamiliar. She was trying to make it fit the only thing she ever knew, which was abuse. About a year ago Joan had a dream in which her father apologized for what he did to her. Joan reacted with anger. "I'm not ready to forgive him!" I suggested she allow herself to be angry as long as she needed to, but with the *intent* to forgive, asking the Holy Spirit to help her. Recently Joan felt strong enough to end therapy, no longer depressed or bulimic, and no longer on medication. Joan was able to forgive her father through her willingness to forgive, and had another breakthrough dream. In it, her father was driving down the street in a sporty convertible, and invited her for a ride. He was young, healthy, and friendly. He showed genuine interest in her life and was the loving father she had always wanted. The dream ended when her father said, "Well, I have to go now. I've got a lot of work to do in heaven!" Joan was elated and in tearful gratitude as she described the dream. "My dad's in heaven?! I thought for sure he'd be burning in hell!" What a beautiful lesson in truth, that even the seemingly worst of us return to heaven, where we've never left.

True forgiveness applies not only to people, but also to circumstances within the dream. We have to forgive ourselves for dreaming the dream. Many spiritual ideologies suggest that we judge nothing as good or bad, merely as neutral events. If we can do this, it helps us step back from the dream more easily. Since it's a dream that's not really happening, it's only our ego judgments of "good" or "bad" that make it "real." However, that's easier said than done, especially with "tragic" events.

My nephew Danny was born with severe disabilities. He suffered an epileptic seizure right after birth, yet was sent home, as the extent of his disabilities was not recognized. Suspicions about his health began to surface when he didn't develop normally, so my sister Patty and brother-in-law Bruce took Danny to a university medical center for an evaluation. I was with my sister when the neurologist gave her the bad news. The nurses had warned us that the doctor didn't have a very good bedside manner, and that was an understatement. The doctor started off with, "Well, Mom, your kid's about as bad as they get." He then proceeded to tell Patty that Danny had severe brain damage resulting in cerebral palsy, blindness, epilepsy, and profound mental retardation. In short, Danny would be a vegetable for his entire life. My sister bravely held her composure until the doctor left, then burst out crying. On her drive home she felt like crashing into a telephone pole and killing Danny and herself, and I went home and cried myself to sleep.

I was extremely angry at that doctor for his insensitivity. Through the years, every time I thought of him I got mad all over again. As I began writing this chapter I realized I was still angry, as my first thought was, "That asshole! I don't care if he's a good doctor or not, he stinks in what he did to my sister. The hospital is idiotic for putting a jerk like that in charge of delivering painful news." However, as forgiveness is a habit for me now, I recognized that I was attacking him. "Oh, my, I haven't forgiven that doctor yet!" Forgiving him before hadn't even seemed necessary—he was just another asshole, deserving of the opinion I had of him. I didn't know before that I needed to forgive every single attack I made on anyone or anything. So, I asked the Holy Spirit for help in seeing the doctor differently. This prayer helped me to see the doctor with compassion instead of judgment. I saw what a painful part of his job it must be to deliver tragic news, and I was able to see that he was not meeting my expectations of a doctor, yet was doing the best he could. This realization calmed my heart so that I could begin the forgiveness process. That process led to even greater peace when the awareness came that this whole episode was not real. The doctor is as innocent as I am for projecting his unskillful words into my dream.

Receiving the news from the doctor was just the beginning of a long ordeal for Patty and Bruce. Danny's impairment was so severe that it was a huge burden for them to keep him home. However, they did so, and lovingly cared for him for the next eighteen years until he died. They couldn't bear to put him in an institution, as they knew he would die from lack of love and touch. It is extremely difficult to understand why some children are born as Danny was, and I wondered why God would allow this to happen.

When Danny was alive I once heard a sermon in which it was suggested that if you have a question for God, write it down, tuck it away, and wait for God to answer. So, I wrote, "Why is Danny the way he is?" I put the note in my wallet, and figured

I'd get an answer sometime in the next few months. About twenty minutes later I was doing the dishes and the word "iconoclast" kept popping into my mind. I was puzzled, but thought perhaps it was related to my question. I knew an icon was a symbol, and I thought of the cross, so figured God might be answering me. I looked up the meaning of "iconoclast" and learned that it is one who destroys religious symbols or attacks socially accepted beliefs. I immediately thought of Jesus, who certainly challenged the beliefs of his day. Did this shake-up of ideas mean I needed a new perspective of Danny's condition? Rather than view his life as a tragedy, was there a positive meaning?

Unable to see the good, I carried this puzzling answer in my head for years, always wondering about it. I somewhat understood it intellectually, but I didn't really get it on an emotional level. Sure, there might be some reason for Danny's impairments that we couldn't understand, but it still did not make sense to me. I struggled with the horrible and unnecessary pain for him and our family.

About eight years later, Danny had to undergo surgery to correct a curvature in his body that was eventually going to press on his organs and kill him. Patty and Bruce were torn about what to do, as surgery would also result in severe pain. They decided on the surgery, and indeed, Danny experienced terrible pain. It was gut-wrenching to watch him moan helplessly. During this period I prayed for Danny, and one day I felt a very strong spiritual connection with him. Suddenly I got it! I couldn't put it into words then and it's hard to put it into words now, but somehow I *knew* that Danny was not his body and that appearances were deceiving. What *appeared* to be a deformity really *wasn't!* There was immeasurable love that flowed from the depths of his twisted body, reaching out and touching the lives of many. A few months later, Danny left his body behind and passed on, and I have been ever grateful for the gift he gave me of seeing beyond appearances, knowing there is a truth behind what meets the eye. Danny apparently strongly affected not only me but many others as well. His memorial service was packed to overflowing and the funeral home had to open up a second room.

A few weeks after Danny made his transition, I came across an article in my *Angels on Earth* magazine that gave me more insight into the fact that our eyes do not catch the entire scene. The story was about a developmentally disabled boy who had limited communication skills. The boy told his mother that there were angels in the ceiling corner of his bedroom, and they played with him. At Christmas, the family had a nativity scene under the tree. The little boy got excited and pointed to the nativity, then to his bedroom ceiling, then back to the nativity. The mother interpreted, "Oh, your angels were there?" The boy nodded his head joyously. As I read this I exclaimed to myself, "Oh, my God! That's what Danny had!" Danny always appeared to be in his own little world, and he frequently laughed out loud for no apparent reason, though he could not talk or see. It felt so good to know that on his seemingly tragic and lonely journey, that all along he'd had the best help and joyful moments one could ask for.

Three Simple Steps

Forgiveness is an act of the will,
and the will can function regardless of the temperature of the heart.
~Corrie Ten Boom

Forgiveness can happen in "a holy instant," which the *Course* calls the moment we accept the Holy Spirit as our teacher instead of the ego. However, it is important to remember that for most of us it is a process that may take years. My lesson with Danny took eight years, and my lesson with my friend Carly took fifteen years. However, once I committed to letting the Holy Spirit do it for me, it only took a few months. Some television shows have featured rape victims and family members of murder victims. The people forgave within a short time. While the intention is good, this leaves many of us with more guilt. Most of us are unable to forgive without making an ego stop for the usual helpings of blame, pride, rage, or whatever portion of turmoil that we feel we need. When we find ourselves in this hostility, the ego happily points out how inadequate we are compared to the really spiritual persons. This is a common ego trap, bashing ourselves for not having forgiven yet, for not feeling better yet, for not being more loving. This is like the fisherman caught in his own net or the dog chasing its tail. The very nature of the ego is unloving and unforgiving, so rather than judge ourselves for not progressing faster, we should commend ourselves for recognizing we got caught in the trap. Our awakening is guaranteed, for in reality there is no such thing as time and it has already happened. Therefore there is no need to beat ourselves up for how long forgiveness appears to take.*

My client Matt forgave his father in an interesting manner. His father was an angry, violent man who committed suicide when Matt was seven. One day Matt brought an African American friend over to play, and his father ordered the child away. "I won't have no niggers at my house!" As part of Matt's therapy I suggested he visit his father's grave and talk to him, spontaneously and uncensored. At the gravesite, Matt hollered, "I hope now that you're dead you realize how horrible you were to my friend!" After getting his anger off his chest, Matt's impish personality surfaced. "By the way, how do you like my Harley, Dad?" Upon leaving the cemetery, Matt rode down the main drag and was stopped by a red light. In the next lane was an African American man who rolled his window down and said, "Boy, I just want to tell you how good you look on that bike! I am really *proud* of you on that bike!"

Visits from beyond the grave help us forgive the appearance of separation in this illusory world. The belief in separation is the cause of all of our fears, pain, and anger. However, all of our physical senses tell us that this world is real, and the ego wants us to believe it is real; therefore, we cannot forgive at first with our logical minds. It does not make rational or logical sense to think that what we can touch, smell, taste, hear, and see does not exist. That's why we need the Holy Spirit's help. After practicing forgiveness we are then able to see the higher logic clearly. It is okay to call the Holy Spirit by another name, such as your guardian angel, guide, master, teacher, Higher Self, Spirit, or whatever is comfortable for you. Use the name that brings the most comfort and the least fear.

---

* Go to my website, http://www.lorricoburn.com, for a free PDF, "Seven Secrets of Forgiveness."

It is not my own strength through which I forgive. It is through the strength of God in me, which I am remembering as I forgive (W-p.I.60.2:2-3).

The process of forgiveness is simple, though by no means easy. To wake up, we have to eventually forgive *everything* that appears in physical form, because the form is not real. We practice forgiving even mundane things such as bee stings, traffic jams, computer glitches, nasty weather, colds, the neighbor's dog. As we practice forgiveness on these little things, we come to see that nothing is real. Then we become more skilled at forgiveness lessons that we think are harder, such as death. With help, however, each lesson is as simple as the next.

The formula for forgiveness is easy to learn, and when practiced it becomes a habit that brings serenity, relaxation, and happiness. The three-step formula is to *recognize, release,* and *replace. Recognize* that you are attacking your brother or a situation, *release* the dream, and ask the Holy Spirit to *replace* it with Its vision. **You are not trapped in the world you see, because its cause can be changed. This change requires, first, that the cause be identified and then let go, so that it can be replaced. The first two steps in this process require your cooperation. The final one does not (W-p.I.23.5:1-4).** A typical request for the Holy Spirit's help is, "Help me to see this Your way, not the ego's way." Your request *will* be answered, in a form that is the easiest for you to understand. The answer may come in a different insight into the situation, from a song, a story, something someone says to you, or a sign. Life becomes quite an adventure when serendipitous, coincidental things happen to help us see the truth. As we release our attachment to separation and our ego identities, forgiveness arises naturally from our Christ Self within. We don't have to *try* to forgive; rather, practicing the steps allows our inner loving nature to surface. Our natural state of being *is* forgiveness, and the practice helps us remember this.

It may be helpful for you to make up your own prayer, affirmation, or mantra. A sample forgiveness prayer might be: "(Name of person/situation), You are a player in the dream I made up and I am a player in yours. In this illusory situation you have appeared to me to be the guilty one, but in truth we are both innocent. Holy Spirit, Thank You for helping us to wake up and remember who we really are behind the drama. Thank You that only love is real, and that we remain whole, complete, and at peace as we choose Your vision."

One way of telling whether we have forgiven is when the person or situation crosses our mind without discord on a consistent basis. Often I have thought I've forgiven someone only to have the thought of him arise some time later and I am right back to being upset, angry, or sad. This means there is more forgiveness work to do. Forgiveness is present when we feel gratitude toward the person or situation for teaching us truth. It is not when we think, "Oh, good, he's out of my life forever!"; rather, "Oh, he's a part of me." I never thought I would feel gratitude around my custody loss, as there was a time when I was constantly hateful and complained all the time. Today I am grateful that the outcome I thought was best was blocked by the people I hated at the time. Opening to gratitude opens the flow of love. We can be grateful for every forgiveness lesson, as it is a golden opportunity to remember who we really are.

My minister, David T. Bell, gave a lesson on the wonderful book *Power vs. Force: The Hidden Determinants of Human Behavior,* by David Hawkins, M.D., Ph.D. Dr. Hawkins co authored *Orthomolecular Psychiatry* with Nobel Prize–winner Linus Pauling, and in 1996 was knighted for his work by the Danish Crown. In *Power vs. Force* he outlines the process of kinesiological (muscle) testing to determine the level of emotion behind a thought. The more love and truth there is, the more powerful the thought. Force comes from anger and negative emotions, and muscles go weak when these emotions are tested. There is a scale from 0 to 1000, in which the highest truth calibrates at 1000. Hawkins' testing shows that Jesus' original teachings calibrated at 1000, but by the time the Crusades began, Christian teachings had dropped to their present 498. Mother Teresa calibrated at 700.

David did a demonstration in which he called my partner, Rod, unaware, up to the front. David first muscle tested Rod by having him hold his arm out, and using two fingers, he tried to push Rod's arm down. As expected, the arm stayed strong and David could not push it down. He told Rod to think of something that upset him, so Rod thought of a fight that he and I had that morning. David was able to push Rod's arm down easily with his fingers. This showed that Rod's discomfort with our fight was a negative force in his system. David then took two envelopes, one that had a picture of Ghandi in it, and the other a picture of Hitler. He held the first envelope close to Rod and asked him to sense the contents, which were unknown to Rod. He then tested Rod's arm, which was strong. David placed the second envelope near Rod, tested, and again Rod's arm stayed strong. Dumbfounded, David apologized to the congregation and sheepishly admitted that his demonstration failed. He said he tested it on a friend and it worked the way it was supposed to, with her arm going weak on Hitler and staying strong on Gandhi.

Two weeks later David grinned as he related that upon further reading of Hawkins, he found that students of *A Course in Miracles* often tested strong on images of commonly perceived villains, because their consciousness had changed from separateness to oneness. Hawkins writes, "By the time the students were up to about Lesson 75, they had lost their vulnerability to negative stimuli. This enables the replacement of the ego's perception and its dualistic positionality with truth which replaces falsehood."[3]

Adolph Hitler is an example of the ego at its most vicious, vile, and vitriolic extreme. How is it possible to forgive him, when many people hope he's burning in hell? The truth about Hitler is that he is the Son of God, and because this is a dream, he is as innocent as his six million Jewish victims. This is *not* to say that what he did was okay or that the suffering of the victims wasn't phenomenal on this level. Further, a forgiving response is not passive, but active, for taking Hitler out in any way possible, including killing him without hate, is the loving thing to do. Forgiveness does not allow abuse to happen nor condone it. It simply does not condemn the person committing the abuse. Forgiveness recognizes that the person forgot he was the Christ Self and acted in error from his ego mind. Had Hitler been in his right mind, able to see the truth about himself and the Jews, he would never have committed those atrocities. What he did to Jews was beyond horrific on this level, and the suffering the Jews experienced was abominable and should never happen to anyone. When we see this as the illusion it is still extremely important to validate the *experience* of profound suffering. However, knowing that ultimately it is an illusion is vitally important to healing. I went to a memorial service for a Jewish woman who was born in a detainment camp in Germany after World War II. She carried the philosophy that if we don't move on with love and forgiveness, we will be consumed with bitterness. She was a loving peacemaker and none of us knew until her memorial service that almost her entire family had been murdered in the Holocaust. She used her personal experience to live a life of love.

I don't know how she viewed Hitler, but he had a right and a wrong mind just like the rest of us. We have to think like God to see Hitler as innocent, and this entails a total change of our usual way of thinking. The ACIM Workbook lessons, as well as prayer and meditation, foster the atmosphere for a paradigm shift in consciousness. It is also helpful to admit that given the right circumstances, we can all become Hitlers. Until we own our shadow sides, we will judge the Hitlers of the world as completely unlike us. My work with addicts and criminals has shown me how basically alike we all are. Any of us can be victimized and turn into a victimizer.

My client Harry, whom I mentioned earlier as feeling very connected to Jesus, said he imagines a banquet in heaven with Hitler at the same table as Jesus. I was astounded! He doesn't read ACIM or any other spiritual literature; it is just his inner wisdom surfacing. *Power Vs. Force* has this to say: "When someone suddenly goes from the influence of a lower attractor field to that of a higher, therefore, it is often acclaimed as a miracle. The unfortunate verdict of human experience is that few escape the energy fields that gradually come to dominate their behaviors. A currently popular spiritual program designed to facilitate such escape is *A Course in Miracles*. The purpose of this course of spiritual psychology is to prepare the necessary groundwork to precipitate a sudden jump in consciousness through encouraging a total change of perception. In more traditional fashion, prayer and meditation also provide points of departure to rise from the influence of a lower energy field into a higher."[4]

These comments about Hitler are likely to offend or upset many people. Others may find them simply absurd. Prior to my study of ACIM I, too, would have found them ridiculous, but my thinking has changed so much that now I can see Hitler as my brother. Previously I would only have seen his victims as my brothers. Seeing Hitler's true Self does not mean I think what he did on this level was right or okay.

Perhaps the most famous and beautiful example of forgiveness is Jesus' forgiveness of those who crucified him. Jesus addresses this in the text of *A Course in Miracles*, stating, **"Father, forgive them for they know not what they do," in no way evaluates *what* they do (T-2.V.16:3).** Jesus was not identified with his body, being fully identified with God. He knew the body was not real; therefore, he did not judge those who erroneously thought they could kill him. Jesus advises us not to judge *anything* on this level of form, because *none* of it is real. Jesus could completely love his murderers because he knew he was one with them. He knew that their actions belied the truth about them, that they, too, were spirits of love. They were afraid of the love within themselves, so projected their fear outward and killed the symbol of love, Jesus. We are all crucifying ourselves daily, as we forget that we are love itself. We hide from this, run away from it, deny it, and try to kill it. But we cannot kill what God created, which is the message Jesus teaches.

This brings us to our next discussion on the role of Jesus as defined by *A Course in Miracles*, compared with his role in traditional Christian views.

CHAPTER SIX

JESUS REINTERPRETED

The new always carries with it the sense of violation, of sacrilege.
What is dead is sacred; what is new, that is, different,
is evil, dangerous, or subversive.
~Henry Miller

Near my home, a church billboard displays weekly pithy messages. "Your decision about Jesus determines your destiny." "Warning! Exposure to the Son can *prevent* burning!" And at Christmas, "Jesus was born to die for your sins." These are meant to encourage us to accept Jesus as our savior so we won't go to hell. The churches mean well and are concerned about us. These churches erroneously interpret Jesus' message of love and forgiveness as coming *only* through him and not other teachers. There are many other teachings that can bring us back to God. My friend saw me reading a book on Buddhism and exclaimed, "But, Lor, I thought you believed in Jesus!" I said, "I do. I just happen to believe in this as well." She feared for my soul and was not reassured until she learned that I'd been baptized of my own volition as a teen. Therefore, my soul was safe for eternity, even if I did read sacrilegious material.

With the message that we have to be saved by the blood of Jesus or suffer eternal damnation, many people are turned off to Jesus, who, in my mind, was the coolest man to ever walk this earth. What did you learn about him? That he was a prophet, the Messiah, God's only begotten son, a master teacher? I learned that he was God's only Son, sent by God to die for our sins, and that I *must* believe this and accept Jesus into my heart. There was no other way to get into heaven. Absolutely no other way!

As a born-again Christian, it was my mandate to save as many souls as possible. I was taught to look down on other religious beliefs as being of the devil. One of our church youth group members broke away and joined a Hare Krishna temple. We thought she was doomed, and we went to the temple to try to convince her to leave the cult and come home. At the temple we harassed one of the members while he was preparing dinner, challenging his Hindu beliefs. He kindly asked us to stop saying negative things because he wanted to prepare the food in a loving atmosphere. I thought this was stupid and jeered at him. These days when I hear preachers proclaim that the Twin Towers fell because of sinful homosexuals and pagans, or that God is mad at us and that's why He sent Hurricane Katrina, I remember my own judgment.

The first time I heard a different interpretation of Jesus than the one I'd learned in Sunday school was from a Unity minister I met at a seminar. He suggested that Jesus voluntarily went to the cross to teach us that death is not real, *not* that he was a blood sacrifice required by a vengeful God. He described Jesus as one who showed the rest of us the way to God. Now, *that* made sense to me, so I found a Unity church and came back to God after a ten-year absence. I heard that God actually wanted me to be happy, and I couldn't believe that. Happy? Remorseful, guilty, and penitent with correct behavior, maybe, but *happy?* It took about two years, but I finally started believing it, and my life began looking up. I felt like I'd come out of a dark forest, and the sunshine was welcoming and warm. Since that time, life has kept expanding with love and joy, with the exception of a few dark periods that I threw in with my ego choices. Knowing what I know now, I could never go back to the darkness I lived in for so long. Before I found the love of God again, I was terrified that I would go to hell if I was wrong about Jesus. Now when my family members challenge me, suggesting I may indeed go to hell, I am simply grateful to feel the total love of God in my heart. My God loves and embraces me and wants only good for me. God is not a God of wrath.

A Course in Miracles is to the Bible what the New Testament was to the Old Testament. It reflects a higher, more loving, and pure vision of God and our relationship with Him. Just as the New Testament brought a message of salvation and mercy in answer to sacrifice and death, the *Course* brings a message of *total* salvation and mercy without *any* sacrifice and death.

This chapter compares Jesus' teachings as written in *A Course in Miracles* to those in the Bible. Some forms of Christianity claim that salvation through the blood of Jesus is the only path to heaven, and this is refuted in ACIM. We look at how Jesus the man became Jesus the Christ when he awakened, and how this was misinterpreted by the church that Jesus was the *only* savior of the world. We see how this fits in with numerous cross-cultural myths that were around for centuries before Jesus ever walked the earth. We also explore expanded definitions of salvation, the Anti-Christ, the second coming of Christ, and the final judgment. Finally, we take a look at some passages from the Bible in light of what we have learned about the ego's thought system of fear as opposed to love.

Myths Surrounding Jesus

> *The nature of Christ's existence is mysterious, I admit;*
> *but this mystery meets the wants of man. Reject it and*
> *the world is an inexplicable riddle; believe it,*
> *and the history of our race is satisfactorily explained.*
> ~*Napoleon*

Jesus was undoubtedly one of the most powerful people to ever walk this earth. His world-reaching influence remains with us today, two thousand years later, and this is testament to his power. The mere mention of Jesus' name continues to evoke healing for those who believe his claims. For these people, Jesus' name stirs something deep within. Likewise, myths inspire and speak to the truth in our being. Somewhere inside of us we resonate with the power and possibility, even though the story sounds impossible for mere mortals.

There are many mythological overtones surrounding the stories about Jesus' birth, life, death, and resurrection. Cross-culturally, there are multiple myths containing virgin births, sacrificed saviors, and resurrections. Jesus was a man who attained the Christ Consciousness, coming into full awareness of his oneness with God. Because Jesus knew his oneness with the power of God, he could easily perform miracles. Because Jesus knew his mission was to help humanity and teach the truth about God, he chose to sacrifice his body. Because he knew he was Spirit and not a body, he resurrected from the dead to show us that death is not real. Jesus completed the mythological hero's journey, the journey back to our inner power. He did what few others had done but what all of us are destined to do. Jesus lived the myth and proved the myth.

Myths spring up around powerful figures after their deaths because they are archetypal stories that describe the hero's journey and help explain the meaning of life. Joseph Campbell was an eminent mythologist and historian. While some historians feel Jesus was strictly a mythological figure who never actually lived, Campbell believed that Jesus was an actual historical figure, as do I.[1] However, Campbell explains, "The recurrent mythological event of the death and resurrection of a god, which had been for millenniums the central mystery of all of the great religions of the nuclear Near East, became in Christian thought an event in time, which had occurred but once, and marked the moment of the transfiguration of history."[2] Without an understanding of cross-cultural myths, it is understandable that early church leaders thought Jesus was the one and only resurrected God. Today we have worldwide communication and knowledge of other cultures' myths, which they did not have. They were not yet equipped to hear Jesus' message that, yes, he was one with God, but so are the rest of us.

Whether Jesus actually lived in a body is not the main point, as the body is unreal anyway. It is his message that is the truth, regardless of the form. The story of the crucified savior harkens to the wisdom within us that knows we must sacrifice the ego to resurrect our Christ Self. There are several myths of crucified saviors, which include Krishna from India, Mithra from Persia, and Tammuz from Babylon. The Persian and Babylonian religions were pagan and are considered heretical to Christians. However, when the Roman Emperor Constantine made Christianity the official religion of Rome in the fourth century CE, pagan rites were incorporated into Christian celebrations. Christmas trees have lights on them to stave off the winter darkness, and this stems from the pagan winter solstice festival of lights. It could be that early Christians used these existing symbols to share and explain their understanding of Jesus, who is called the "Light of God." Likewise, the pagan fertility festivals of the vernal equinox may have explained the resurrection of Jesus. The pagans celebrated the rebirth of spring and used eggs to symbolize fertility. This corresponds with renewed life from the resurrection.

There are virgin birth myths in addition to the crucified savior myths. One Christmas I listened to a call-in radio show and the host said, "If you could ask God one question, what would it be?" A frequent question arose: "Was Mary really a virgin?" The word "virgin" as used in the Bible meant "a young girl" or "a young maiden," according to Biblical scholars. Matthew 1:23 reads, "Behold, a virgin shall be with child and shall bring forth a son, and they shall call his name Emmanuel, which being interpreted is, God with us." Another way of interpreting this passage is that the pure, "virgin" spirit within us will bring forth the Son of God, our true Self, which is God within us. Interpreted esoterically, symbolic of internal truths, the Bible reads very differently than when it is interpreted exoterically, literally.

Ancient Aztecs had a savior whose mother was called a virgin. He also died and resurrected. Cortes and the Catholic Spaniards who traveled to Mexico were astounded to find their religious themes repeated. They thought Saint Thomas must have reached America with Jesus' message, or that the devil was using the Mexican myth to play havoc with their Christian faith.[3] Again, without the knowledge of the world's cultures that we have today, their bewilderment is understandable.

The Christmas story is my all-time favorite, and I am not concerned with whether the events happened exactly as the story goes. I am filled with awe and reverie as I read about the bright star shining a message of love and hope. I imagine myself with the shepherds as the angels sing "Glory to God in the highest, and on earth, peace, goodwill toward men." I adore *A Charlie Brown Christmas*, which depicts commercialism with gaudy decorations on Snoopy's doghouse. Charlie Brown bemoans that nobody seems to remember the true spirit of Christmas, and Linus answers him by reading from the Bible. "For unto you is born this day a Savior, which is Christ the Lord" (Luke 2:11). Linus softly says, "That's what Christmas is all about, Charlie Brown." I get chills every time.

Perhaps because of the mythological overtones, early Christians debated vehemently the divinity of Jesus. Was he a man or was he God incarnate? Most people, especially his disciples, had never met anyone like him and easily assumed him to be an avatar, an incarnation of God. The Apostle Paul and the earliest Christians were on fire to spread the message of Jesus, receiving their energy from Jesus' love. They believed his claims of oneness with God. God had come down to mix with men, and this was unheard of. Jesus' presence was phenomenal, indescribable, and electrifying. When Saint Anthony was called on to defend his belief that Jesus was God, all he said was, "I have seen him!" Anyone who has *experienced* Jesus can relate to what he said, and words and theology are secondary. I, too, have experienced Jesus, both when I was a Christian and now as I study *A Course in Miracles*. The experience of Jesus awakens in us the knowledge that we are loved, we are magnificent, and we are destined for greater things. Thus, I can understand why Christians who feel the love of Jesus can mistakenly think he is the only way back to God. We view the world based on our experience, and if we resonate with Jesus but are repelled by Hindu gods, then we may falsely assume our way is the only right one. Jesus certainly is a powerful path to God, but he is not the only one.

Official church doctrine regarding Jesus' divinity was established at the Council of Nicea in 325 CE. The Apostles' Creed was adopted, which declared that Jesus was God but had also walked the earth as a man.[4] Following the council, all writings suggesting that Jesus was an ordinary man or a prophet, rather than God in the flesh, were condemned as heretical and burned.[5] Belief in Jesus as simply a great master teacher later became punishable by death. To this day, orthodox Christianity judges as blasphemous those who see Jesus as a teacher rather than a deified savior. The Jewish orthodoxy cried for Jesus' death for blasphemy when he said, "I and the Father are one" (John 10:30). New ideas appear frightening and have been routinely condemned throughout history, just as many have already condemned *A Course in Miracles*.

Church history is replete with renunciations of teachings that differ from the currently accepted model. In 1633, Galileo was denounced for his discovery that the earth orbits the sun. The doctrine of the church was that earth was the center of the universe, and they claimed the Bible supported their interpretation. Under threat of his life, Galileo was forced to recant his scientific findings:

> I, Galeleo,Galilei, . . . kneeling before you, most Eminent and Reverend Lord Cardinals, Inquisitors general against heretical depravity throughout the whole Christian Republic . . . swear that I have always believed . . . all that is held, preached, and taught by the Holy Catholic and Roman Apostolic Church. But whereas—after an injunction had been judicially intimated to me by this Holy Office, to the effect that I must altogether abandon the false opinion that the sun is the centre of the world and immovable, and that the earth is not the centre of the world, and moves. . . and after it had been notified to me that the said doctrine was contrary to Holy Scripture—I wrote and

printed a book in which I discuss this doctrine already
condemned . . . with sincere heart and unfeigned faith
I abjure, curse, and detest the aforesaid errors and
heresies, . . . should I know any heretic, or person
suspected of heresy, I will denounce him to this Holy
Office.[6]

Only recently, almost four hundred years later, did Pope John
Paul II officially acknowledge that Galileo was right.

When we read the Bible as if it were literal truth rather than
metaphorical, misunderstandings arise. Granted, there are a lot of
historical facts mixed in with the metaphors, but we can read it in
the *spirit* of truth. This way, we will get the message of God's love
for us and learn how to restore our connection with Him.

The Only Path to Heaven?

Every real thought on every real subject
knocks the wind out of somebody or other.
~Oliver Wendell Holmes

I read a book on religions and cults written by a Christian
author. It was very well done, balanced and nonjudgmental. When
the author expressed why he believed Christianity was the one
true religion, he stated that when it came to eternity, he wanted to
make sure he was making the right choice. He stated Christianity
was, in his opinion, the only true religion because the Bible is the
only verifiable and inspired word of God, and that Jesus declared
that he was God Himself. Jesus said, "I and the Father are one"
(John 10:30). He was crucified in part for blasphemy, for he dared
to claim he was God. This passage is cited by Christians as a
primary reason that Christianity is true while other religions are
not.

Jesus is quoted in the Bible as saying, "I am the way, the truth,
and the life; no man cometh unto the Father, but by me" (John
14:6). This statement is part of traditional Christian doctrine that
belief in Jesus is the only way to get into heaven. Protestants and
Catholics seem to differ slightly in their interpretations. Catholic

theology states that Jesus was the atonement for our sins and we should have a relationship with him; Protestant theology agrees, but it goes one step further and states that we need to also accept Jesus into our hearts as our personal Savior, turning our lives over to him.

> *"No man cometh unto the Father but by me"*
> *does not mean that I am in any way*
> *separate or different from you except in time,*
> *and time does not really exist*
> *(T-1.II.4:1).*

In *A Course in Miracles*, Jesus interprets this statement differently. When Jesus states "I Am," He is talking about his very Being, His Self, which is the Truth. This is the Self in all of us, the love that we are. The Christ is the way, the truth, and the life. Jesus realized his Christ Self and gave us the *example* of how we, too, can realize It. Thus, the doctrine that states this is the only way to heaven is essentially true, because the only way to heaven is to understand our oneness with God. We *do* have to believe, but in the Christ within us. Jesus' statement was not about his particular body, but about the Beingness of Christ within each of us that is heaven. Heaven is not a place we arrive at after having lived a sanctified life. It is a state of mind, a state in which we have returned our minds to the oneness of God. It is the choice of God over the ego's false thought system. In heaven, in eternity, there is no time, only the present moment. Jesus states that there is no difference between him and us except in time, because in the illusion, in time, it appears that he returned to God first. Jesus was the first one to awaken fully from the dream. The truth is that none of us has ever left God to begin with.

Jesus further clarifies the above passage. **When I said, "I am with you always," I meant it literally. I am not absent to anyone in any situation. Because I am always with you, *you* are the way, the truth and the life (T-7.III.1:7-9).** Once again Jesus is saying that we are all the Christ, and the Christ within us is the way, the truth, and the life.

Another scripture on which Christianity bases its belief that Jesus is the only way to heaven is John 3:16: "For God so loved the world that He gave His only Son, that whoever believes in Him should not perish but have eternal life." However, in ACIM, Jesus repeatedly interprets the one Son as being *all of us*, innocent of any sin. **God has not many sons, but only one (T-29.VIII.9:1).**

The Gospel of John continues in verses 3:17–19: "For God sent the Son into the world, not to condemn the world, but that the world might be saved through him. He who believes in him is not condemned; he who does not believe is condemned already, because he has not believed in the name of the only Son of God. And this is the judgment, that the light has come into the world, and men loved darkness rather than light, because their deeds were evil." Interpreted differently, if you do not believe in the Christ Self within you, you are lost and in darkness. The ego loves the darkness and knows not the light. Jesus the Christ was sent into the world, not to condemn it if it did not believe in him, but to awaken it to the truth of the Christ Self in each of us. We are saved when we remember the truth about ourselves as the Son of God.

There is nothing about me that you cannot attain.
I have nothing that does not come from God.
The difference between us now is that
I have nothing else. This leaves me in a state
which is only potential in you (T-1.II.3:10-13).

Jesus reiterates in this passage that he is no different than we are, and that we are fully capable of realizing our oneness with God. The only difference between him and us is that he no longer identifies with the body or the ego. The hallmarks of the ego are separation, fear, and guilt. The ego cannot possibly accept the idea that we are one with God, for then it would no longer exist. Therefore, it labels this idea blasphemous and instills guilt and the fear of punishment by God for daring to think this way. The ego did this with the apostles and is still doing it today with each of us. I notice that often when I own my Christ Self, it's followed with a migraine headache. It's as if I'm punishing myself for daring to know the truth. A friend of mine also experiences this, as she gets a bad cold after she shines. She is a minister and delivered a beautiful message at her first funeral. Many complimented her, and the next day she was in bed sick. This is our unconscious guilt showing up, and it also appears in the letters of Apostle Paul.

Much of the doctrine of the church comes from the Apostle Paul. Paul was certainly one of the most influential men in history, and his love for Jesus and motivation to spread the message of God's love gave rise to Christianity. He was clearly filled with Spirit, and many of his letters are poetic and beautiful. He was transformed by the love of God, and any person who taps into the love of God, regardless of the form, is transformed. Prior to his conversion, Paul persecuted the Christians. He wrote that Christians are worthless sinners in need of salvation, and this seems to come from the ego thought system of fear. Could it be that Paul's guilt, his belief that he was a sinner who needed saving, was his own projection rather than the correct teaching of Jesus? It is quite possible that remnants of his guilt affected his preaching, as guilt affects many preachers today. The TV evangelists who have shouted loudest about the sins of the flesh have been caught with their pants down or their hands in the cookie jar. Usually what we're most vehement about is what we're most guilty and afraid of. It is vital that we not judge these preachers, for we have the same ugly ego as they do. Yet the ego loves to jump up and scorn, as if it is innocent while others stink of guilt.

There are many people who insist that the Bible is the *only* inspired word of God and the *literal* word of God. They get very angry when this is questioned. When people are angry, fear is always underlying. Perhaps these people are afraid that what has given them love, hope, and structure will be taken away from them. The ego is afraid of anything that breaks out of the box, which finds the truth within rather than from rules and regulations. Following strict rules and not questioning authority is what led ordinary people to follow an insane leader like Hitler. If we were to literally follow the Bible today we would have to execute a sizable number of sinners, for in Leviticus 20:10 it is written: "If a man commits adultery with the wife of his neighbor, both the adulterer and the adulteress shall be put to death." Yet in the chapter right before this, Leviticus 19:18, God is allegedly quoted, "You shall not take vengeance or bear a grudge against your countrymen. Love your fellow as yourself. I am the Lord." This incredible contrast highlights the ego's severity with God's mercy. It shows how the ego tries to contaminate the total love that God has for us.

Any scripture can be interpreted in numerous ways, and each version reflects the personality, which is the ego, of both the author and the reader. God may inspire some ideas, but they still come through fallible humans. As we progress in our understanding, our views expand and change and our interpretation of scripture does as well. Do you still believe everything the same way you did twenty years ago?

After I wrote the first draft of this book, an odd coincidence occurred. I ran into a friend from my church youth group when I was a teen. Dave was one of the group leaders and acted as a guest preacher on occasion. His sermons compelled me to come forward to the altar and confess my sexual sins with my boyfriend. We also had parties at his lake cottage, and he forbade us to wear bikinis because he said it gave him lustful thoughts. Dave was also the first person to ever let me drive his car. I had run into Dave a number of times previously, but I was guarded because I assumed that he still practiced the religion we were raised with. I assumed that he would disapprove of my alternative beliefs. Dave's sister is one of my lifelong best friends, and she is a devout Christian. We have agreed to disagree about religion, and we don't discuss it.

When I ran into Dave this time, somehow the conversation got around to how he'd been interested in Eastern thought since he was fourteen years old. I told him he had me completely fooled. I realized I had judged Dave and had been completely wrong. I told him about my book, and he offered to read it. Before this encounter, he probably would have been one of the last people I'd want to read it. However, I listened to my inner voice which said to go ahead, and when Dave read the book he was very supportive. He gently noted my judgment toward fundamental Christianity, and showed me how our church had been good for us. He pointed out that different people need different paths, something I'd been fond of saying, but in my judgment I had not been able to apply the idea to evangelical Christians. I felt like a huge burden was lifted off my shoulders, as I had been praying for release of my judgment toward fundamentalism. Dave's presence was an unexpected and incredible gift that once again taught me not to presume and judge.

In my town there is an interfaith council in which representatives from all religions are invited to share in building community together. It is a wonderful sight to see members of Christian, Jewish, Hindu, Muslim, Buddhist, and other spiritual paths honoring one another's beliefs. It is a very loving group with no judgment that one path to God is better than another, and the focus is love and peace. I have a friend whose husband is a Methodist minister. She has read ACIM and her husband is open-minded, loving and non-judgmental. The majority of Christians are loving and nonjudgmental toward other religions. An August 2005 Beliefnet/*Newsweek* survey showed that the vast majority of Christians believe that people of other faiths will indeed go to heaven.[7] However, in our media the right wing is the most vocal, so many think that they represent mainstream Christianity. The view that all other faiths are wrong if they don't believe in Jesus is simply not what most people believe.

Salvation

If pain could have cured us we should long ago have been saved.
~George Santayana

My childhood church taught that we need the salvation of Jesus' blood because we are sinful, and that we are all condemned to death because of Adam and Eve's original sin. I wondered about infants who died and didn't get a chance to know Jesus, as well as people from other cultures who never even heard of Jesus. I was taught that these souls would be introduced to Jesus at some point, however brief, and would then have the opportunity to accept him. I worried, "What if they just couldn't buy the story of the cross and as a result had to spend eternity in hell?" I was told that was God's justice, but I never believed it in my heart.

Salvation is nothing more than "right-mindedness"
(T-4.II.10:1). For salvation is the end of dreams, and
with the closing of the dream will have no meaning.
Who, awake in Heaven, could dream that there
could ever be need of salvation (T-17.II.7.4-5)?

Fear condemns and love forgives.
Forgiveness thus undoes what fear has produced,
returning the mind to the awareness of God. For this
reason, forgiveness can truly be called salvation. It is the
means by which illusions disappear (W-p.I.46.2:2-5)?

The original Greek meaning of the word "saved" is "whole." *A Course in Miracles* teaches that our true Self does not need salvation because it is already whole. Salvation is "right-mindedness," choosing love over fear, choosing the Holy Spirit's voice over the ego's. The moment we choose God, we are saved from the illusion. The moment we truly forgive, we are saved. However, once we recognize that we have made up this illusion, we realize that there has never been anything to be saved from. Another word for salvation might be "enlightenment." We become enlightened to the truth of our Being.

The hallmarks of the ego are guilt, fear, and separation, while God is love and oneness. What are your beliefs about Jesus and God? Do they contain fear or guilt? Is there any worry that if you or your loved ones don't behave or believe a certain way that you will go to hell? If so, that's fear. Love says that you are safe, loved, and protected no matter what. Do you think God is a Being or a Force somewhere out there, apart from you? If so, that's separation.

Salvation comes through seeing the Christ Self in our brothers, which then awakens the awareness of our own Christ Self. We are unable to return to God without our brother's help, for it is through forgiving him that we ourselves are saved. This is why the *Course* calls our brother our "savior." There is not one savior named Jesus; there are billions of saviors. Deep down we long to connect truly with our brothers, to dissolve the illusion of separateness.

We can see the Christ in everyone's eyes when we look deep into them. Determine to look directly at people and note, "I behold the Christ in you." As you do this, you will start seeing the Christ in the store clerk, in strangers on the street, and in everyone.

The Crucifixion

If you are distressed by anything external, the pain is not
due to the thing itself but to your own estimate of it;
and this you have the power to revoke at any moment.
~Marcus Aurelius

There is a positive interpretation of the crucifixion
that is wholly devoid of fear,
and therefore wholly benign in what it teaches,
if it is properly understood.
The crucifixion is nothing more than an
extreme example. Assault can ultimately
be made only on the body. I elected,
for your sake and mine,
to demonstrate that the most outrageous assault,
as judged by the ego, does not matter.
As the world judges these things,
but not as God knows them,
I was betrayed, abandoned, beaten,
torn, and finally killed.

When you hear only one Voice you are
not called on to sacrifice. You are not
persecuted, nor was I. I will with God
that none of His Sons should suffer
(T-6.I.1:5; 2:1; 4:1; 9:1-2; 10:4; 11:1, 7).

The guiltless mind cannot suffer. The sane mind
cannot conceive of illness because it cannot conceive
of attacking anyone or anything (T-5.V.5:1, 3).

155

The Passion of the Christ was a wildly successful movie that powerfully depicted Jesus' apparent suffering on the cross. Many viewers were stunned and came away with a heightened appreciation of Jesus' love for us. My friend felt that Jesus certainly must have been God to endure that torture and forgive his murderers. Indeed, in the above passage, Jesus acknowledges crucifixion is one of the most gruesome ways to die that the ego invented. However, Jesus teaches that assault can only be made on a body, and that he did not identify with his body. He therefore did not suffer on the cross. **The Self which God created cannot sin, and therefore cannot suffer (W-II.330.1:5).** The wrong mind projects the body, and the body is the illusory image on our movie screen. Jesus was totally identified only with God, and thus could watch the illusion from outside of the dream. He did not believe in the dream, and he volunteered to manifest a body to teach us that the dream wasn't real.

In meditation, yogis can slow down body systems so they are barely breathing, their pulse rate drops close to zero, and their minds are floating outside the body. They are perfectly aware and alive, but the body appears almost dead. They are capable of not feeling pain in the body. Hypnotists train people's minds so they can undergo surgery without anesthesia.

Lester Levenson was a modern day master who also identified with mind instead of body. Lester was a physicist and successful entrepreneur, who, in spite of worldly success, was emotionally and physically miserable. At the age of forty-two, he had had two heart attacks and doctors sent him home to die. This was in 1952, prior to bypass surgery. Lester decided he had nothing to lose, and he began letting go of all emotions that were unloving. In other words, he gave up the ego. He intensively released fear, guilt, and all other forms of negativity for three months, whereupon he experienced a conscious awakening. For the rest of his life he was in a complete state of peace. Lester lived for another forty-two years and dedicated himself to sharing his process through the Sedona Method®. He died of cancer in 1984. During the process of his body's degeneration, he experienced no pain, because he did not identify himself as his body, and his mind, having awakened, was free of guilt. Lester's dear friend Hale Dwoskin took care of him and witnessed his profound peace during the dying process. Hale has carried on Lester's work and is the author of the New York Times bestseller *The Sedona Method.*

I know a man who wears a necklace with a stake rather than a cross, symbolizing the nails driven into Jesus' hands and feet. This man feels tremendous gratitude and love for Jesus' willingness to suffer and die for him. He is on the right track about the love, if not the suffering. Many churches these days seem to focus on Jesus' love rather than God's wrath and judgment. They are kinder and gentler than in the past. These churches are a blessing, as people blossom and love themselves through accepting Jesus' love for them. However, this love is for *everyone,* not just those who follow the rules of the church and accept Jesus as their savior. Many of us stay away from spiritual communities and Jesus' teachings out of guilt. We worry that if we take a drink or smoke a cigarette or have sex with the wrong person that we'll go to hell or be cast out of the church. Indeed, many churches preach against the indulgences of the flesh, so people don't attend, as they feel uncomfortable. However, the more we are filled with the love of God, the less likely we will harm ourselves with unloving behaviors. Guilt-tripping people only produces fear-based compliance; real change comes from love.

> *The message of the crucifixion is perfectly clear:*
> *Teach only love, for that is what you are.*
> *If you interpret the crucifixion in any other way,*
> *you are using it as a weapon for assault*
> *rather than as the call for peace*
> *for which it was intended. The Apostles often*
> *misunderstood it, and for the same reason*
> *that anyone misunderstands it. Their own imperfect*
> *love made them vulnerable to projection,*
> *and out of their own fear*
> *they spoke of the "wrath of God"*
> *as His retaliatory weapon (T-6.I.13:1-2; 14:1-3).*

If the apostles misunderstood Jesus' lesson, it is easy to understand how most of us would. We are all under the grip of the ego and that's why it has taken us so long to hear the message that God is within all of us. The secrets of enlightenment have been around since the beginning of time, yet very few have been capable of comprehending them. Thus, they have been made available to the privileged few in secret societies, until our recent age of intellectual openness. We are very fortunate to now have the secret teachings readily available to all, and *A Course in Miracles* is one explanation of the mysteries of the universe.

The apostles misunderstood Jesus' basic teachings because they projected their own guilt and fear onto his crucifixion. They wondered how Jesus, who was one with God, could be killed. He had powers to heal the sick and bring the dead to life, so how come he did not escape his own gruesome death? The apostles were steeped in the Judaic tradition of sacrificial atonement for sin, so they appear to have translated Jesus' death within this framework. Here was someone who was innocent, being put to death. Jesus was the perfect metaphor for the sacrificial lamb placed on the altar before God. However, this is quite different from Jesus' explanation in ACIM. Jesus says he gave us an extreme example that persecution, attack, betrayal, and abandonment cannot occur except in a dream. None of these exist in the mind that is awake, the guiltless mind that does not identify with the body. The apostles understandably made the body of Jesus special, for they had no other paradigm in which to understand him. However, Jesus' innocence was given as an example of everyone's innocence.

Jesus states in ACIM that we crucify ourselves every time we feel guilty, every time we choose the ego over God. He says that we no longer have to go through daily crucifixions, for he has shown the way, and we can learn from his example. **The Holy Spirit never asks for sacrifice, but the ego always does (T-7.X.5:5).** God does not need a sacrifice, but most of us feel so worthless that *we* need one.

Many people believe that we can only learn through suffering, and I used to believe this as well. Today, however, I ask only for gentle lessons, through receiving love instead of causing myself pain. The belief in suffering is the belief in fear, guilt, and pain. My friend Sarah, who is one of the most joyous people I know, overcame the sudden death of her husband when she was thirty-four, childhood sexual abuse, and an eating disorder. She taught me that the hardest thing is to *receive* all of the love God has for us. It's easy to deal with our problems; we're used to that. It's harder to open up to the truth that the joy, love, and peace are within us. Once we break free, however, it is a wonderful ride! For Sarah, it's literally a wonderful ride. She has become so trusting, free, and open with life, that she rides her horses with her hands in the air, exclaiming with joy. I have watched her transformation with interest and have valued her as a role model. She has taught me to let my good in, to believe that God is ready and willing to pour out blessings if only I can receive them. This is the joy that Jesus wants us to have. He is joyous; he was not the suffering, sad image so frequently portrayed.

The Resurrection

No man can pass into eternity, for he is already in it.
~Frederick William Farrar

The importance of the resurrection is emphasized in both Christianity and ACIM. The resurrection was the whole point of Jesus' life. It is the whole point of our lives. There is no death! There is no separation! Therefore, we have nothing to fear. Christianity emphasizes the resurrection of the body and our thinking, while ACIM focuses solely on the resurrection of our thinking. **The resurrection is the denial of death, being the assertion of life. Thus is all the thinking of the world reversed entirely. Life is now recognized as salvation, and pain and misery of any kind perceived as hell (M-28.2:1-3).** The promise is that once our thinking is resurrected we will see this world completely different. Gone will be the pain and suffering, and we will embrace love in stead of fear.

The Second Coming of Christ

He who does not see God in the next person he meets,
need look no further.
~Gandhi

Believers have been awaiting the return of Jesus Christ to the earth since the early days of Christianity. Recently in our own country we have seen increased interest and anticipation of this event, which is called "the rapture." Unexpectedly the faithful will be taken up to heaven, while unbelievers will be left behind to face a seven-year period of war and tribulation. One painting depicts overall chaos and multiple car accidents, as Christian drivers vanish into thin air. There is an immensely popular book series titled *Left Behind* that chronicles the prophesied events, which include the rise of the Anti-Christ and an apocalyptic war. The Anti-Christ is a leader who makes a deceptive peace pact with Israel, while his ulterior motive is power and war. The forces of God will ultimately win the war of Armageddon, followed by one thousand years of peace on earth.

When I was a teenager my church showed a movie about the rapture called *A Thief in the Night*. I invited my girlfriend to come, hoping she would become saved. My girlfriend left without going up to the altar, which disappointed me. The movie terrified me, even though I was saved and would be one of those lifted in the clouds.

The Second Coming, as defined by Christian doctrine, paints a frightening scenario for non-Christians, who get left behind to face war and tribulation. However, the Second Coming as defined by *A Course in Miracles* offers a different explanation. **The First Coming of Christ is merely another name for the creation, for Christ is the Son of God. The Second Coming of Christ means nothing more than the end of the ego's rule and the healing of the mind (T-4.IV.10:1-2).** When we awaken to the Christ within us, this is the Second Coming. The word "Christ" refers to the higher Self of man. It is the Greek word for "Messiah," "the anointed one." Jesus became the Christ when he recognized his oneness with God; Krishna became the Christ; Buddha became the Christ. ACIM states that we all will become the Christ when we forgive and see Christ in all our brothers. **The name of *Jesus* is the name of one who was a man but saw the face of Christ in all his brothers and remembered God. So he became identified with *Christ*, a man no longer, but at one with God. Is he the Christ? Oh, yes, along with you (C-5.2:1-2; 5:1).** If the word "Christ" is uncomfortable for you to use, use a word such as "Spirit," "Higher Self," "Divinity Within," "True Self," or whatever else works for you.

I had a discussion about God with a client of mine, Kathy, who is active in her Presbyterian church and reads a lot of mainstream Christian literature, including the *Left Behind* series. To my surprise, she expressed acceptance of several ACIM ideas, including Jesus not being a sacrifice. She said she'd had a number of psychic experiences that her church would judge as her imagination at best and the devil at worst. But, she knows they happened because *she* experienced them, and they were helpful. Thus, "I keep an open mind," she says.

Kathy loves Jesus and her church is extremely good for her mental health, so when she spoke of leaving her church I encouraged her to return, which she did. She has been a member of it since childhood, so it is quite important to her.

I told Kathy that I saw the *Left Behind* series as invoking tremendous, unnecessary fear of God. She saw it differently and said that when she first started reading them, she needed the fear to get back on track with God. She felt she would have been too complacent without it. She made the point that while God does not want or need us to be afraid, when we're in the ego, *we* may need fear as a motivational prod. She had punished herself by marrying alcoholic men, and allowing them to emotionally abuse her. She lent money to people who never paid her back. She took people into her home when they were homeless, then they ripped her off. As Kathy progressed, she related to God through love instead of fear and guilt. She faced severe financial challenges with equanimity and stopped loaning money to people who used her. In a crisis when she was falsely accused and threatened with legal charges, she calmed down and enveloped herself with the peace of God. She stopped attracting alcoholic men. Kathy has let go of the ego's need to learn through fear, struggle, and sacrifice.

Kathy came up with an intriguing thought after reading *The Disappearance of the Universe*. She compared the concept of disappearing in the rapture to the concept of the disappearance of the universe when we awaken from the dream. According to ACIM, when we awaken to our true Self, we are saved and awaken from the dream. The world as we know it disappears, for we are home with God. According to the rapture concept, those who are saved by the blood of Jesus disappear and return home to God. The end result is the same. The common theme is belief in Jesus' teachings, even though those beliefs are somewhat different. There is a kernel of truth in many thought systems; it's just how they are expanded and interpreted that demonstrate the difference between fear and love.

The Anti-Christ

All great ideas began as blasphemies.
~George Bernard Shaw

Christian doctrine states that in the final days before the war of Armageddon a false leader called the Anti-Christ will arise. He will deceive by appearing to come in the name of peace, but his underlying motive is to bring war. ACIM suggests a different definition of the Anti-Christ from that found in the Bible. The Anti-Christ is any idol that hides the truth of your Christ Self. Idols, as discussed in chapter 4, are akin to addictions, and are anything that we value more than God. This is the meaning of the Biblical commandment "Thou shalt have no other Gods before Me" (Exodus 20:3). Idols can be money, bodies, relationships, sex, sports, hobbies, or anything else depending on whether they are used appropriately or as addictions. Most of us have several idols. These are things we think we cannot live without. As the *Course* says, **Let not their form deceive you. Idols are but substitutes for your reality. In some way, you believe they will complete your little self, for safety in a world perceived as dangerous. . . . They have the** power to supply your lacks, and add the value that you do not have (T-29.VIII.2:1-4). An idol is a false impression, or a false belief; some form of Anti-Christ. . . . All forms of Anti-Christ oppose the Christ. This world of idols *is* a veil across the face of Christ (T-29. VIII.3:1; 5; 4:1). Since *nothing* in physical form is real, placing undue emphasis on it is idolatry.

As I wrote this I met a very loving, caring minister at, of all places, the casino! I was reading the Bible in the cafeteria, and we struck up a conversation when he commented that the Bible was his favorite book. Pastor Don was filled with the love of Jesus, and I could tell by his manner that he was an inspiring, uplifting preacher. He had been a militant bodyguard for Malcolm X and the Nation of Islam in the early sixties. He used to hate white people until the love of Jesus healed him. Later, God, or Allah, also healed Malcolm X, who no longer saw the white man as the devil. Pastor Don needed the path of Christianity while Malcolm X needed the path of Islam. Both paths offered the necessary healing of their racism.

I asked Pastor Don what he thought of the cross-cultural myths around crucifixions of saviors and virgin births that are found even in places where no one has ever heard of Jesus. I told him that I could no longer see Christianity as the only true religion after discovering these. Pastor Don had read a book on myths about crucified saviors, so was familiar with the folklore. He turned to I John 4:1–3 in my Bible and read: "Beloved, do not believe every spirit, but test the spirits to see whether they are of God; for many false prophets have gone out into the world. By this you know the Spirit of God: every spirit which confesses that Jesus Christ has come in the flesh is of God, and every spirit which does not confess Jesus is not of God. This is the spirit of antichrist, of which you heard that it was coming, and now it is in the world already."

The Anti-Christ is defined by the church as any teaching that denies either the deity of Jesus or that Jesus is the only way to salvation. When the idea doesn't fall in line with church teachings it is seen as blasphemous, heretical, or in the spirit of the Anti-Christ. Actually, the Anti-Christ is any thought we have that denies the Christ Self within us, thus keeping us from our wholeness. Pastor

Don's response to the mythological overtones speaks to the main mistake the church made around Jesus. The ego tried to keep us from God, as it always does. The church indeed captured the idea that Jesus was showing us the way to God, but it fell into the ego's trap to limit heaven to a few select believers. That way the followers of Jesus could feel the power of his transformative words but still remain in fear that the rest of the world was going to hell. The insistence that Jesus is the only way is guaranteed to offend many people, thus effectively shutting them off from the most influential teacher in history. Score another point for the ego.

In the Bible the ego is referred to as Satan. The biblical story is that God and Satan are at war for control of the earth. Every religion has allegories to explain the presence of evil and our perceived separation from God. *A Course in Miracles* says the ego is a myth, a story devised to help us understand our situation. Yet it is just a story, for the ego is not real. Every time we think we have to war against Satan or the ego, we are making it real. Every time a preacher rails against sin, he is making the ego real.

New Testament Teachings

When all beliefs are challenged together, the just and necessary ones have a chance to step forward and to re-establish themselves alone.
~*George Santayana*

There are a number of New Testament teachings ascribed to Jesus that parallel his words in *A Course in Miracles*, and there are many that do not. None of us knows what Jesus really said, because we weren't there. To discern what he might have said we can look at whether the teachings are based in fear or love. Jesus taught only love. In recent years there was a fad in which people wore bracelets with "WWJD" on them, signifying "What Would Jesus Do?" This could easily be rephrased, "What Would Love Do?" Jesus never judged or condemned, yet there are many verses in the New Testament that suggest a harshness that could not have come from Jesus. What appears to have happened is that the Bible, inspired by Spirit, got contaminated with the ego fear of the human channels. That is why so much of the Bible invokes love and truth, while other parts make us shudder.

Most religions contain a form of the golden rule, "Do unto others as you would have them do unto you." They also have allegories to explain our apparent fall from grace or our separation from God and paradise. Most religions stress the importance of love and forgiveness. Love and forgiveness are *the* keys to happiness and finding God, and that is why most religions offer a path to truth.

Christianity and *A Course in Miracles* have a number of similarities, but also have some significant differences. An exhaustive review of these is beyond the scope of this book, so only a few verses will be examined. The main similarities are forgiveness and the love of God. Both Christianity and ACIM state that "the kingdom of heaven is within you" (Luke 17:21), rather than outside of you, although most people still think of God as a Being far away in heaven.

Other similarities include the mind of Christ. St. Paul's letters encourage us to take on the mind of Christ, and ACIM states that the mind of Christ is within all of us. The Bible refers to us as heirs to the kingdom and sons of God, just as ACIM does, though Christian doctrine separates Jesus out as the one special Son of God. When the Bible is read symbolically, it becomes easier to ascertain the heart of Jesus' message. Interpreted esoterically, referring to the inner spirit of man, the message of Jesus Christ in the New Testament is one of awakening the Christ within all of us. This metaphysical view of Jesus' message is particularly apparent in the Gospel of John. When Jesus says, "He who hath seen me hath seen the Father" (John 14:9), and "I and the Father are one" (John 10:30), he delivered one of the core messages of *A Course in Miracles*.

The main differences are that ACIM says God did not create this world; rather, this world is an illusion, and the ego (Satan) is only a thought without any power of its own, since it is not real. Christianity states that God created this world, that Satan is real, is the ruler of this world, and is in a battle for power with God. ACIM states that the only true reality is God's heaven. We are still at home with God, and our dream of separation from Him is a mental hell. Protestant Christianity teaches that those who accept Jesus Christ as their savior are the only ones who will get to heaven, and everyone else will burn in eternal hellfire.

Jesus was raised a Jew. He loved God and learned from the Old Testament. Because Jesus knew intimately the total love of God, he saw how the ego makes God and the Bible fearful, when they were not intended that way. The *Course* says, **Not only does the ego cite Scripture for its purpose, but it even interprets Scripture as a witness for itself. The Bible is a fearful thing in the ego's judgment. There are many examples of how the ego's interpretations are misleading. "The wicked shall perish" becomes a statement of Atonement, if the word "perish" is understood as "be undone." Every loveless thought must be undone, a word the ego cannot even understand. To the ego, to be undone means to be destroyed (T-5.VI.4:4-5; 5:1; 9:1-3).** This means that everything that is not love will be corrected, undone, for only love is real. The "wicked" shall not perish in eternal damnation because their unloving actions are not part of true reality.

The above reinterpretation is refreshing, and reading the New Testament in light of Jesus' love is also enlightening. Jesus said, "You are the light of the world" (Matthew 5:14). This does not sound like he's calling us sinners who need to be saved. This sounds similar to the ACIM message that we are the Christ light. "You have heard that it was said, 'You shall not commit adultery.' But I say to you that everyone who looks at a woman lustfully has already committed adultery with her in his heart" (Matthew 5:27–28). The mind is the maker of our world. The mind projects its thoughts outward, and that is what shows up in physical form. Here Jesus is not saying that lust is bad, he is saying there is no difference between physical action and thought because only the mind is real. The body is the illusion.

"But I say to you, Love your enemies and pray for those who persecute you, so that you may be sons of your Father who is in heaven; for he makes his sun rise on the evil and on the good, and sends rain on the just and on the unjust. For if you love those who love you, what reward have you? Do not even the tax collectors do the same? And if you salute only your brethren, what more are you doing than others? Do not even the Gentiles do the same? You, therefore, must be perfect, as your heavenly Father is perfect" (Matthew 5:44–48). Here there seems to be a mix of Jesus' teachings with the author's projection of fear. In ACIM Jesus calls those who persecute us our brothers and our saviors. Jesus, knowing us all as one, does not see anyone as an enemy. God extends only love, and all receive equally of his blessings, even "wicked" people. He does not judge anyone as evil, and therefore does not send sunshine to the "good" people and rain to the "wicked." The call to be perfect could be read as, "You, as an extension of God, are already perfect. You must accept this to awaken to your perfection."

"Judge not, that you be not judged. For with the judgment that you pronounce you will be judged, and the measure you give will be the measure you get" (Matthew 7:1–2). This does not mean that God will judge you and deliver punishment if you harm others. God does not judge or condemn; however, the ego does. Since we are one, what we do to others we do to ourselves, and when we judge others we judge ourselves. Identifying with the ego always brings self-punishment.

"But to all who received him, who believed in his name, he gave power to become children of God" (John 1:12). When we believe in Jesus' name, Christ, which is also our name, all the power of God is ours. We have to receive and believe in order to tap into the power that has always been there.

"I have yet many things to say to you, but you cannot bear them now. When the Spirit of truth comes, he will guide you into all the truth" (John 16:12–13). Could Jesus have been talking about the dream nature of this world? When people are steeped in misguided notions, they cannot hear messages that are radically different. People in Jesus' day were not ready for the whole truth. We usually understand truth gradually, taking in bits and pieces as we can handle it. Today the global consciousness is higher than when Jesus physically walked the earth. War is no longer considered acceptable or the first option for conflict resolution. Abuse, whether verbal, emotional, sexual, or physical, is no longer silently condoned, at least in the United States. The world has changed and is ready for Jesus' message in *A Course in Miracles*.

What Type of God?

> *The populace drag down the gods to their own level.*
> *~Ralph Waldo Emerson*

Pastor Don, whom I met at the casino, was blessed by the love of God, and his joy radiated it. His opinion of God was that He is a God of love. "But," he said, "He is also a God of justice . . . *and a God of wrath if you piss Him off!*" This is where I thought he was mistaken. God is *only* love, and unconditional love does not condemn. Man has made God in *man's* image. Man has mistaken God as Someone to be feared and from whom we will be separated for eternity if we don't accept Jesus. The Bible is replete with messages of fear, guilt, punishment, and separation—hallmarks of the ego. The ego projects; that's its job. Therefore, it is no wonder we have conceived of a God who mirrors our own self-hatred.

What the writers of the Bible correctly sensed was that without God we are lost, alone, and bereft. The original definition of the word "sin" was an archery term that meant to "miss the mark." We indeed miss the bull's-eye when we choose with the ego mind instead of the Christ Mind. We completely get off track, miss the point of life, and lose our way. The need to accept Jesus misses the mark somewhat, but not completely. As long as we don't accept our Christ nature we will *feel* separate from God, though in actuality we *cannot* be separate and are with God for eternity.

My pastor from my teen years shared a life-transforming experience in which he was suicidal and Jesus appeared to him. The power and love he felt was profound, and this gave him reason to live. He dedicated his life to God and to spreading the teachings of Jesus as found in the Bible. This was the perfect path for him. The Holy Spirit guides each of us to our unique path. However, contrary to church doctrine, the loving experience of the Christ Self can be had with or without knowing Jesus as our personal savior. I needed a relationship with Jesus as a stepping stone to discover the Christ within me. Therefore, the church's emphasis on developing a *personal* relationship with Jesus was very helpful to me. However, not everyone requires this.

These are the questions we have to ask ourselves: "What do *I* think God is like?" Is He or She angry or loving or both? Do I believe in one God, many Gods, an impersonal God, a personal God, One who actively participates in this world, or One who leaves man to his own devices? Furthermore, do I think God created this world with all its wonders as well as its horrors? What would Love think?

The Final Judgment

Knowledge is two-fold, and consists not only in an affirmation of what is true, but in the negation of that which is false.
~*Charles Caleb Colton*

The biblical Book of Revelation is filled with horrors about the final battle between God and Satan. After the battle, we will all be judged worthy or wicked on Judgment Day, and the wicked will be thrown into a lake of fire. However, there are metaphysical interpretations of Revelation that convey positive messages, quite in contrast to the frightening interpretations of traditional Christian doctrine. *A Course in Miracles* elucidates Judgment Day this way:

> ***This is God's Final Judgment:***
> ***"You are still My holy Son, forever innocent,***
> ***forever loving and forever loved,***
> ***as limitless as your Creator,***
> ***and completely changeless and forever pure.***
> ***Therefore awaken and return to Me.***
> ***I am your Father and you are my Son"***
> ***(W-p.II.10.5:1-3).***

What more needs to be said?

169

CHAPTER SEVEN

DEVELOPING A RELATIONSHIP WITH SPIRIT

Follow your bliss.
~Joseph Campbell

If there is no God, then why has virtually every person on this planet, who's old enough to reason, wondered about it? When you think of God, what do you get? Do you think of Nature? Do you sense a formless void or an energy field? Do you see an image of an old, white-bearded judge sitting on a throne? Do you picture many different gods and goddesses? *A Course in Miracles* defines God this way: **We say "God is," and then we cease to speak, for in that knowledge words are meaningless (W-p.I.169.5:4).** Words and symbols on this level cannot even come close to describing All That Is. God, or Love, is all there is; there is nothing else. Everything else we think we experience is just illusion. This is why the *Course* states, **Nothing real can be threatened. Nothing unreal exists. Herein lies the peace of God (T-in.2:2-4).**

In our present human state, God is unknowable. However, perceiving ourselves to exist on this level, images and metaphors help us connect. In my church we say "Mother/Father God" to encompass both the masculine and feminine natures. Yet God is neither male nor female. Use whatever images are most helpful for you, such as angels, gods or goddesses, animals, Jesus, or other masters. Meditate and get an image of your own higher Self, the part of you that is wise, calm, and has all the answers. You can ask this part of you for help at any time.

Think of the most unconditionally loving person you know. Now multiply that person's love by infinity. That is like God. Who is the most joyful, exuberant person you know? That person's joy is but a fraction of God's laughter. Jesus tells us that our illusory separation occurred when **into eternity, where all is one, there crept a tiny, mad idea, at which the Son of God remembered not to laugh (T-27.VIII.6:2)**. This is why I erupt into laughter so often these days, as I am remembering my true identity. I can now see how silly I was to conjure all sorts of separation scenarios.

What brings you joy? What was the happiest moment of your life? Who are the people you love spending time with? What are the hobbies, sports, or interests you love to do? What excites you? This is where God is! Reading makes me feel God's presence, but for you it may come from baseball, gardening, music, art, yoga, golf, car racing, and so on. One of my clients feels God's presence when he's playing soccer. In that arena he gets in touch with his higher Self, his love, his passion, his ability to soar beyond limitations. He feels in command, as he allows his intuitive Self to play the game. He's not thinking, he's *being*. Another client of mine is enchanted with scuba diving. She doesn't really believe in God, yet she feels a powerful presence with the ocean. It awakens and enlivens her, and it makes her feel connected to life. This is what God is. We don't have to call it God or encapsulate it in a religious context to feel it. God is whatever inspires you, harkens you to greater heights, and speaks to you of something bigger, grander, and more awesome.

Spend as much time as you can doing what you love. Notice how you feel about yourself and others when you're immersed in that special activity. You will probably feel expanded, connected, and blissful. The ego will try to keep you busy with work or other distractions to keep you from your happiness. In our hectic, fast-paced culture, it's hard to slow down, but slowing down and being in the flow or in the zone is what gets us in touch with God. It's when our chattering minds stop for a moment that our inner voice can be heard. Tapping into Spirit is how we charge our batteries, and unless we recharge regularly, we'll go dead to life. If we don't follow our inner voice, we lose energy, feel less powerful, and lack enthusiasm.

A friend of mine is a physicist and says he is an atheist. We belong to the same environmental group, and he loves nature and has a strong desire to protect the planet. We discussed our spiritual beliefs and he said he didn't believe in God, but he felt awe with the mysteries of life. He expressed wonder and amazement at the stars and galaxies, and inspiration from the intricate way the ecosystem works so perfectly, down to the most minute detail. I replied, "That's what I call God." Although ACIM says that God did not create this planet, God gave us free will and ingenuity to do so. The phenomenal intelligence and beauty on this earth is a symbol for the love, power and imagination God bestowed upon us.

When I was younger I related to God as someone "out there." As my spiritual journey has progressed, God has become a force, an energy, inside of me. This power beckons me to go higher, to expand. It tells me there's more to life than meets the eye, and it urges me to look beyond surface appearances. There is expansiveness in my heart center, a radiance and serenity that feels spacious, free, and uncluttered. The mind is still, released from constant chatter. I have found that what I seek is seeking me, and I couldn't get away from it if I tried. It is the essence of my Being, and the more I surrender to it the more it reveals itself. It is total love, and it always seeks to engage me. I am it and it is me.

Learning to Hear the Inner Voice

The only real valuable thing is intuition.
~Einstein

When you are still an instant . . .
then you will hear his Voice (W-p.I.182.8:1).

God is something we *feel* or *sense*, and that is why many scientists do not trust that there is such a force as God. They want concrete, outer proof of an invisible force that is at the center of our Being. The word "inspired" comes from "in spirit." When we listen to our inner spirit, we are *inspired* to do those things which are for our highest good. Following this inner guidance smoothes our way and softens our paths, making life gentler and easier. As we feel this Presence in our lives and begin communicating with It, so many interesting and wonderful "coincidences" happen that we become aware that something bigger is at work. We *experience* God's love *inside* of us, and outer events show our rational minds that a force is acting in our lives. For those who have had mostly negative life experiences, it's hard to believe in God. Yet that is another ego trap, for we choose the fear and negativity over love, and negativity is what then keeps showing up in our lives. We are trapped in the outer illusion of this painful world. Even in the worst circumstances, we all have the still small voice that beckons us to listen.

There is a touching scene in the movie *Contact* in which a scientist, Ellie, played by Jodie Foster, is debating the existence of God with a former priest, Palmer, played by Matthew McConaughey. Ellie's mother died during childbirth with her, and her father died when she was nine. Devastated by her emptiness, Ellie has spent her life searching for extraterrestrial intelligence, in hopes of finding out she's not alone. Ellie challenges Palmer, noting that God has not given any proof of His existence, and suggests that we have created the concept of God so we won't feel alone. She says she needs proof before she can believe. Palmer asks her if she loved her dad, and she says she did. He tells her to prove it, and Ellie is rendered silent.

I ran into a former client the other day, and she said that one of the most important things she learned in her therapy was to listen to her inner voice. That voice is the Holy Spirit. Another client said she didn't want to pray to someone out there, because she has a hard time believing in God because of her negative childhood. I told her the Holy Spirit is really her higher Self inside of her. She related better to that. It usually *sounds* just like our own voice, but it *feels* different, calmer. This inner voice is gentle and loving, guiding us to what's good for us. Like the voice in automobile navigating systems, it gently corrects us when we get off course. It doesn't berate; it just corrects. In our daily activities, it tells us when and how to slow down and when to get busy. It advises on career decisions, what to eat, when to contact someone, what activities to engage in, and every little detail of our lives. I instruct my clients to continually stop, be still and breathe, and ask, "What should I be doing now?" or "What do I really *feel* like doing now?" Be quiet and listen for the answer. Then *do* it. So often we say, "Not now, I want to do this other thing." Resist this tendency, for our lives run more smoothly and we feel much more at peace when we turn every single decision over. Jesus encourages us to affirm: **Today I will make no decisions by myself (T-30.I.2:2).** As I have released the ego, I don't make concrete plans nearly as much as I used to, and I am more spontaneous as I listen to what the Holy Spirit guides me to do each moment. I am still focused and productive without being frazzled.*

> *A healed mind does not plan. It carries out the plans that it receives through listening to wisdom that is not its own (W-p.I.135.11:1-2). His Voice speaks for Him in all situations and in every aspect of all situations, telling you exactly what to do to call upon His strength and His protection (W-p.I.47.3:2).*

Making no decisions by ourselves is especially important for our constant forgiveness lessons. We need to practice forgiveness continually, making it a habit. Every single thing that bothers us needs to be forgiven, *every single thing.* This is the way we will wake up from the dream. *"Recognize, Release, Replace"* can be a mantra, reminding us to get into our right mind. Judging is such an integral part of the ego nature that it gets us at every turn and we need continual guidance. Whenever we catch ourselves judging or being angry, we can use this prayer:

---

* Go to my website, http://www.lorricoburn.com, to download the audio *Time Non-Management*, which will teach you how to get things done from the peaceful voice of inner guidance rather than frantic busyness.

> *I must have decided wrongly, because*
> *I am not at peace. I made the decision myself,*
> *but I can also decide otherwise.*
> *I want to decide otherwise, because I want*
> *to be at peace. I do not feel guilty, because the*
> *Holy Spirit will undo all the consequences*
> *of my wrong decision if I will let Him.*
> *I choose to let Him, by allowing Him to*
> *decide for God for me (T-5.VII.6:7-11).*

A word of caution is necessary here. Sometimes we do what we think our inner voice is telling us to do and the result harms us. This is the ego voice disguised as the Holy Spirit. That is why it is helpful to specifically talk to the Holy Spirit and ask that you be shown Its way, not the ego's. The ego voice will always eventually lead to guilt, but initially it may feel good. The Holy Spirit's voice tells us not to feel guilty for anything, because once we ask for help, It will undo the consequences of our wrong decision.

A good rule of thumb to discern the ego's voice from the Holy Spirit's is that **the Voice of the Holy Spirit does not command . . . it merely reminds . . . remaining quiet even in the midst of turmoil (T-5.II.7:1,4,6).** The Holy Spirit's voice is patient, giving things time to work themselves out in the assurance of love. It knows that love is never lost. In contrast, the ego's voice feels like a compulsion, something we just have to do *right now*. It contains a twinge of tension, unease, or negativity, if not outright anxiety. The ego's compulsive and impulsive voice is particularly acute in romantic relationships. We feel we just *have* to contact our lover to fix things, when letting him be is usually the healthier route. I suggest to my clients that they count to ten before picking up the phone or e-mailing, and try to divert themselves in any way they can, preferably by journaling feelings or doing something to nurture themselves. The compulsion often feels absolutely overwhelming, and the ego voice convinces us we'll feel better when we talk to the lover. We may or may not feel better in the short run, but eventually we feel worse. The ego deceives us with short-term gratification for long-term pain. In Alcoholics Anonymous it's called "stinking thinking," the idea that just one drink won't hurt, and it may even help, because it will take the edge off. The ego is so sly that it gets us thinking that our addiction is actually good for us!

We often hear the advice, "Follow your heart." This can be great advice or awful advice, depending on the situation. If our heart has a still, calm sense of rightness and it is beckoning us in a new direction, the suggestion is probably beneficial. But if our heart feels empty, yearning, or despairing, then the answer will lead down the wrong road. A lot of us go after love affairs that are all wrong for us because our hearts are broken. We feel desperate without our beloved, yet when we get back with that person our lives become chaos. The inner voice is the "still, small voice," not the crying, anxious plea. When we're not sure what the right answer is, we should wait. That's usually the hardest part.

Spontaneous writing can be a tool for accessing Spirit. Don't be afraid that this is weird "channeling," for we are all channeling Spirit every day. We are the channel for that inner voice. To do spontaneous writing, sit down, get quiet and still, and ask a question of Spirit. Speak a prayer of protection, such as, "Only love and light may enter my thoughts." Then wait for the thoughts to come to you, and write them down.

Try not to censor them, and once done, put the paper away for a day or two. Then reread what you wrote. You will know if it is Spirit speaking by the loving quality of the advice. If something feels wrong or could lead to harm, discard it as from the ego.

When I have done spontaneous writing, I knew it was from Spirit because it told me surprising things I had not thought of before. When I applied the advice, it worked. For example, I was once told that the problem I thought was someone else's was really mine, and it was up to me to change my attitude. That was not the answer I expected, or wanted, to hear. Another time Spirit challenged a long-held assumption I had about someone, reminding me that I **never see my brother as he is (W-p.II.335.1:2)**.

Answers may come in a variety of forms, through songs, overhearing a conversation, several people telling us the same thing, a striking line in a book, movie, or CD. If we have asked a question, we *will* get an answer, but we have to be alert to perceive it. Sometimes it's not the answer we want, so we ignore the repeated signs. Even if it's a good answer, we may have trouble receiving it. I received an unsolicited mailing from an ACIM group, and enclosed was a card with the *Course* quote, **There are many answers you have already received but have not yet heard (T-9.II.3:6).** So, I said, "Okay, God, what is it you're trying to tell me?" I quickly got the answer, which was "I love you." I wrote it down and stuck it smack center on my desk. I'd had trouble receiving God's love directly, from the Holy Spirit's Voice. I could feel God's love indirectly through meditation, loved ones, events, my clients, and nature, but I was blocked on clear, verbal answers. After I got this card, I was able to open, and hearing God say "I love you," now feels as real as when my partner says it. Sometimes we need to get the same answer hundreds of times before it sinks in, but Spirit is infinitely patient.

Fear can actually be the Holy Spirit's voice when it is a gentle warning to avoid a dangerous situation. An acquaintance of mine was warned not to take the subway home from work. She actually heard a small inner voice say, "Don't take the subway." She ignored it and found herself alone in a car with a demented-looking man who came after her. Fortunately she got away, but she could have prevented the terrifying episode altogether if she had listened. I often coach my daughter to pay attention to her "vibes" around men. If she gets any sense at all of danger or discomfort, she should get away as fast as she can. Too many women are raped by dates or strangers because they don't listen to their gut senses.

What about when the ego shrieks so loudly that we can't hear the inner voice at all? Sometimes we are in the midst of severe anxiety and depression, and try as we might, we don't feel connected with God. At these times, do the best you can to behave loving toward yourself; do something comforting, give yourself tender loving care, perhaps call a friend, and wait. Summing up gratitude for all our blessings will often put us back on track. We can also ask ourselves, "What do I *feel* like doing now? If the answer is, "I don't feel like doing anything," or "I absolutely *have* to eat this Twinkie, get away from here, drink this beer," and so on, we can be sure it's the ego talking. Double check to see if the answer is coming from love or fear. As we answer the loving voice, we will eventually feel connected again.*

When we are in total despair it may help to remember that despair is just a *feeling*, it is not the truth. This is where a meditation practice is helpful, to detach from identifying with passing feelings. When in despair, remember this reassurance: **Do you really believe you can make a voice that can drown out God's? Do you really believe you can devise a thought system that can separate you from Him? Do you really believe you can plan for your safety and joy better than He can? You need be neither careful nor careless; you need merely cast your cares upon Him because He careth for you (T-5.VII.1:1-4).** We can ask ourselves, "Am I making this situation real? Can I remind myself that I am safe at home with God?"

Simple affirmations repeated as mantras are also helpful when we can't seem to pull out of the ego's madness.

> *I cannot be guilty because I am a Son of God.*
> *I have already been forgiven.*
> *No fear is possible in a mind beloved of God.*
> *There is no need to attack*
> *because love has forgiven me (W-p.I.46.6:3-6).*

My friend Diane experienced the ego's madness as it tricked her into thinking it was the Holy Spirit's guidance. She had to move from her beloved house on ten acres in the country, because she got divorced and could no longer afford it. She felt under pressure to move because she had an offer on her house, so she chose a home that she didn't like. She ended up sinking $50,000 into the

---

* Go to my website, http://www.lorricoburn.com, for a free PDF, "Fifteen Ways to Identify and Listen to Your Inner Voice."

new home just to make it comfortable for her tastes. Everything that could go wrong did, from the wrong sink being delivered, to crippled floor joists, to the broken furnace. Now, two years later she is moving again because the furnace is so loud she can't sleep. Her previous frame of mind was that she could not get the house she wanted because she could not afford it.

She chose the new, unpleasant house because she got a shiver when she walked in the family room, and she took this as an intuitive sign that it was the right house for her. The ego was laying another trap. It was the right house all right, to reinforce her ego belief that she could not get what she really wanted.

Our intuition may feel like higher guidance when actually it is propelled by the subconscious ego belief that we are unworthy. Our intuition compels us to what we *really* want deep down, and if we do not heal ego guilt, we actually *want* to punish ourselves.

In the meantime, Diane has decided to make a more loving decision this time, asking for the help of the Holy Spirit. She and I have discussed how God only wants us to have joy and peace, and only the ego tells her she can't find a house that is beautiful and comforting as well as affordable. When she decides with the Holy Spirit she will find a house that she *loves*. She shouldn't settle for anything less. If a house feels bad, it's not the right one. If she feels afraid, it's not the right one. The guidance of the Holy Spirit feels right and peaceful and *only* results in our joy.

Psychotherapy

Your vision will become clear only when you can look into your own heart. Who looks outside, dreams. Who looks inside, awakens.
~Carl Jung

My client Marjory provides the perfect example of following the Holy Spirit's direction. Marjory was in therapy to help her change dysfunctional patterns with her partner. Her image of her higher Self was a wolf. She howled with her dog and this was one of her connections to Spirit. I went on a trip out west and in the gift shops were numerous wolves made of porcelain, wood, metal, and glass. I wanted to get Marjory a wolf and went into many shops. I complained to a friend that I just couldn't find the right one, and she said I'd know it when I saw it. Finally I found a coffee mug with two wolves howling at the moon. Back home I gave it to Marjory and she exclaimed, "Oh, I love it! It has the perfect colors and the wolves are great!" She then read the slip of paper tucked inside the mug, "Pottery by Mara." "I've always wanted to change my name to Mara!" she said. I never knew that, nor had I ever bought a present for a client before, yet felt compelled to find Marjory a wolf. We chuckled at the serendipity of the universe, and in her subsequent sessions she worked on trusting the higher power that was at work in her life. A year later, Marjory was in the market for a house. She lamented that she'd lost her chance, as housing prices had risen $20,000 and she could no longer afford it. I reminded her of the "Pottery by Mara" coincidence and said that if she acted on what her inner voice told her to do, that the perfect house would show up. Marjory did end up with a beautiful house that was priced $35,000 less than comparable houses. This is what happens when we are on the right track. Doors open, miracles occur, and life becomes interesting.

Often coincidences and unusual events will show us that we're on the right track; they are a way the Holy Spirit talks to us. We can ask for signs that we are doing the right thing, and they often reassure us. Dreams speak to us as well. I've had several prophetic dreams that have assured me I was in the right place, including a dream about my current partner that I had seven years before we got together. Intriguing episodes increase our trust that a higher force is working in our lives. Recently I sent a letter to an old friend, Jim, with whom I had ongoing conflict. I told him that I finally recognized that he was so hostile toward me because of my judgment of him. He leaned toward verbal abuse, but my unspoken judgment was every bit as attacking as his spoken words. I told Jim that forgiveness allowed me to see only his good qualities, and that I no longer held him out of my heart. I asked him to call me to let me know he got the letter, and he left a curt message to never contact him again under any circumstances. At first I was hurt and befuddled, since I had expressed love and forgiveness and he just barked back. A few days later in meditation I burst out laughing for about a half hour. It was his growling mask! That's not who he really is! The next day I got a strange voice mail message. There were background voices and then a man growled into the phone! I said, "Okay, Holy Spirit, what was that about?" I realized that it was confirmation that Jim is simply growling and I can look past his behavior to the love behind it.

Learning to love ourselves is another way of getting closer to Spirit. Since God is love, any way we increase love in our lives builds our awareness of God's presence. As a psychotherapist I have been blessed with witnessing hundreds of people improve their self-love. There are a handful of techniques that I have found particularly helpful and proficient for emotional and spiritual growth. These are EMDR®, the Sedona Method®, mindfulness meditation, cognitive-behavioral therapy (CBT), twelve-step support groups, and inner child work. EMDR is a powerful tool that was first used with combat veterans who had post-traumatic stress disorder. It uses bilateral stimulation of the brain to heal the trauma and can be used on any number of issues in addition to severe traumas. The Sedona Method is a powerful, efficient, and quick method of releasing negative emotions that does not require dredging up the past. Along with insight meditation, it is one of the methods most effective for releasing ego negativity and awakening from the dream. Insight meditation entails observing the mind's thoughts from the position of the witness rather than the owner of the feelings. For example, when anger arises we note, "There is anger," rather than "I am angry." This releases ego judgments and accesses the higher Self.

Cognitive-behavioral therapy changes our thinking, thereby resulting in behavior change. Fear thoughts are replaced with realistic thoughts, in addition to taking reasonable action steps. For example, "I'll never get the job I want!" is switched to, "I keep applying myself, and the perfect job shows up for me." This is combined with a goal such as sending out ten resumes per week. Twelve-step groups for addictions are so powerful that I tell clients if they are only going to go to one thing, therapy or a twelve-step group, go to the group. The process of surrendering to a higher power is the same as listening to the inner voice of the Holy Spirit. It undoes the ego and heals the addiction. Inner child work is especially helpful for victims of childhood abuse, as it focuses on letting go of shame and loving oneself instead. As shame is released, the ego is released. The book *Healing the Shame that Binds You*, by John Bradshaw, is a classic in this field. Resources for these techniques are located in the appendix.

My client Wesley demonstrated how therapy can help spiritually awaken us. Wesley is sixty-eight years old and describes having a knot in his chest from strong anxiety his entire life. He came to therapy following the death of his wife. Shortly after he began therapy the knot in his chest went away for the first time in his life, and it has only surfaced briefly a few times since. Wesley started studying the Kabbalah, the mystical path of Judaism. Prior to his wife's death he never went to church or thought much about his spirituality. He had a profound experience in a therapy session while we were doing EMDR. He stopped abruptly and said, "Something weird just happened! I saw myself from across the room and I was watching myself." We discussed how this was his witnessing Self, the Self beyond the personality and body. He was astounded and exclaimed, "This changes everything! I can no longer look at myself in the same way anymore! Everything I needed I already had. What you said helped me find it. I'm not looking for anything outside of myself anymore."

Prayer and Meditation

> *Tension is who you think you should be.*
> *Relaxation is who you are.*
> *~Chinese proverb*

Prayer is when we *talk* to God, consciously or unconsciously. Meditation is when we *listen* to God. We are always praying, because every thought is a prayer. Every thought is creating the world that shows up for us. *A Course in Miracles* indicates that true prayer is the realization that we are one with God and need nothing else. It states that until we recognize this, however, we tend to pray for certain outcomes. When we think we need a certain outcome, we are making the dream real. ACIM gives specific instruction on how to pray:

> *The secret of true prayer is to forget*
> *the things you think you need.*
> *To ask for the specific is much the same*
> *as to look on sin and then forgive it.*
> *Also in the same way, in prayer you overlook*
> *your specific needs as you see them,*
> *and let them go into God's Hands.*
> *There they become your gifts to Him,*
> *for they tell Him that you would have no gods*
> *before Him; no Love but His (S-1.I.4:1-4).*

This prayer applies to what we want for ourselves as well as for others. The only true prayer for another is to see only his Christ Self and to overlook any appearance of sickness or harm. If we perceive anything less than his perfection, we are making the illusion real.

Why is it that sometimes our prayers seem to go unanswered? Often we are supplicating from the ego instead of surrendering from our Spirit. Our Spirit needs nothing. However, we do need things to survive on this earthly level. If our prayer does not get answered in the way our ego thinks it should, it's because that is not what we really want or need deep down. All we ever really want deep down is to remember our oneness with God, but we *think* we want the illness to be healed, money to come in, or the conflict to be solved. Sometimes when we get what we want it keeps us focused away from the true goal of knowing God, while other times it serves to increase our faith. Our higher Self is giving us exactly what we need at all times, even if it doesn't seem that way. Most of us are not ready to be home with God except for brief moments within our lives, because we are scared to release our attachment to earthly things. It's not that we have to sacrifice earthly pleasures, but when we experience God, they will pale in comparison and we won't care about them anymore. Thus, our path back to God is usually slow but sure, as we are ready to receive it. **All the help you can accept will be provided, and not one need you have will not be met. Let us not, then, be too concerned with goals for which you are not ready (M-26.4:8-9).**

Meditation is an extremely valuable tool for quieting the mind so the inner voice can be heard. One of my ministers used to say that twenty minutes of meditation per day would change your life, and he was right. There are hundreds of different ways to meditate, and there are many good books and audios available. Some of us experience God in meditation, but many of us try to meditate and don't really feel anything. Our mind wanders to the list of tasks for the day or the troubles we're having; we don't feel that peaceful bliss we're told comes with meditation. I have been meditating for twenty years, and I still can't calm my mind except for brief moments. In spite of this, spiritual growth has proceeded. We need to find what works for us individually, for there are no rules to finding God. For me, reading and pausing to reflect works far better than meditating. I used to think that if I didn't meditate I wouldn't become enlightened, but then I came upon a liberating book by Jed McKenna, *Spiritual Enlightenment: The Damndest Thing.* Jed states that meditation can help calm the mind and possibly help in conscious awakening. However, enlightenment is simply waking up from the dream, and we can awaken *without* meditation. The idea that enlightenment is some far-off achievement that comes only after we've perfected ourselves through lifetimes of meditation is an insidious ego trap. So is the belief that we have to go through trials and initiations to prove ourselves worthy of spiritual mastership. Since we are one with God and have never left heaven, what is there to prove?

The Sedona Method instructor Hale Dwoskin is fond of saying, "There's nothing to do and nowhere to go." I love that line, for it highlights that we already have all that we need inside of us. In truth we are already enlightened and need but recognize it. Eckhart Tolle in *The Power of Now* states, "The word enlightenment conjures up the idea of some super-human accomplishment, and the ego likes to keep it that way, but it is simply your natural state of felt oneness with Being."[1] *A*

Course in Miracles says, **Enlightenment is but a recognition, not a change at all (W-p.I.188.1:4); I need do nothing (T-18.VII.h).** The *Course* Workbook lessons are designed to bring about the shift in consciousness so we can awaken to God, but the *Course* says it is not the only path to God. **A universal theology is impossible, but a universal experience is not only possible but necessary (C-in.2:5).** ACIM also states that one day we won't need the *Course* itself, for we will have gone beyond it. All paths provide guidance, but the guidance should not be confused with the end result, which is the universal experience of God.

The value of any spiritual teaching lies in its practical application to our lives. Does it increase our connection to God? Does it bring us joy and peace? Does it make us feel safe and loved? Does it help us to think and act more lovingly to our brothers and ourselves? Does it help us forgive? Does it help us wake up? The goal of the curriculum, regardless of the teacher you choose, is **"Know thyself." There is nothing else to seek. Everyone is looking for himself and for the power and glory he thinks he has lost. Whenever you are with anyone, you have another opportunity to find them (T-8.III.5:1-4).** My former minister used to tell visitors to our church that if they didn't like what they found there, keep searching. Don't stop looking for a place where you can experience the love of God. Every path has some value. *A Course in Miracles* is a self-study course that can be learned while engaging in any other spiritual practice. While it is not an organized religion, individuals hold study groups, and resource information is listed in the appendix.*

Joining a spiritual community is extremely valuable in keeping us on the loving track. Not everyone needs a community of people, however, as some feel God's presence far more powerfully from a walk in the woods, a stroll on the beach, or a hike in the mountains. Find what works for you and do it regularly. Stay ahead of the ego, for just as an untended garden becomes strangled with weeds, negative thoughts will choke out love.

---

* Go to my website, http://www.lorricoburn.com, to download the audio *Moving Toward Enlightenment*, for a more detailed explanation of the path to enlightenment, as described in ACIM.

Going Home

Where Thou art—that—is Home.
~Emily Dickinson

There is nothing, absolutely nothing, that can keep us from the love of God. Our return to God is assured; in fact, it has already happened and is awaiting our recognition. **You are as certain of arriving home as is the pathway of the sun (W-p.II.ep.2:1). We but undertake a journey that is over (W-p.I.158.3:6).** However, desire to be released from the illusion has to be stronger than the desire to stay before it will happen.

In *The Wizard of Oz*, when Dorothy has had her fill of scary dream experiences, Glinda, the Good Witch, tells her she has known the way back home all along. The answer was within her. Dorothy questions why she didn't tell her this sooner, and Glinda says because she wouldn't have believed it. Dorothy had to follow the yellow brick road of her illusions before she could accept the truth. Likewise, we tend to go through many illusions before we are ready to return home. However, we have a choice, and we can return home right here and now. I invite you to click your heels three times (wearing ruby slippers helps) and affirm, "I'm already home. I'm already home. I'm already home."

I leave you with a prayer from the *Course* and wish you many blessings.

Hear, then, the one answer of the Holy Spirit
to all the questions the ego raises:
You are a child of God, a priceless part
of His Kingdom, which He created as part of
Him. Nothing else exists and only this is real.
You have chosen a sleep in which you
have had bad dreams, but the sleep is not real
and God calls you to awake.
There will be nothing left of your dream
when you hear Him, because you will awaken.

Your dreams contain many of the ego's symbols and they have confused you. Yet that was only because you were asleep and did not know. When you wake you will see the truth around you and in you, and you will no longer believe in dreams because they will have no reality for you. Yet the Kingdom and all that you have created there will have great reality for you, because they are beautiful and true (T-6.IV.6:1-8).

NOTES

Introduction

1. *Newsweek*/BeliefNet.com survey, August 2005.

Chapter Two

1. As a psychotherapist, I am well aware that many people need medication to overcome depression and anxiety, and I took medication when I was unable to pull out of the abyss on my own. I continue to recommend medication when it is appropriate for my clients.

Chapter Three

1. Brian Greene, *The Fabric of the Cosmos* (New York: First Vintage Books, 2005), ix–x.

2. Ibid., x.

Chapter Four

1. This book refers to "our mind" and "our Self," in the singular form, since there is only one mind and one Self, rather than "our minds" and our Selves. Further, ACIM defines "ego" differently than Freudian psychology. ACIM groups all aspects of our separate, individual identity together and calls them "ego." Freud separated personality into the superego, ego, and id. The superego is the conscience and functions to keep our thinking and behavior appropriate. The ego has the rational, problem-solving,

and decision-making functions. The id contains animalistic drives such as sex and aggression.

2. Michael Mirdad, *"A Course in Miracles,"* audio CD, Grail Productions (360) 671-8349, available at www.grailproductions.com.

Chapter Five

1. Jon Mundy, *"A Course in Miracles*: It Isn't Easy," *Miracles* 4 (July–August 2005): 6.

2. Mirdad, *"A Course in Miracles"* audio CD.

3. David Hawkins, *The Eye of the I* (Sedona, Ariz.: Veritas Press, 2001), 315.

4. David Hawkins, *Power vs. Force: The Hidden Determinants of Human Behavior* (Sedona, Ariz.: Veritas Press, 1995), 222.

Chapter Six

1. Joseph Campbell, *The Masks of God: Occidental Mythology,* (New York: The Viking Press, 1964), 347.

2. Ibid., 334.

3. Campbell, *The Masks of God: Primitive Mythology,* (New York: Penguin Group, 1972), 9.

4. Campbell, *The Masks: Occidental,* 389; Michael Baigent, Richard Leigh, and Henry Lincoln, *Holy Blood, Holy Grail* (New York: Dell Publishing Co., 1982), 368.

5. Baigent, *Holy Blood, Holy Grail,* 368.

6. University of Missouri-Kansas City Law Department, Faculty Projects, www.umkc.edu.

7. http://www.beliefnet.com, *Newsweek*/Beliefnet Poll Results, August 2005.

Chapter Seven

1. Eckhart Tolle, *The Power of Now: A Guide to Spiritual Enlightenment,* (Novato, Calif.: New World Library, 1999), 10.

APPENDIX

ACIM Notation

A Course in Miracles has three volumes within one book: Text; Workbook; Manual for Teachers. There is a section called "Clarification of Terms" at the end of the Manual for Teachers. There are two supplements: *The Song of Prayer* and *Psychotherapy: Purpose, Process, and Practice.*

Notations are in bold print and, for example, are to be read as follows:

T-7.V.2:4-5: Text, chapter 7, section 5, paragraph 2, sentences 4-5.

W-p.I.100.3:7: Workbook, part I, lesson 100, paragraph 3, sentence 7.

W-p.I.31.h: Workbook, part 1, lesson 31, heading.

W-p.II.13.1:1-3: Workbook, part II, question 13, paragraph 1, sentences 1-3.

M-11.5:6: Manual for Teachers, question 11, paragraph 5, sentence 6

C-3.4:1: "Clarification of Terms," term 3, paragraph 4, sentence 1.

S-2.I.5:3: Song of Prayer, chapter 2, section 1, paragraph 5, sentence 3.

Psychotherapy Techniques
from Chapter Seven

The Sedona Method: www.sedona.com; Hale Dwoskin, *The Sedona Method*.

EMDR: www.emdr.com

Meditation: There are many good audios and books, and the one I use is Holosync, from Centerpointe Research Institute. This one is good if you have difficulty focusing and stilling your mind, as it slows the brain waves even when you can't stop thinking: www.centerpointe.com. An excellent book on mindfulness meditation is *The Heart of the Buddha's Teachings*, by Thich Hnat Hahn. Another is *A Gradual Awakening*, by Stephen Levine.

Twelve-Step Groups: Alcoholics Anonymous and Al-Anon are often in the phone book. A Google search on Alcoholics Anonymous brings up meetings in your vicinity.

Cognitive-Behavioral Therapy: When you call a psychotherapist, ask if he or she does cognitive-behavioral work. Go to www/nacbt. org for the official site of the National Association of Cognitive-Behavioral Therapists; however, many therapists who do excellent cognitive-behavioral work do not belong to this organization.

Inner Child Work: John Bradshaw is a pioneer of inner child work. www.johnbradshaw.com

While ACIM is extremely helpful in the process of waking up, it clearly states that it is not the only path to God. If the spiritual teaching you follow has adequately answered your questions about the world's suffering and given you a sense of peace, then be grateful and stick with it. All religions contain valuable teachings, and there are common threads among them. You should follow the path that resonates best with you, the one that makes you feel God's love and peace. In fact, you can practice your own religion and also study ACIM.

<u>Books</u>

A Course in Miracles contains the Text, Workbook, and Manual for Teachers all in one book. It can be purchased at any bookstore or from many of the resource centers listed below. *The Song of Prayer* and *Psychotherapy: Purpose, Process, and Practice* are contained in the latest ACIM Combined Volume, published by the Foundation for A Course in Miracles. If you find that you are interested in studying ACIM further, it may be helpful to read some of the following books. The actual *Course* itself can be rather difficult to understand at first, and these books may keep you from misunderstanding it as I did. They should be seen as adjuncts to the *Course*, rather than replacements, for it is necessary to study the text and do the workbook to gain the full experience of ACIM.

- Gary Renard, *The Disappearance of the Universe*
- Jon Mundy, *Living A Course in Miracles*
- Marianne Williamson, *A Return to Love, The Gift of Change*
- Kenneth Wapnick, *The Message of A Course in Miracles*
- Robert Perry, *Path of Light, Return to the Heart of God*
- Gerald Jampolsky, M.D., *Love Is Letting Go of Fear*

<u>Websites</u>

There are many helpful websites. Most of these have free e-mail newsletters, listings of events, and explanations of ACIM concepts. Among these are:

- **www.facim.org** Foundation for *A Course in Miracles.* This site offers an excellent question and answer section under "Electronic Outreach." It covers virtually every question you can think of about *A Course in Miracles.* Bookmark it! Kenneth Wapnick is the most intellectual of the *Course* teachers and knew Helen Schucman and Bill Thetford.
- **www.miraclecenter.org** Miracle Distribution Center. This site has a listing of *Course* study groups, and a catalog of ACIM materials.

•**www.garyrenard.com** Gary's website contains excerpts from one of my favorite books, *The Disappearance of the Universe*.

•**www.miraclesmagazine.org** Jon Mundy is a witty, interesting teacher who is one of the few remaining people to have personally known Helen Schucman and Bill Thetford.

•**www.miracles-course.org** Community Miracles Center. Reverend Tony Ponticello's site has an extensive catalog of bargain priced books and audios, and a list of ACIM study groups.

•**www.circleofa.com** Robert Perry, Allen Watson, and Greg Mackie have made extensive scholarly contributions to *Course* studies. Their daily commentaries on the Workbook lessons are excellent, and are free by e-mail.

•**www.awakening-mind.net;** **www.teacherofteachers.net** David Hoffmeister's websites are dedicated to help us reach enlightenment.

•**www.attitudinalhealing.org** Gerald Jampolsky, M.D., and Diane Cirincione, Ph.D., run a center based on *Course* principles to assist those dealing with life-threatening illnesses.

•**www.marianne.com** Marianne Williamson has probably introduced more people to the *Course* than anyone, with her articulate, flowing style of speaking.

•**www.grailproductions.com** Dr. Michael Mirdad is a dynamic speaker—if you get a chance to hear him, do!

•**www.thevoiceforlove.com** DavidPaul and Candace Doyle have written books and offer teleseminars on learning to listen to the Holy Spirit.

•**www.pathwaysoflight.org** Reverends Robert and Mary Stoelting offer home study courses, counseling, books and other resources.

•**www.lorricoburn.com** This is my website, where you can view my speaking schedule and latest books and audios.

ACKNOWLEDGEMENTS

I feel like the wealthiest person on earth in terms of loving family and friends. As I started thinking of everyone who has helped me along the way, the list grew too long, so only the people directly related to producing this book are mentioned.

My parents and my sisters and brothers are the most loving, accepting family in the world. My mom, Darlene Slocum, has demonstrated the miracles of faith and forgiveness. My daughter Cassie has been what the *Course* calls my "savior," and our special relationship has become a holy one. Pat and Bruce Hess have gone way beyond the call of duty with their loving hospitality. I am truly blessed.

Many friends read this manuscript and offered helpful feedback. Thanks to:

Nancy Biehn, for lifting me up in my darkest hour; Rev. David Bell, for clear and direct feedback that gave me focus; Rev. BJ Erngren, for being my biggest cheerleader and the midwife of this project; Margo Hansen, for showing me the power of beholding the Christ; Kate Ferris, for speaking *Course* to me instead of coddling my negativity; Rev. Paula Lawrence, for being one of the most powerful spiritual healers I've known; Michael McClair, for laughter and pointing things out; Edie McKnight, for being open-minded, honest, and supportive; Mark Mullerweiss, for teaching me how to laugh and let go; Catherine Munro, for being yourself, free and honest; Cynthia Peele, for your generous feedback and helpfulness; Jim Raleigh, for your sincerity and dedication to our mutual path;

Rod Rodriguez, for being the most wonderful partner anyone could ask for; Ken Slumpff, "Bro," for the bond we've shared since we walked to grade school together; Walter Slumpff, "Dad," for telling me I could accomplish anything I wanted; David Winfree, for your incredible support and helping me release judgments.

My Master Mind partners Ada Cowan and Cathy Dyer have pulled me through many dark nights.

My psychotherapist peer support group was together for over a decade, and supported me through much growth: Edie McKnight, Kate O'Brien, and Stephanie Veling.

My spiritual family at Interfaith Center for Spiritual Growth includes too many wonderful people to list. Andrea Brisson, Ed Clark, Melanie Fuscaldo, Amy Garber, Steve Lyskawa, Susan Major, Scott McWhinney, Alex Penn, Fred and Judy Sauer, Malcolm Shaffner, Mary Siebert, Patrice Sauve, Lisa Smith, and Jeff White have directly impacted this project.

I have been blessed with a coach, par excellence, Adoley Odunton, a warm, nurturing energy healer, Diane McLean, and a therapist who made me feel lovable, Susan Liddy.

There are many other friends who have supported me through the years. Thanks to: Jill Carel, for believing in me and encouraging my ministry; Nancy Cottingham, for being the best clinical supervisor ever; Sarah DesJardins, for teaching me to trust myself and receive God's good; Pat Haber, for reflecting truth to me so I could make a major shift in my relationship; Heather Harder, for letting me know the power of my intuition; Linda Matter, for being my Sedona Method® releasing partner; Ingrid Sekhon, for many years of sharing; Diane Schmidt, for sticking by me through all my travails; Jacqueline Wolf, for being a soul sister.

Ron Cohen, Tracy Small, and Doug Dagley are people who saw the light in me and told me so without ever having met me face to face.

Thanks to Nancy Custer for the idea of earth suits, Rev. Scott McClintock for *The Lion King* analogy, and Betty Kercher for encouraging the use of *The Lion King* story.

Ken Daliege was an angel with his graphic design and formatting work in the initial project.

196

Katherine Faydash edited the initial manuscript with incredible efficiency.

All of my clients, study group members, and workshop participants have been my teachers. You are gifts to me.

John Shank, thank you for giving me the forgiveness opportunity that let me find what I was really looking for: God. You taught me the meaning of "Nothing real can be threatened. Nothing unreal exists. Herein lies the peace of God." I will always love you, deeper than the deepest ocean.

CPSIA information can be obtained at www.ICGtesting.com
Printed in the USA
LVOW071931121211

259058LV00008B/144/P